WORKHORSE

MY SUBLIME
and
ABSURD YEARS
in
NEW YORK
CITY'S
RESTAURANT
SCENE

WORK HORSE

KIM REED

hachette
BOOKS

New York

Author's Note: Most names and some identifying characteristics have been changed. Time has been compressed. Where dialogue appears, some is verbatim, and for some, the dialogue has been approximated or completely arranged to re-create the essence of conversations. Great care has been taken to tell my truths. This is my story and how I remember it.

Hachette Books
Hachette Book Group
1290 Avenue of the Americas
New York, NY 10104
HachetteBooks.com
Twitter.com/HachetteBooks
Instagram.com/HachetteBooks

First Edition: November 2021

Published by Hachette Books, an imprint of Perseus Books, LLC, a subsidiary of Hachette Book Group, Inc. The Hachette Books name and logo is a trademark of the Hachette Book Group.

The Hachette Speakers Bureau provides a wide range of authors for speaking events.

To find out more, go to www.hachettespeakersbureau.com or call (866) 376-6591.

The publisher is not responsible for websites (or their content) that are not owned by the publisher.

Print book interior design by Amy Quinn.

Library of Congress Cataloging-in-Publication Data

Names: Reed, Kim, 1978– author.
Title: Workhorse : my sublime and absurd years in New York City's
    restaurant scene / Kim Reed.
Description: First edition. | New York : Hachette Books, 2021.
Identifiers: LCCN 2021021597 | ISBN 9780306875106 (hardcover) | ISBN
    9780306875083 (ebook)
Subjects: LCSH: Food service—New York (State)—New York. | Reed, Kim,
    1979– —Career in food service. | Food service employees—United
    States—Biography. | Social workers—United States—Biography. |
    Administrative assistants—United States—Biography.
Classification: LCC TX930 .R44 2021 | DDC 647.95747/1—dc23
LC record available at https://lccn.loc.gov/2021021597

ISBNs: 978-0-306-87510-6 (hardcover), 978-0-306-87508-3 (ebook)

Printed in the United States of America

TR

10 9 8 7 6 5 4 3 2 1

For all the little Kims

CONTENTS

Contents

one

AUTHENTIC ITALIAN BLOODLINES

"You goin' to see my boyfriend at 101 Clark Street?" Rosie called out.

I flashed her a smile as I scooted fast out the door of our office, glancing back just long enough to catch a glimpse of her frosted bangs and kohl-rimmed eyes peeking over the stack of papers and overstuffed manila folders on her desk. Rosie was the office manager at Heights and Boerum Council, and she knew damn well who I was going to see because she listened in on ninety-nine percent of the calls I made to our frail, elderly clients. All the old men were her boyfriends.

"Tell him Rosie's askin' why he don't come in to see me no more."

Mr. Stein was my last client of the day, and the sooner I got to his apartment, the sooner I could leave and get back to the office. It wasn't that I didn't want to visit him—I liked my job as a social worker looking after Brooklyn's homebound seniors, most of whom were past ninety and in varying states of decline. The folks who, on the rare occasion they were able to venture out of their apartments, made their way down the sidewalk slowly pushing a mini shopping cart that doubled as a walker, just a few inches at a time. Their belabored state made it hard to look away: rail-thin arms and legs, backs that rounded over like the hook of a coat hanger, each breath forced and shallow. Their bony wrists and hands were covered in veins—thick and protruding ones, like mountain ranges on a globe. I never used to be squeamish about these things, but since I discovered a few mountain-clusters on my own shins and behind my knees, the sight of them bothered me.

Most of my clients were teetering on the edge of being forced into an assisted living facility, which would mean in exchange for forking over their entire monthly income, they'd live in a tiny, dressed-up hospital room with a total stranger for a roommate. It was my job to see that they had what they needed to keep hanging on at home. Often it wasn't much: grab bars in the shower, a pantry stocked with food that hadn't spoiled, one of those Life Alert bracelets. Maybe a home attendant who came a few times a week to help them bathe and, perhaps most importantly, scour their place for any seemingly harmless everyday objects that could suddenly turn into life-threatening hazards the minute mobility went out the window.

One particular danger was throw rugs, which most of my clients had strewn all over their floors, even though it was common knowledge among the over-eighty set that throw rugs were a one-way ticket to a broken hip, wrist, femur, or some lethal combination of the three. I also watched for any signs of cognitive impairment. The lone shoe on the bottom shelf of the fridge next to yesterday's half-eaten meatloaf in the Meals on Wheels tin was not a random mistake. It meant someone probably had a mild stroke within the past few days.

Mr. Stein usually came by the office once a week. He flirted with Rosie and stocked up on tickets for the Heights and Boerum Council senior shuttle bus. Sometimes he attended the Tai Chi for Seniors class held every Friday in the conference room. But a few days prior, we'd received a call from his longtime doctor asking if we'd dispatch one of our social workers to his patient's apartment. Apparently, Mr. Stein was a no-show for his last two appointments. Rosie was quick to chime in that it had been at least a month since he'd come to the office.

Most social workers were stuck working out of a dingy, window-less church basement on the worst corner of an already run-down neighborhood, but thankfully, Heights and Boerum Council was perched three flights up in a clean and bright building with decent-sized windows overlooking Montague Street—the main drag of Brooklyn Heights, one of the oldest old-money neighborhoods in New York City. The catchment area only stretched as far as the adjacent Cobble Hill and Boerum Hill, and aside from a few sketchy pockets that bordered the Gowanus Canal, it consisted of quiet, tree-lined residential streets with rows of well-kept brownstones worth about five million dollars apiece. Boerum Hill had made headlines recently when Michelle Williams and Heath Ledger bought a town-house over on Dean Street.

Celebrities choosing to settle down here didn't surprise me at all. I walked these streets every day—*all* day—and most of the area was as precious as a Norman Rockwell painting. In fact, I usually set out early for a home visit just so I could wander up and down for a while before surrendering to whichever client I was seeing. I got lost in the details: old-fashioned wrought-iron gas lanterns, ornate brass door handles, matching flower boxes hanging from every windowsill, wide limestone staircases with thick, curved banisters stretching from the street up to the parlor floor. The drapes were often left wide open in the homes along the less-trafficked, more moneyed streets near the promenade, set so close to the road that you could see clear inside and admire the eleven-foot ceilings, dangling crystal chandeliers, grand pianos, and works of art on the walls. I always feared the owners would catch me staring or realize that I'd walked by their home four times in ten minutes, but I couldn't help it.

But every few blocks, tucked between these manicured beauties, I stumbled upon an eyesore covered in dead vines, with dirty windows. The number on the crumbling façade was usually the one I was looking for. I never knew what I might find once inside: decades of unchecked hoarding, signs of elder abuse or severe neglect, other evidence of longtime dysfunction made worse by the ravages of dementia. I once walked into a massive brownstone overlooking the promenade and found the floor of the ground level missing. It had caved into the basement years earlier, leaving a gaping hole in the middle of my client's home. She never had the money to replace it but instead worked out a system of holding on to the wall and other semistationary objects as she made her way along the four-foot ledge of wood paneling left around the perimeter. Like a fool, I set out after her, turning back only after the tamped-down layer of newspapers and magazines lining her narrow path began to slide beneath my feet. She wasn't my only client who was property-rich and cash-poor.

I wanted to get back to the office quickly to have five minutes to freshen up in the bathroom and swing by Hot Bagels & Deli, which sold bagels with butter for $1.09, before trekking off to job number two in the Village: moonlighting as a hostess and reservationist at Babbo, one of New York City's busiest restaurants. I didn't know I'd be hostessing when I left my apartment in the morning; I only agreed to cover the shift about an hour before my visit to Mr. Stein, when George, the maître d', called and asked me to come in, so I wasn't wearing my most comfortable hostess shoes. I had on dumpy, cream-colored pumps with soles like flimsy cardboard, and after a full day of running around Brooklyn, it felt like someone had taken a mallet to the balls of my feet. The skin on the back of my right heel was already red and tender—it would break soon, but far be it from me to pass up earning an extra seventy bucks.

"I'm going up to see Mr. Stein," I announced to the doorman at 101 Clark as I breezed past him and into the elevator.

He looked up from his newspaper and said, "I haven't seen that one come down in a long, long time."

That was never something you wanted to hear as you were about to enter an elderly stranger's home for the first time.

When I reached the eighteenth floor, the door to apartment 18F was ajar. Many clients propped open their front doors when they knew someone was coming. Much more terrifying than the potential of being robbed was the very real threat of falling and breaking a hip as they rushed to answer in what was considered a reasonable amount of time. Breaking a hip was no joke. At best, it meant a three-month stint in some Medicaid-funded hellhole rehab center, probably the one way out past the last stop on the L train with the low ceilings, fluorescent lighting, and shit-brown carpeting so matted that it looked wet. At worst, a broken hip meant never coming home.

I leaned in close to peer through the crack in the door, and the smell hit me hard. This was a Tiger Balm visit, and I did not come prepared.

Tiger Balm, a potent ointment used by athletes to relieve sore muscles, was so chock-full of camphor and menthol that if you put even the smallest dab of it under your nose, it was all you'd smell for hours. It was similar to the stuff used by morticians when working on cadavers, and I hoped to God by New York City sanitation workers. A single swipe on your Cupid's bow was like being forced to breathe with your nose stuck inside a jar of Vicks VapoRub, and there were times in life when it was the preferred state, like at Mr. Stein's home. Except I didn't bring any.

Dumbass, Kim. I should have known better but was too concerned with showing up to job number two semi-fed and somewhat put together. I missed all the obvious clues. He sounded all right over the phone, but what had I expected him to say? It wasn't like a man old enough to be my grandfather was going to tell the chipper, twenty-six-year-old social worker who called him up out of the blue, "*Sure*, you can come over—but enter at your own risk! The place smells like urine, the laundry hasn't been done in months, and the pile of rancid garbage bags stacked up in the kitchen is now covered with a smattering of baby roaches. I can barely get out of this wheelchair, which makes transferring to the toilet nearly impossible, so I've taken to relieving myself into a mop bucket filled with kitty litter, and I don't remember the last time I was able to climb into the tub for a bath. I haven't the strength to so much as crack a window, so I'm at a loss as to how all the flies got in, but sure, *little girl*, come on over!"

I was still standing in the doorway when I spotted Mr. Stein sitting in his wheelchair toward the back of the dark apartment, patiently waiting for me. Between my first inhale and my first look into his stoic blue eyes, I knew there would be no time for that bagel or for brushing my teeth, my hair, tapping some concealer under my eyes, even dashing to CVS to spray my clothes with Febreze.

It was early fall 2005. This was not what I imagined doing when I came to New York. I moved from Clifton Park five years earlier, in 2000, to get a master's in social work. I never stopped to think about what job I might land, or how much I'd be paid. I just wanted to get to the big city, and continuing with school made for the cleanest exit from the upstate suburbs. The deal I made with my parents was that after graduation, I'd stay for one year to get that "living and working in New York City" experience to pad my résumé. But I knew before I even arrived that I was never going back.

Social work didn't require a Mensa membership, but it wasn't easy. Nothing about standing up for a forty-five-minute visit to avoid the bedbugs that had infiltrated every porous surface of a client's apartment was easy. Especially when trying to maintain my composure, not insult my client, particularly when their dignity might be hanging on by a thread. It called for a fair amount of empathy, a bona fide backbone, a strong stomach, and the patience of a saint. I wasn't exactly locking myself into a rigorous intellectual commitment, just an emotional one, and more pressingly, a financial one. I might not have been good at math—I borrowed forty thousand dollars at 6.25 percent interest to attend one of the most expensive schools in the country, to earn a degree for a job that paid thirty-five thousand dollars a year—but getting a good read on people and helping them maneuver out of whatever mess they'd gotten into came natural to me. I was good at helping people figure out their shit, usually with enough time to stop them from getting evicted, having their gas and electricity shut off, or breaking a leg after tripping on a goddamn throw rug, only to be found two days later by their doorman, lying on their kitchen floor, dehydrated and half-conscious.

I'd always felt a pull toward people in haphazard states. When faced with someone in trouble I often found myself operating on autopilot doing what others couldn't do, wouldn't do, or were smart enough to avoid in the first place. I'd been like that for as long as I could remember. When I was five, I'd watched from the curb as the older kids in the neighborhood raced their bikes down the steepest hill in our development. One kid lost control as he flew down the hill—his pedals began to spin wildly, forcing his legs out spread-eagle—and I witnessed at eye level as his front wheel split a small bird in two. Shrieks, giggles, and *eeeewwws* erupted as the kids fanned out from the kill zone, but I went over to it. I could barely bring myself to look at the mess of rusty-red guts and feathers, but I didn't want the little guy to be alone. Who knows how long I would have stayed crouched down beside him had not my older sister, Kelly, stormed over and yanked me up off the pavement.

People in need never failed to pick up on this emotional radar. Even complete strangers seemed to have zero qualms about pouring their hearts out to me, unsolicited. A Vedic astrologer once told me, "Perhaps others find it easy to confide in you because you are so secretive with regards to yourself." I could get anyone to divulge their deepest fears and most guarded secrets as though asking them for the time, but nobody—*nobody* knew anything about me.

On the nights I covered the hostess shift, I needed to get to Babbo by 5:30 p.m. at the latest. We opened to the public at 5:00 p.m., and thirty minutes of running the door solo was all George had patience for. Every night, even on the most frigid and miserable Monday in January, a line of would-be diners formed outside as early as 4:15 p.m. and quickly stretched down the block. Ice storms, the blackout of 2003—didn't matter—they were out there. When George asked me to hostess on a weeknight, he was desperate. And I always said yes because I was desperate.

However, I couldn't leave Heights and Boerum Council before 5:00 p.m., and social workers were not to leave directly from a client's home—the workday had to end at headquarters and not a minute before five. This was a direct result of a yearslong silent feud between Barbara, the executive director, and Rosie, because Rosie snuck out of the office every day at 4:55 p.m. Some days it was more like 4:50 p.m. Every so often, early in the morning before Barbara arrived, Rosie slipped off her tiny canvas boat shoes and climbed onto the couch in the lobby, stretching her five-foot-nothing frame up the wall, pulling down the clock, and turning the hands forward five minutes. So this left me just thirty-five minutes to ride nine stops on the R train from Court Street to West 8th Street in the Village, speed-walk across Washington Square Park, and pull back the two heavy wooden doors of 110 Waverly Place, where the sea of densely packed bodies clogged up the entryway to Babbo.

Tonight was no different. I yanked open the second door and managed to plant my right foot down on the restaurant floor while checking my phone. It was 5:31 p.m., but it would be 5:34 p.m. before I was able to squeeze my way through the clusterfuck space we affectionately referred to as "the pickle"—a narrow strip running the length of our ten-seat bar from the front door to the maître d's podium, where George was guarding the entrance to the dining room and waiting for me. The look on his face told me that he knew I wouldn't make it over until 5:34 p.m., too. His bare head and dark-suited shoulders formed a little mound atop the podium. His big blue eyes protruded a bit, and he kept them halfway closed as he watched guests make their awkward way toward him. This was his poker face when working the door. It was only when you got him talking about something he truly loved like his pugs, Roxanne and Oberon, or the theater, that you'd see his eyes all the way open.

"Thought you said you could get here by 5:15, Kim?"

"You know I can't get here before 5:30 on a weeknight, George."

I threw my jacket and bag in the empty coat closet, then stood inside it for a moment to catch my breath before taking my place beside George. He rummaged around in the podium's top drawer and after a few seconds pulled out a small, crinkly bag of Swedish Fish. The night almost always went better if George was kept happy, so we hostesses and coat checkers began bringing him treats. He was partial to the Dove chocolates with the inspirational messages printed inside the foil wrapper, but Swedish Fish were by far his favorite. Without taking his eyes off the door, he slid his hand toward me and dropped a single fish into my open palm.

Babbo was no ordinary restaurant and in general was not for the faint of heart. It wasn't much to look at from the outside. All that set it apart from the other carriage houses lining the south side of Waverly Place was its pale yellow paint and the black and red iron lettering screwed into the facade above the ground-floor windows. It was the sort of spot easily missed. The building sits on the northwest corner of Washington Square Park, just down the street from NYU, and I must have schlepped past it fifty times, lugging my backpack stuffed with a copy of *Ego Psychology and Social Work Practice*, the *DSM-IV* pocket guide, and dirty coffee cups before a classmate pointed it out as the place where she'd just found part-time work as a hostess.

"The chef there—the one with the red ponytail—is famous. He has his own show on the Food Network. The restaurant pays eleven dollars an hour and Gwyneth Paltrow had dinner there with Luke Wilson last week," she boasted. "They still need to hire one more person."

I'd never heard of the Food Network, but I certainly knew who Gwyneth Paltrow and Luke Wilson were. And $11.00 an hour was a big step up from the $6.90 I made cataloging microfiche at the Bobst Library as part of my university's work study program, so I walked into Babbo the next day with my résumé.

I met with the day manager, Brad. He had long, wavy hair pulled back in a ponytail and wore a tie-dyed T-shirt. He looked out of place sitting among the tables draped in white linen, as fast-moving waiters wearing ties set the tables with candles and silverware. He asked me if I wanted "an espresso or cappuccino." I didn't drink either but said cappuccino to come off as sophisticated. Then he left to go make my cappuccino himself. He was treating me more like a guest than someone on a job interview. In the forty-five minutes that we spoke, he didn't once bring up the job I was applying for—part-time reservationist and hostess. He talked only of the owners: Mario Batali—the chef with the TV show—and Joe Bastianich, who handled the restaurant's wine program and whose family owned two vineyards in Italy. Brad made a point of telling me twice that both men were Italian, and when I asked him when they came to the United States, he clarified that he meant "authentic Italian bloodlines," as though they were racehorses. He spoke of them, and the restaurant itself, with a kind of over-the-top reverence. All I'd thought about before I walked in was the money, but as Brad continued, I found myself wondering, *Where the hell am I?* But it was drawing me in.

I had a stint waiting tables at the Denny's in Clifton Park until my parents made me quit—I made the mistake of telling them that a few of the managers were known for trying to sleep with the servers—but Babbo was not Denny's. It wasn't exactly Tavern on the Green or The Russian Tea Room either. Brad said Ruth Reichel of the *New York Times* gave them a three-star review shortly after Babbo opened in 1998. I nodded and pretended that I knew who Ruth was and understood why the review was important. I sat up a little straighter and self-consciously ran my hands through my hair. Working at Babbo was starting to seem much more serious than I imagined, but I was already hooked on the idea of $11.00 an hour and getting to see what Gwyneth Paltrow wore in person.

"Nobody cooks like Mario. Nobody does what we do. Everyone wants to eat here. We don't serve things like chicken parm—that's not Italian."

I wanted to come across as educated and worldly, so I told him, "I'm going to be a therapist eventually. I'm getting my master's degree across the street and might attend the Gestalt Center for Psychotherapy after."

Brad nodded, shrugged. He said, "I'm really a masseur, but I injured my hand, so now I'm here."

There was a *Maximum Occupancy* sign hanging on the wall next to the coat closet, but nobody cared what it said because it was of zero importance to everyone in the room. More people were lined up outside than could actually fit in the pickle. For the rest of the night, fresh bodies foisted themselves inside every few minutes, like a club—one in, one out. To maneuver through the only way in and out of the restaurant, people were forced to press up against complete strangers, sliding past random chests, breasts, shoulders, hips, the warm protruding bellies on the sweaty guys in suits who rushed down from Midtown to be first in line for a walk-in table. Everyone got close enough to smell what was typically detected only in more intimate scenarios—shampoo, deodorant, freshly applied lipstick, whether it was Altoids they were sucking on or Tic Tacs. The guests smelled pretty good; like fabric softener and Cool Mint Listerine. It was Babbo, after all. Most folks made a real effort.

The people crammed in the pickle were willing to wait for two-plus hours—sometimes in four-inch stilettos—for a seat at the bar or for one of the few small tables kept for walk-ins. The walk-in tables weren't very high off the ground, so eating a meal at one meant enduring random pocketbooks, asses, and plates of other people's food intermittently lopped onto yours—a rare piece of real estate worth its weight in gold. The servers and back waiters ran plates and tall, wobbly flutes of expensive bubbly on trays in and out of the area all night.

Sometimes when stuck in place and waiting for the bodies to shift, I thought up possible escape routes should there be a fire, or more likely a stampede. My best bet would be to haul it down the staircase in front of the coat closet that led into the basement, push open the garbage hatch, and climb out into the street.

Something odd always happened about twenty minutes into working the hostess shift. Time had a way of passing strangely on the floor, as if it slowed down and sped up simultaneously until it was impossible to keep track. This happened even though we watched the clock obsessively: *Are the 7:30s down? Who does the 9:00 six-top think they are, showing up thirty minutes early with an extra person? Where the hell is the 8:15 Ben Stiller four-top?* I would forget myself—my worries, cares, whatever I was doing tomorrow, the fact that my feet were swelling up out of my shoes—I was nothing except for the task I was doing the very moment I was doing it: running a check from the bartender up the steep staircase to a server on the second floor; taping a little orange coat check ticket securely onto a guest's shopping bag; helping Kate Hudson slip out of her ivory, floor-length coat; arguing with George.

At some point during the night, I remembered. It happened in an instant: the music stopped, and I snapped back into being myself again. And even if it was a rough night where nothing went according to plan and my feet were pounding, my T-zone looked like I swiped it with cooking oil, and I couldn't shake the sense of being dirty—as one would after working a fifteen-hour day—I was always left with an overwhelming sense of feeling *good*. Like there was nowhere else I'd rather be.

I had done the two-job shuffle for more than four years. When Brad offered me the hostess job, I told him I only needed to work at Babbo for six months, until graduation, after which I'd get a "real job in social work." Brad knew a naïve and ignorant NYU kid when he saw one, but instead of putting me in my place, he gave a hearty laugh and said, "You might want to keep a shift or two and make a little money on the side."

Fast-forward, and I didn't *want* to make a little money on the side, I needed to. Badly. I often still came up short at the end of the month. I'd panic and start calling my fellow hospitality workers, looking for shifts to pick up. I'd sit down and figure out what could be paid late—just like I did with my clients who lived off a ridiculously small amount of money, like $637 a month from social security. I'd think about how much free food I could get from Babbo before my next paycheck. Maybe it wasn't the rib eye I was eating each night, but I made the most out of what was in the walk-in. Sometimes when I worked the evening phone shift down in the basement, the guys in the kitchen would send down the "mistake" plates, like when a new server fired the wrong dish and we ended up with a plate of beef cheek ravioli or braised octopus that no one ordered.

But I did stupid things, too, like heading to the bar at Balthazar after my last shift of the week and blowing sixty dollars on two glasses of wine and an appetizer, even if I had to put it on my Visa. It was hard watching guests do that sort of thing all night. Some nights it was all I wanted to do, even after working fifteen hours.

I had an ulterior motive for taking the shift after my visit with Mr. Stein. Craig Bierko, who played one of Sarah Jessica Parker's boyfriends on *Sex and the City*, was on the reservation book, and I was off-my-rocker crazy about him. He always came in with Ryan Reynolds and Robert Sean Leonard, and the trio was hands-down the friendliest bunch of guys from the Hollywood crowd. They flirted with the hostesses and coat check girls incessantly, talking to us as though we were actually important, with absolutely no hint of douchebag entitlement. They always showed up happy, like they knew how lucky they were to live the way we all imagined they did as successful actors.

Craig always teased me about my sweater—I was usually wearing the same one when he came in, as I only had two good tops: beige, fitted cashmere with magenta flowers and a trail of tiny rhinestones running down the front. Craig, Ryan, and Robert insisted on carrying their drinks from the bar to their table so as not to burden me, totally unaware that nothing irritated Mario more than the sight of a guest carrying their own glass through the dining room. "Just *take it* from them," he said to me once, all patience lost. So I began doing just that—pulling the cold, wet crystal right out of their hands before they had time to protest. I usually kept crushes close to the vest, but since there was no chance of anything actually happening with Craig, I didn't feel compelled to hide it—so everyone knew that I adored him. Even George.

Even the guests who weren't famous but were somehow different from me, I found intriguing. Trim, older European men in perfectly tailored suits who bore no hint of a middle-aged waist and sat with their legs fully crossed. Brazilian families with little ones under the age of six, dining on a 10:30 p.m. table; the children always ordered straight off the menu. You could spot the super-wealthy native New Yorkers dead-on. They looked like they belonged on a film set: done up, but with a subtlety to their put-togetherness that was evidence of a certain kind of lifestyle, one that required long-term maintenance. Their skin was poreless. Their fit, toned bodies were sculpted to near perfection. Every hair in place. Their black clothes didn't look like my black clothes—when they wore black, the pigment was so rich, it looked like ink that hadn't dried. These people ate at restaurants like

Babbo for no particular reason. Just dinner on a Tuesday. The men showed up in Ascot Chang dress shirts, the women in Chanel tweed and pearl earrings the size of Ping-Pong balls. The women might be in their fifties but had thirty-something faces and chiseled, size-two bodies. I'd never seen anything like them before. People like that didn't exist where I came from.

Not that I came from nothing. Clifton Park was a middle-class suburb—a bedroom community in upstate New York between Albany and Saratoga. It was my parents' idea of a great place to live, and they were quite content, puttering all over town in their matching red Volvos. They went to the Shop 'n Save, where my sister Kelly bagged groceries all through high school and college, or Boscov's, a discount department store where my mom was on a first-name basis with the saleswomen. She popped in every few days looking for deals on socks, underwear, bath towels, reduced-price Jones of New York knitwear, Nautica pajama sets, Tommy Hilfiger golf shirts for my dad—he loved them so much, he often spontaneously pointed to the logo across the chest and announced, "It's Tommy Hilfiger," as if from the ready-to-wear collection and not the bargain-basement staples produced for the masses. My mom's motivation for buying up all these items so cheaply was to justify spending eighty-five dollars on her favorite Lancôme night cream. I once pointed out that if she added up all the money spent on the socks, shirts, and pajamas, it would cost the same as if she sprang for the really good stuff, which I'd recently learned was Crème de la Mer from a salesgirl at Saks with skin like a newborn's, but she didn't hop onboard with my logic.

"Don't you take out that kind of money to go to New York," my mother said.

But that was precisely what I did.

I worked the day phone shift on Saturdays in addition to picking up hostess and evening reservation work, and there were worse places to be on a Saturday morning than Babbo. Though considered small by restaurant standards, when you were in Babbo's open, three-story space, you got a sense of what a grand old home it had probably once been. There was a six-foot-wide steep center staircase anchoring the room and separating the kitchen in the back from the first-floor dining room and the pickle. The second-floor dining room had a massive skylight, so in the morning we kept the lights off and let the sunlight pour down the staircase as though it were a big tree trunk. Mario and Joe wanted to keep the lights off to save on the electricity bill, but I'd have kept them off regardless. The rays picked up all the tiny dust particles in the air, adding to the twinkling effect of the space.

I rented the smallest of three bedrooms in a walk-up in East Midtown that might or might not have mice and came complete with a neighbor who thought it perfectly fine to operate his woodworking business on the landing between our units, his buzz saw whirling not two feet from my front door. So the mornings at Babbo were a bit of luxury. Outside, Greenwich Village hummed, but inside I sat in relative quiet. All I heard was the faint clanging of pots, the pulse of the dishwasher's hose, and some muffled Spanish from the guys in the kitchen at my back. The guests had all been gone for hours, but a bit of their energy remained, like embers left over from the raging wildfire of excitement and desperation just seven hours earlier.

One Saturday morning, Mario scared the ever-living shit out of me. He'd been lying on the banquette by the windows, out cold, still in his chef whites. I mistook his broad back for the daily delivery from White Plains Linen. There was nothing more terrifying than being alone in that calm, quiet space and suddenly seeing what you thought was a stack of freshly laundered white tablecloths and napkins rise up like a ghost and walk out of the restaurant without saying a word.

On Saturdays, I tried to come in around 9:00 a.m., an hour before we opened the phone lines, to grab a grapefruit from the walk-in, put on a pot of coffee, spray down the phones with Lysol, and get a plate of whatever the overnight porters prepared for their version of family meal. Family meal was when the entire staff sat down and ate together before the start of service, and it usually flowed into the pre-service meeting where George gave everyone the scoop on who was coming in that night. The overnight porters broke for a meal in the early morning, right around the time I arrived.

Most importantly, I locked the front door. Otherwise, people from the park came in and swiped a bottle of whatever was on the end of the bar. I suspected they were all MICA (mentally ill, chemically addicted), and because I was a mental health worker they didn't scare me, but being the sole witness to their brazen thievery did. We had a saying in social work: "Never let the client get between you and the door," but that was exactly the setup at Babbo. Someone could put a knife in me and be back in the park before Mario so much as rolled over.

Prospective guests also showed up before 10:00 a.m., and I wasn't so sure some of them wouldn't stab me either if I couldn't give them a reservation. Some drove in from the suburbs of New Jersey or Connecticut, hoping to make a reservation for whatever date we were releasing that morning—always one month from that exact date. What kind of person would drive all the way into Manhattan from Jersey on a weekend just to make a dinner reservation? A smart one. Because that was what you had to do to get a table. Some of the more zealous folks resorted to banging on the windows. Everyone assumed that our lack of open tables was a publicity stunt and that we were intent on shutting out the average person, which was ridiculous—the more bodies we pumped in and out every night, the more money the front of the house made.

It took less than sixty seconds to book a single reservation. If I skipped the pleasantries and got right down to business, I was done in thirty-five seconds. That meant I could fill an entire night—down to every last 11:15 p.m. for two—in under forty minutes. By 10:40 a.m., less than an hour after letting them fly, all reservations for the corresponding night exactly one month out were gone. And for the next seven hours and twenty minutes of my shift, I went back to doing social work—more specifically, crisis intervention. Once, I got a call from a woman named Deborah, area code 201, who, when I told her we were already full that Christmas Eve, lost her shit completely and belted out, "Well, fuck you—*FUCK OFF!*"

I slammed down the phone fast on that one. Not out of anger, but because I didn't want our pastry chef, Gina, to see how badly my hands were shaking. Gina had been sitting across from me on table twenty, quietly stewing while she pretended to tally up the receipts from her morning purchases at the Green Market.

"*Fuck* Mario and Joe," she said, pouring me a glass of blood orange juice, which was off-limits to the staff. "Do they know the shit you put up with all day?"

She turned and headed into the kitchen before I could answer. Not that I wanted to, because getting into a Mario-and-Joe-bashing session with Gina took a certain amount of skill and effort if I wanted to come out alive. Tip the scales too far in alignment with her and I might ignite that dormant loyalty she still had for Mario, but scratch the surface too lightly with my grievances and I ran the risk of being branded a traitor to my fellow line workers. She told me once that she'd thought about going to law school before becoming a chef, and she would have made a great litigator.

I heard the swing of the kitchen door and Gina returned, carrying a plate piled high with scrambled eggs, buttered toast, half a roasted tomato, fried potatoes with green peppers and onions, sausage, and one of the flourless chocolate hazelnut cakes she was famous for, still nice and cold from the walk-in. On days when I'd been thoroughly raked over, Gina made me breakfast. She was the de facto mother of Babbo, and even looked the part of a caretaker—plump, with doe eyes that gave the false impression of being mild-mannered. Like any good Italian mother, she had a talent for sleuthing out everyone's business. Gina was completely piped in to Babbo's subterranean layer of gossip, half-truths, and surreptitious happenings. She always knew who was sleeping with whom, who was about to get fired, which server was skimming from the pooled cash tips, who was about to leave to work for rival restaurateur Danny Meyer, and she was absolutely convinced that one of our chefs sold drugs out of the second-floor apartment that Mario and Joe kept for out-of-town friends and employees who came over from the winery in Italy.

Gina was smarter than me, and for this reason it took us years to become friends. When I started at Babbo I was twenty-two, fresh from the suburbs and pretty ignorant of life outside of them. I had nothing remotely interesting to say to her. But she spent an hour of her Saturday sitting across from me, planning her menu and making grocery lists, and over the years she warmed to me. We bonded over crazy would-be guests who barged in yelling, "Your phone lines are broken! I've been calling for hours and I can't get through!" as though I were a 911 operator. Our friendship had an uneven power dynamic, but because I was the baby in my family, her authority didn't bother me. Back when I first started working at Babbo, she loathed my wide-eyed, optimistic view—of the restaurant, the city itself, the big show we all put on when celebrities came in. She'd been the pastry chef since the place had opened and was now disillusioned with the mystique of Babbo as a hangout for rock stars and Mario's famous friends. We all saw through it to some degree, yet it didn't stop us from falling for it every night. In what other scenario would you remember with laserlike accuracy the five or six arbitrary words that some stranger threw out to you as a formality—"Ooohh my God, everything was *amazing*! Loved, loved, loved it—we'll be back! You guys are *the best*!" A kind word from the likes of Diane Keaton, Jake Gyllenhaal, or Elton John made even the most disinterested heart thump wildly. Their presence alone was disarming, but their individual attention, however fleeting, became crystallized in my brain—I clung to each memory as though God himself came down from heaven and shared the secrets of the universe with me. Even Gina had her favorites. She stuck around all night when the Black Crowes came in, just to visit with them after bringing out their dessert, whether they ordered any or not.

Sometimes, I looked around at my colleagues' faces when a celebrity walked through the door and began their Everest-like trek through the pickle. Some servers looked down at the floor. Others pretended to be absorbed in their work. These coworkers didn't dare demean themselves with stares of unearned admiration, but they didn't seem able to treat celebrities like regular guests either. It was almost as if these coworkers wanted to hide, avoiding the famous guests altogether. When it was over, the whole charade left me feeling a bit uneasy, similar to when I did something wrong as a kid but never got caught. Because the very thing that created unease was also what made being at Babbo so much fun. It was a lot easier to surrender to the excitement and accept the part I got to play, especially after a day spent helping clients like Mr. Stein. Being a part of this place—*an insider*—was what really kept me working there. I could have gotten a part-time job anywhere, and truth be told, I was not a good hostess. I was afraid of carrying trays. I didn't even know the positions on the tables—"table fifty-one, position two," one of my coworkers would say as they shoved a tray with a Negroni into my hand. I had no clue which guest was sitting in position two; I hovered the tray over their table and watched for someone's eyes to pop.

I was allowed to work hostess shifts for two reasons: I was reliable, always willing to cover a shift when someone called out sick because I always needed the money; and I was decorative. Restaurants hired pretty hostesses. We had to look neat, put together, but we were never to overdress the guests—fat chance of that. When hostessing, I had to appear sweet and pleasing, even when an asshole guest well into his sixties grabbed my arm, hard, and pulled me in close as he spat out, "They don't make you wait fifteen minutes for your table at the French Laundry, my dear." Once, a well-known punk band came in, and some jackass at their table patted another hostess on the ass as she was trying to set down their drinks. They thought it was pretty funny until Nina, the floor manager, stopped by. Whatever she said to them did the trick because they behaved like they were in church the rest of the night. I always felt like a bit of a dolly, prancing guests through the floor to their table, looking back midway to ask, "Is this your first time here with us?" with a vacant smile, trying not to grunt as I pushed in the chairs of fully grown adults as far as they'd go, which was essential in keeping the pathway from the dining room to the kitchen and the bathrooms clear.

The servers, the back waiters, George, they could scan the dining room and collect all the clues left by inanimate objects like a stale plate of untouched chickpea bruschetta, a half-empty bottle of wine or a dessert plate wiped clean with a finger, and in five seconds they could tell you exactly how much longer a party would remain at their table. I could never do that. I didn't notice these things.

I saw the four-top who berated George for giving away their table, even though they showed up thirty minutes late, wedged in place at the podium and unable to move away from him. They started to quiet. The color drained from their faces. Then there was a beat: a decision being made. Whether to mellow or hold fast to their self-righteous indignation. I saw Kate Winslet and Sam Mendes, relieved to be sitting upstairs and away from the prying eyes of those packed into the pickle. Beats me how they convinced George to put them up there—all celebrities were seated downstairs, no matter what, so everyone who came in had a chance to gawk at them. I saw the middle-aged tourists from the Midwest—no doubt big fans of Mario's Food Network show *Molto Mario*. They likely planned their trip around whatever date they were able to nab a reservation. My coworkers and I poked fun at them a little—they showed up in T-shirts, shorts, and fanny packs, and yelped with delight at the sight of Mario's red ponytail swinging in and out of the kitchen window. But their joy was contagious. I couldn't help but feel good, even if they embodied everything that made me run from Clifton Park like it was on fire.

And then suddenly I saw no one. The last of the 11:15s were down. The pickle had emptied, save for our bar regular, Tall Paul, and the drunk couple still working their wine on positions one and two (I knew the bar seats). Jimmy Day, the bartender, was filling up a couple of plastic quart containers with beer for the guys in the kitchen. I scanned the dining room and slowly realized that Craig Bierko and his pretty blond girlfriend left hours ago. The only evidence of how I felt when I came through the door at 5:31 p.m. was when I got home after midnight and took off my clothes, pried my cream-colored shoes from my feet, and noticed all the blood on the inside of my right heel.

two

KICK THE CABINET

"*Fah-lahn-ghee-nah*," Cillian sounded out slowly. He grabbed the first of three glasses lined up on the bar, each one filled a third of the way with a pale gold wine. He gave it a swirl, scraping the glass base against the white marble bartop, and then sniffed before handing it to me. I put my nose all the way into the glass, like he did. It smelled like peaches—all white wine smelled like peaches to me, but I didn't dare tell Cillian that.

"Now you say it, Kimmy."

He might as well have asked me to say something in Chinese. Even though by December 2009, I'd worked at Babbo for almost nine years—one while still at NYU, another seven after graduation in tandem with my social work—I still didn't know a thing about Italian wines, including how to correctly pronounce their names.

"*Come on*," he coaxed, his blue eyes hungry.

Otto's big red barroom was quiet. The usual soundtrack was a medley of drunk NYU students, thirty-somethings fighting to hear one another on their first date, and the clang of silverware hitting the floor. But it was after 11:00 p.m. Cillian and I practically had the bar to ourselves.

I wasn't supposed to be there. Employees had to ask permission from Mario or Joe if we wanted to eat at one of the sister restaurants within the B&B Group. Mario knew we were all friends and that employees charged each other for half the food and wine we actually ordered. Cutting items off the bill was easy to do at Otto—it was casual, was always packed, and served easy-to-prepare, low-cost items like pizza, salumi and cheese boards, and little ramekins filled with chilled side dishes like marinated cuttlefish and eggplant caponata.

The GMs—general managers—unofficially sat above this rule, and since I was with Cillian, the GM of Babbo, I wasn't worried. Besides, we were on an important mission: get me up to speed on Italian wine as soon as possible.

"Say it once more? Or give me the quartino list so I can see how it's spelled." I squirmed in my high-top chair.

"Nope." He shook his head playfully. He was in his element, teaching me his favorite subject. I had to give him something.

I eked out, "Fil—anne—gin—ce—o?"

"Ha!" Cillian smacked his hand down on the bar as his upper body bounced in his chair. His eyes squeezed shut, and his face filled up with his crooked bottom teeth. He was nearing fifty, though you'd never know it save for the buzz cut he wore to make the most of his thinning, light brown hair. Every night, he swept up and down Babbo's steep staircase like a man of twenty-five, and even farther down into the basement to fetch one revered bottle after another. He had once been the wine director, and talking to guests tableside about wine was where he really shone—he was one of the best teachers I ever encountered. But when the old GM burned out, Cillian was christened to the top job and now dealt with the grease trap backing up and flooding the basement, the POS system crashing, the HVAC breaking in the middle of service on a ninety-five-degree night in July, Christmas decorations falling from the ceiling and crashing onto guests' heads as they stood waiting in the pickle, people passing out in the single-occupancy bathroom, and lead-footed firefighters storming up the staircase with axes in hand. But Babbo had become the undisputed pinnacle of Italian food and wine in New York City, and he was in charge of the show. He loved his appointed role.

Cillian was never not working. He probably hadn't had a day off in months but agreed to help me that night regardless.

"How can you be this bad at pronouncing Italian?" he teased, his eyes tearing.

It was four years after my first visit to Mr. Stein's apartment. I was still working two jobs—social worker by day and hunkering down in the Babbo basement making reservations by night. But a few months prior, I had finally stumbled upon something that could maybe rescue me from both. I was in the running to become Joe's new executive assistant, hence the desperate need to finally get schooled on Italian wine.

The previous year, in 2008, I came close to breaking out of the two-job shuffle. I'd taken a new job as a social worker/paralegal at an elder law firm whose founding partner had close ties to Heights and Boerum Council. My then-boyfriend, Liam, came from a family of lawyers.

We decided I'd become an elder law attorney—this was the best way to get down to one job, aside from us eventually moving in together and getting married. The position paid slightly more than Heights and Boerum Council, but not enough to give up my Babbo shifts.

Liam and I knew each other from college. One night in the summer of 2005, years after graduation, we ran into each other at the Ginger Man bar in Midtown. I knew when I saw his familiar, safe face, and the way his brown eyes shone when he looked at me, that we were going to start dating. I knew I was going to let him in.

I had a hard time connecting with random guys in bars in New York. I didn't know how to do my part to keep things moving along. I hadn't had a lot of boyfriends growing up—I wanted to be in a relationship but was terrified of getting that close to someone. Some people couldn't handle intimate scenarios with strangers, like client/social worker relationships, but I couldn't handle intimate scenarios in my personal life. And it didn't help that social work was practically devoid of eligible young men.

Liam knew how to be a boyfriend. He took on the responsibility of molding us into a couple and I was happy to come along for the ride. He was *fun*. We ate too much, drank too much—he coaxed me to McSorley's Old Ale House at noon on a Saturday, turning me into someone who begged coworkers to cover my shifts, and a few hours later we'd spill out into the sunlight on East 7th Street, buzzed, forearms sticky from the grimy wooden tables. We reveled in our shared history and mutual friends. We were a good couple on paper, but part of our attraction was that we were both miserable when we reconnected. He'd just failed the bar exam for the fourth time, and I was drowning in student loan debt and juggling two jobs.

We fell apart once ring shopping came up. He ended up leaving me for an older female colleague at the DA's office, who left him for a cop shortly afterward. When our relationship ended, so did the notion of my going to law school and my plan for how to pay for it, and my exit from the Babbo basement. Coming so close to getting out of my rocky financial situation only to have it yanked away was the most distressing part of the situation. That, and I lost my best friend.

Before I'd left Heights and Boerum Council, I went to see one of my favorite clients, Ms. Keller, who'd been admitted to the Cobble Hill Health Center. Her gray-blond hair looked yellow and dirty against the white pillow. She lay on the hospital bed, moving her arms, legs, and head spasmodically, trying to get comfortable. Snapped onto her neck like a Lego was a square plastic knob. I'd never seen anyone on a ventilator before, but could tell she was in pain. Her gaze bored into mine as if begging me to pop that hard, unnatural thing off her throat.

It wasn't easy seeing Ms. Keller like this. Before, she had needed little help, maintained a neat and orderly apartment owned by the Jehovah's Witnesses—"very kind landlords, and awfully good at fixing things." She'd served in the WACs as a young woman. She was an *easy* client; a pleasure to visit. Just required weekly assistance with grocery shopping and preparing meals. On the walk back to the office, I started crying uncontrollably, but was completely confused as to why. Even though I had just seen a person I cared about in the throes of suffering during what I knew would be her last days on Earth, I didn't understand why I was crying. What I did know was that I felt horribly guilty. What had I failed to do for her? But that wasn't quite the extent of it, because under all that was relief that I was able to walk in the other direction.

"You're sizzled," Rosie said, when I told her. She said it a few more times as the year went on. She was right; I was burned out. Social workers, especially when new to the field and lacking experience, took pride in their ability to handle tough situations. But looking back, I'm not sure how well I was really handling encounters. Perhaps I was just disassociating.

I began to spend more time at Babbo after the breakup. Aside from my job at the firm, I had nothing else to do. I came in to work the evening phone shift one night and was stopped by George at the podium. He kept his head down and looked at the floor as he said softly, "Did you hear about Gina?"

While I was busy ditching my Saturday phone shifts and downing lights and darks at McSorley's with Liam, Gina was diagnosed with cancer. The doctor knew it was bad and scheduled her for surgery immediately. They opened her up and found tumors everywhere. It was a nine-hour operation. They said it was stage IV, and that thirteen percent of people with her diagnosis would live past five years.

The phone lines rang unanswered half the night; I was useless. Gina was only twelve years older than me.

Gina returned to her shifts thin and gaunt, a glass of dark green, pulpy juice always in hand. She said it was puréed kale, and drank while pinching her nose. We talked a little about what she'd been through, her battles with the insurance company, but mostly she asked about me, so I told her about Liam.

"I never liked him," Gina said, as she pushed the phone away—almost out of my reach—to make room for a plate of jiggly saffron panna cotta and a warm blueberry crostata. By now, it was more important to her that I eat properly while at Babbo than actually answer the phone lines. "Don't stop eating over a loser who can't pass the bar."

We talked about what was next for me, now that Liam and attending law school were no longer options. I couldn't believe I was back to square one, facing the same dilemmas I'd been wrestling with for some time: to make more money, get the hell out of social work and the Babbo basement, and be around men my age.

I could have killed all three of those birds years ago by training to be a server. Servers worked four nights a week and made $90,000–$95,000 a year, almost double my current salary. Even the back waiters who barely interacted with guests earned $50,000 or more. It was all in pooled tips, so it wasn't like if one person got stuck with a table who stayed half the night, that server would take home less than everyone else. Everyone hustled, and all front waiters made close to six figures a year.

But something about being a server didn't sit right with me. I bought into the stigma too much. In Clifton Park, being a server or waiter was for people who dropped out of high school and had no other viable career options. It was acceptable only as an after-school or summer job. I told myself that I didn't look down on my friends who worked that position, my Babbo family. But I did. If I didn't think that their job was good enough for me, even if it would've allowed me to pay off my student loans in four years instead of fifteen, what else did it mean? I thought about it a lot, usually when I was checking my bank balance or canceling yet another outing with friends because I'd run out of money. These were coveted and lucrative roles that required real skill—being a server, sommelier, or manager at a place like Babbo—but my ego won out over my wallet every time. I didn't mind being poor so long as I had a professional degree to hide behind.

Besides, people who worked in restaurants began their day in the midafternoon and finished their shifts at midnight or later. What was there to do when you got out of work in the middle of the night?

"It all goes right up their noses," Gina said once, midway through a rant about how little the kitchen staff was paid compared to those who worked the front of the house.

Some of my coworkers lived a little harder than I did. The hours they kept practically called for it. What *did* you do when you finished work in the middle of the night? You drank. You went to a restaurant like Babbo. You ordered food and wine you surely still couldn't afford, and this became your every-night normal. I was sure it would've been mine, had I chosen that path.

It wasn't true of all servers. Some were mothers and fathers supporting families, rushing home to get a little sleep before rising early to drop their kids at school. Some had side dreams they nurtured. But within the industry, blowing that big paycheck on a bottle of wine that you polished off solo before doing lines of coke at Juno in between karaoke songs until the sun came up was definitely a thing. Or so I'd heard. The punishing nature of the work practically screamed for a reward at the end of the night. If I had to deal face-to-face with even one 201-area-code Deborah each night, I'd probably have lived like this.

I felt the same way about the guys who worked at Babbo as I did about being a server: some were great friends, and some were great fun, but I didn't like the idea of seriously dating them—the thought of being tied down to someone who had to hump it for Mario and Joe every night, just like me, turned my stomach. Anchoring myself to one of them felt like further weight in favor of the two-job shuffle. I saw them all as Mario and Joe's yes-men. I never gave the guys at Babbo a chance. That was really stupid, especially when the other industry I spent my time in had zero young men.

There was one exception.

Jesse was a floor manager seven years my junior. He came up from New Orleans after Hurricane Katrina made it impossible for him to finish school at Loyola, and was hired first as a server at Esca, our sister restaurant in the theater district. Jesse was young and beautiful. You either wanted him, wanted to be him, or wanted to be his friend. He was the only man I saw Joe take to like he did the female employees. A few months after things fizzled with Liam, Joe plucked Jesse from Esca and made him a floor manager at Babbo.

I'd had been showing up for my Saturday morning phone shifts (the only shift I took outside of the basement) unshowered, dressed in flannel pajama bottoms, wearing mismatched socks slipped into Liam's rubber Adidas flip-flops. I shuffled in and locked the door, barely conscious of what I said to guests on the phone or anything happening around me. It was Jesse's incessant tapping that caught my attention.

Tap-tap-tap-tap-tap went Jesse's right leg under table twenty, as though plugged into a socket. I'd seen him come through the restaurant before but hadn't given him a good look. He was filling out the service chart that assigned the servers and back waiters to their stations. He wore a black suit and purple tie and had a head of sandy-brown curls. His olive skin had a flush across his cheeks that made his eyes appear as blue as turquoise gemstones. The suit was likely cheap, but everything looked good on Jesse. Tall and slender, his body had that effortless tone that came free in your late teens and early twenties but could never be replicated in a gym after that.

When he wanted, Jesse made the most mundane gestures feel significant, even sacred. He could ask me the simplest question, like whether I could hostess on Saturday, and bathe it in the kind of subtle intimacy that made me feel like we were the only two people on Earth. But he was not a sweet talker. He promised nothing verbally. There were sporadic invitations to play games of Scrabulous on Facebook. Text messages that began with asking me to cover a hostess shift and ended hours later in the middle of some conversation about nothing that meant everything. Sometimes during family meal, he chose to sit alone with me on table one while I answered the phones instead of eating at the bar or up on the second floor with everyone else. We ate in relative silence, but he always sat close enough to let the leg that wasn't tapping gently press against mine.

My Saturdays soon revolved around the moment he'd walk through the door, always with a copy of the *New Yorker*, a thin

Sudoku workbook, and three lottery tickets. I knew when he was early and I knew when he was late. On days he was late, the anticipation of his arrival would trigger a spike of adrenaline that caused me to feel my heartbeat in my face. I'd become self-conscious and head to the bathroom to check if my coloring had changed for all to see, which it had. Jesse was not the kind of crush you admitted to, like Craig Bierko. This was something else entirely. I guarded it like my life depended on it. I didn't dare reveal it, lest I crumble and cease to exist. I didn't eat. I didn't need to. I was fully sustained by my delusions. I needed to get a handle on it first before anyone else found out, but I was never able to. Because it wasn't real.

Jesse's first stop was usually the kitchen to see Kendal, Gina's protégé, who worked the pastry station. Gina initially had reservations about offering her the role on account of how pretty she was.

"Kim, she's a gorgeous half-Thai, half-Italian nineteen-year-old," she said, exasperated. "The kitchen will eat her."

Then Jesse would swing around to me on table one where I'd be juggling the phone lines, and stay a few minutes before heading down to the wine cellar where Elizabeth, a petite, pixie-faced somm with a head of golden-brown tresses that she always wore tied-up in a thick ponytail, would be pulling bottles.

I never actually saw him sidling up to Kendal's stainless-steel nook of a pastry station as she churned away on some mascarpone mixture or as he appeared to Elizabeth from behind one of the ten-foot wooden shelves in the wine cellar as her slim arms struggled to heave a case up to her chest. But I noticed the pattern after a while.

I could always tell who else he might be working on by the way they looked at me. We generally avoided looking at each other altogether. If I did get caught in an unwanted eye-lock with another one of his girls, the exchange, though quick as lightning, felt like being injected with a deadly poison that threatened to kill the very root of one's joy.

The game that Jesse and I played rarely ended in us hooking up, but it peppered my life with such psychological intrigue that I let it go on for almost a year. It finally ended on Halloween night in 2009 at around 4:00 a.m. in Jesse's railroad apartment, one floor above John's Pizza on Bleecker Street. After using his very tiny bathroom to brush my teeth and take off my Blair Waldorf wig and the tartan headband that had been digging into the sides of my head, I walked in on him in his bedroom, struggling to remove the thick red tights that were part of his costume as Ruffio, the leader of the Lost Boys from *Hook*.

I got out of there early the next morning. I stood outside the Grey Dog coffee shop on Carmine Street with stringy hair greasy from Jesse's hands and from being underneath that hot wig all night. All my friends from college were probably awake, already tending to their babies in their not-too-recently purchased houses, while I stood on the sidewalk, cold and gummy, calling the number on the back of my Visa to see if I had enough credit left for an egg and cheese on a croissant and a hazelnut coffee to go. I felt as though after finally getting what I wanted, suddenly, I didn't want it anymore. It felt like the end of something, not the beginning. But I was also relieved, like I could at last let this whole absurd charade with Jesse go, and get into a real relationship.

Cillian was right to laugh at me that night at Otto. It *was* odd and even a little embarrassing that I was this unfamiliar with Italian wine varietals and how to properly pronounce them because wine was a huge deal at Babbo. We had one of the largest and most sought-after collections of Italian wine in the country—a "million-dollar cellar." It made up a significant amount of the restaurant's profit. Sommeliers from all over the world would've killed to work there. We had one guy, Toby, come on as a junior sommelier and stay only six months—just long enough to get the goods on our operation—before he left to open his own Italian wine–focused spot on the other side of the neighborhood. No one suspected that he was in it just for the access. He was young; he came to us straight out of NYU. His departure was spoken of sparsely and in whispers. As though it were an act of treachery, but no one would come right out and say it. Words were chosen carefully. He was an owner now. Someone poised to be on equal footing with Mario and Joe. But no one celebrated it either. Being part time, I hadn't realized the politics. When I heard the news, I practically skipped into the restaurant pleased as pie and told anyone who'd listen how I couldn't wait to go to Toby's new place. I was greeted with raised eyebrows and a curt "yep."

We had bottles that wine geeks didn't know existed before working at the restaurant. They got to pour vertical tastings, which I learned was when each course was paired with the same type of wine, made by the same winery, but produced in different years—the older the winery, the more the wine team's eyes sparkled. Maybe the table began with a bottle from the '90s, but they were drinking one from the '70s or older by dessert. A somm's whole demeanor and physicality changed when it happened—their walk morphed into a stride as they moved purposely through the dining room with a bottle tucked in their arm like a treasured football. Their faces read all business as they spun their wine key into the cork and pulled it out and poured themselves a little taste (to test it, of course) before priming the guests' glasses. This was all done with the thoughtful intensity of someone disarming a bomb. One look at them and I thought, *Quiet! The master craftsman is at work.* But if you watched closely, you saw them fighting to temper their glee.

Almost every role required a fair amount of knowledge about the wine program—the only carve-out was the hospitality department, because no one who reached a live human being on the Babbo reservation line cared about the menu and wine list. They just wanted to know if they were getting in.

The wine program was one hundred percent Joe's domain. He and the early somms meticulously built it up during the restaurant's first few years. He even cowrote a book on the subject, which became something of a bible within the industry, and his family had two wineries in Italy. I didn't know how much I'd need to know about the wines as Joe's assistant, but common sense told me I should learn what he assumed I already knew.

I first heard that the role might be opening a year earlier, in 2008, right after I took the job at the law firm and things were getting shaky with Liam. While working the phones, I came across an email in the hospitality inbox from our HR department at Corporate, and read that Joe was looking for help in his office. Natalie, his current executive assistant, was looking to leave.

A thrill shot through me. And then immediately my heart sank. I couldn't leave a brand-new job two weeks in without damaging that connection. I felt regret that the opportunity had slipped past me, but I also felt something return to me that had been missing for years, as though the mere idea of this job had shaken me loose. It was hope. Hope that the New York that I'd blindly, almost automatically packed up and left everything for might still be attainable. I didn't know exactly what Natalie did, but if the perks that came with the workload were anything like the one's from Meredith's job, then I wanted it.

Meredith was Mario's assistant, and she seemed to have just as much sway at the restaurants as the managers did. She was his little lieutenant. Even Fred, Mario's sous chef who listened to no one, listened to Meredith. She didn't throw her weight around—she didn't need to. The role's proximity to an owner conjured up a certain respect. She was an insider among insiders. A few times, I came up from the basement during my evening phone shift and saw Meredith sitting at table twenty with Mario while he held court with the likes of James Gandolfini and Mariska Hargitay. Meredith worked coat check with me once during her first year on the job, and that night, every single one of our VIP guests greeted her like an old, dear friend—grasping her hand, pulling her in for a hug.

Restaurants had similar group dynamics to families and gangs, except we didn't kill people when they tried to leave. But if you didn't get fired and you didn't quit, eventually your loyalty was rewarded. I knew Joe liked me. He liked the women at Babbo better than the men. Joe usually swung by Babbo once a night in the middle of service, always in a suit and tie, his round face expressionless. Sometimes when we were all boxed in together at the podium, he pulled out a stack of Post-its from the side drawer and started playing tic-tac-toe with the hostesses and coat checkers. Whenever he had to correct me on something I didn't do right, like grabbing the bulb of a guest's wineglass instead of the stem or keeping my hands in my pockets, it always seemed to pain him.

I'd told my mother that I'd never work for Mario and Joe full-time.

"I thought you liked them?" she'd snapped.

"I *do* like them," I reassured her. But then I told her about the rumor I'd heard a while back. That Joe had made the former general manager of Del Posto—the group's fancy, four-stars-from-the-*New York Times* ambitious restaurant in the meatpacking district—come home early from his honeymoon in Italy just to fire him on the spot.

"You didn't tell me that," she gasped in a hushed voice generally used when playing with a baby or shaming a puppy for peeing on the carpet. "He wouldn't!"

Joe practically force-fed my mother free Vespa Bianco, the Bastianich Winery's flagship wine, each time she and my dad took the train down from Albany to have dinner. That, in her eyes, rendered him incapable of such harshness.

A big deal was made when any staff member's family came in—plate after plate of pasta dishes, salumi or antipasti that hadn't been ordered flew out of the kitchen and were quickly slipped onto the table until they could barely pick up their wineglasses, which got refreshed every few sips so they were never sure how much they'd had to drink, and only half of it showed up on the bill. My parents didn't know that the whole restaurant industry was volatile, and I wasn't stupid enough to tell them, save for the slip about the old Del Posto general manager. It wasn't just Joe or our group. I heard chatter from the servers about people at other places getting fired—*just like that*. Chefs were known to scream—literally—like angry babies when something didn't go their way.

But none of that mattered anymore.

Things were getting bad in the Babbo basement. I was too tired to hostess on my feet for seven hours after having already spent eight hours visiting clients all over Brooklyn. Earning money while sitting down, not having to summon the mental energy required to handle guests face-to-face, was ideal. So I sat down there. Waited to be brought bread and butter or an occasional mistake plate from the kitchen, and did my work in relative peace—if you could say that about the reservation line at Babbo. I answered it most nights on autopilot. After the first few years of playing gatekeeper, it became rote.

Conditions in the basement took a turn for the worse when we began an excavation to make room for a twelve-foot-high wine cellar. There had been a small one-person office in the western end, with dial-up Wi-Fi and good heat. But once the excavation started, we relocated to the east end, setting up a makeshift desk on top of a metal filing cabinet. In the winter, two space heaters turned up high were essential. Our new station put us only a few feet from the two-door hatch that opened up to the street, which let the cold air in.

We were welcome to go upstairs and answer the phones sitting directly behind the maître d's podium during service, but it was hard to make out "the thirteenth of January" from "the thirtieth of January" while the Rolling Stones were playing at club-level volume, and it meant sitting at eye level and about one foot from George's backside as he directed traffic in and out of the dining room—an equally awkward setup for both parties. Even a subtle bend at the waist resulted in an uncomfortable ass-bump to the side of your head, so most of us toughed it out in the basement.

But with the excavation mice might have come, which I only discovered on the night I accidentally left my Ugg boots behind at Heights and Boerum Council—the ugliest but warmest shoes. I showed up for my evening phone shift in red ballet flats. I was pretty sure I felt a tickle and subtle weight skitter across the top of my foot. Afterward I started hearing what sounded like squeaks, and each one, real or imagined, triggered a swift kick to the cabinet, creating a thunderous blast that hung in the air as the sound reverberated off the quivering metal. Surely, I thought, this would send any mouse within a ten-foot radius fleeing back toward the southern end.

When the squeaks stopped altogether a few weeks later, I was surprised that George came down to ask if I was *sure* I didn't want to answer the phones upstairs, seated behind him.

"I think there are no more mice down here," I said.

His cue-ball eyes opened wide. "Yeeeeesssss," he began, before breaking into a grin. "But what's eating them is . . . "

"Oh." I knew what he meant instantly but fought hard for a few seconds before allowing it to sink in. Then I listened carefully to the hodgepodge of sounds coming from the southern end and could just make out the sound of faint shrieking.

I got in the habit of kicking the cabinet even if I didn't hear any-thing, just for good measure. It became something of a nervous tic. I couldn't go two minutes without doing it.

Cillian came down one night to check his voice mail and stayed long enough to witness my new system of defense. "What is that noise? Is that *you*? What are you doing?"

I began to explain my perfectly logical way of keeping my work-space pest-free, but before I could finish, he doubled over, his head hanging down by his knees, overcome with laughter. When he re-covered, I grabbed the reservation book and followed him upstairs without a word.

Someone had the bright idea to adopt two cats from an animal shelter and let them loose to "live" in the basement. All this did was leave us with two traumatized kitties who would disappear down in the darkness for days and reappear more terrified with each sighting. Gina put her foot down one day and said the cats had to go—to real, loving homes. Cillian had developed a soft spot for them since being dispatched to fetch them, so he volunteered, naming them Satchmo and Bird.

Eventually the basement office was finished, and we started calling it "the cantina." The cantina had exposed brick walls, amber sconces, and its own adjoining bathroom. It doubled as a private dining room that we offered to VIP friends of the house—you had to write for *The Sopranos* or be Liam Neeson or Uma Thurman if you wanted to eat down there. But I still caught myself listening for signs of life and won-dering how on earth I was still down there a couple nights a week.

"What would you do if you could do *anything*, not something just because it fits on your résumé?" my mother asked me during a visit back home. We were discussing my way out of the dual-job dilemma over a glass of Toasted Head chardonnay. We sat at my parents' kitchen table overlooking the blue-gray deck my father had painted to match my mother's menagerie of cement bunnies and a turtle. The question dredged up the memory of the email I'd come across in the hospitality inbox the year before. It occurred to me that Natalie, Joe's assistant, was still there, in the same role. She had never left. But maybe she still wanted to.

I couldn't just call her up and ask if she still wanted her job. I really didn't know her. But I knew someone who did.

Jesse had learned that Natalie did, in fact, want to leave and had been working to ease her way out these last few months. Jesse was now the GM of Otto, and one night when Joe was making his usual rounds to the restaurants, it was Jesse who broke the news to him that I wanted the job.

"*Kim* Kim? You mean *our* Kim?" Joe allegedly said, letting slip a rare show of emotion. That was a good sign. Joe didn't usually say much at all, and when he did speak, it was almost entirely without inflection.

Of course, Gina had an opinion.

"Are you crazy? He won't pay you shit. You'll be lucky if you get fifty thousand dollars out of him. Besides, do you know what time Natalie calls the restaurant at night to put in VIP reservations? After 8:00 p.m.—and she calls from the office line." Gina flipped open the lid of one of her jars of homemade fruit-infused grappa and let two skinned pears slide from her hand and plop into the jar one at a time. "No. I'm not contributing to the exhaustion of Kimmy." Softening slightly, she asked, "Well, have you met with him about the job yet?"

"I'm going to. Friday at six at the Del Posto bar."

"You'd better be prepared to perform verbally."

We looked at each other, both realizing I did not know what she meant.

"When you're talking to him, you have to come up with answers quickly. You have to respond confidently—know what you want to say. Don't go on and on like you do. Stick to the point. He's going to ask you questions one after another. He's going to hit you hard."

He is? I thought. That didn't sound like tic-tac-toe-playing Joe.

Each time I walked into Del Posto, I never knew where to look first; the ceiling was so high, it took my eyes a moment to find it. It was dark in there, the windows always shaded. Everything was made of light gray marble or rich mahogany wood and leather, and the white linen tablecloths created gleaming pops of white in the dining room. The first thing I heard was the tinkling of piano keys, and it felt as though I'd arrived at some clandestine midnight ball like the one in "The Twelve Dancing Princesses." I was glad I didn't work there; that way I'd never get used to it.

I spotted what looked like Joe's bare head in the back of the dining room, leaning over a table; but that guy couldn't be Joe, I thought. He was too thin. And what was with the sweater? I'd never seen Joe in anything other than a suit. But it *was* Joe—looking even thinner than the last time I'd seen him. He had recently taken up running and lost sixty pounds. The gang at Babbo suspected that his trans-formation had to do with a rumored falling-out between him and Mario back in 2008—*little brother* trying to one-up *big brother*, since Mario was heavy too.

We took a seat on one of the leather banquettes in the lounge.

"So, you want to be my assistant?" Joe asked. He let me talk, but I was mindful to follow Gina's advice of keeping things concise and clear.

Joe then told me about his appearances on *The Today Show* and how I'd help plan them. About the winery in Italy and the events he put on at restaurants in Connecticut and New Jersey to sell the wines. The Batali & Bastianich Group—the B&B Group—had just gotten involved with something called Eataly, and I'd be working on that too. He spoke as though the job was already mine.

This wasn't going at all as Gina had predicted. In fact, Joe said more to me in twenty minutes than he had in ten years, and he actually smiled a few times.

"You'll have to get along with Mario's team . . . and my mother, Lidia, and my wife, Alice."

Lidia was not involved in most of the B&B Group's restaurants, but she was a successful restaurateur and TV star in her own right. She'd hosted a wildly successful cooking show on PBS for the last two decades.

"I get along with everyone—"

"I know you do; that's why you're sitting here," he said, cutting me off.

And then he asked me how much money I wanted.

I told him I had to make at least what I was currently making, which was fifty-five thousand dollars a year.

And just like that, daggers flashed in his eyes. It came and went so fast, I almost thought I imagined it. It was a look I'd never seen from him before. Sharp, like the newly formed angles on his once-chubby face.

The interview wrapped quickly after that. Joe promised to be in touch, and I exited the restaurant feeling unsure about how it all went down.

A month or so passed. I'd been following up with Natalie, who kept saying she didn't have any news for me. Joe hadn't decided what he wanted yet. "Don't worry," Natalie said. "He's like this." But I couldn't help thinking I somehow blew it.

My employers at the law firm didn't want me to go. I'd been there just under a year and they'd already given me a small raise and a bonus, but I thought they'd understand in the end. The partner who hired me was a woman named Mabel, who, while scanning my résumé suddenly gasped and blurted out, "You work at Babbo?" We were only ten minutes into the interview, but my tales of celebrity sightings and badly behaved guests dominated the next thirty. Mabel was in her early seventies and was even shorter than Rosie, but she commanded that firm like we were all her kids, marching in dressed in her signature skirt suits and pearls. I liked working for her. But I was already hooked on the idea of being Joe's assistant, of being like Meredith. Diving into the glamour of the restaurant world and less of the grind. Or so I thought.

One night in late December, Joe came into Babbo while I was working coat check. Deliberately meeting my eyes, he leaned in to George at the podium and said, "So, I see you've met my new assistant, Kim."

I smiled, and then pulled open the door that led down to the basement. I knew we weren't quite done yet. "You want to go downstairs and talk about money?"

"No, I don't," he said quickly, but still smiling. "We'll figure it out—call Natalie tomorrow." Then he was through the pickle and out the door before I could even say thank you.

It seemed to be a done deal for Joe, but he had no clue how much debt I still owed Sallie Mae or the mounting balance on my Visa that never seemed to go down. I needed to make at least what I was making at the firm because I knew becoming Joe's assistant meant I wouldn't be able to work evening shifts anymore; I'd never get to the restaurant on time. The plan was to work in Joe's office during the week, and only keep my Saturday shift at Babbo.

Natalie arranged for me to meet Joe at Otto one night the following week. I walked in and spotted Mario at the end of the bar, his feet in his Converse and pink socks dangling off his usual high-top chair.

"What are you doing here?" he asked, looking stern as he watched me walk toward him.

"I'm meeting Joe about becoming his assistant."

"Ahh, I've heard about this." He patted the seat of the chair next to him.

I sat down.

"It's not a particularly hard job," he said. "But it's an important job."

I nodded, starting to feel nervous. His interest made me realize that if I screwed up somehow, I might have to answer to him too. I hadn't thought about that.

"Basti is a big 'idea man.' He dreams up all kinds of great things. But he needs someone who can pull it all together." Then he just looked at me.

It always scared me a bit when Mario went still and stared like that.

He continued, "Basti is a little strange. But then again, so are you, so maybe this will work. Natalie's gone batshit crazy. . . . I think it was the job that did it to her."

three

BABY BLUE
BUTTON-DOWNS

As soon as the elevator reached the tenth floor of 45 East 20th Street, I heard the *ding* of a bell and then a rumbling as its metal door jerked open and slid into the wall. What sometimes followed was the quick *clap-clap* of heavy footsteps hitting the hardwood floor, providing a mere one-second warning. Noises that, in this exact order, had already proved a useful pattern: Joe was coming.

Three short steps and he was squarely in our small, bright yellow office. It was the lone workspace on the tenth-floor entryway. The rest of Corporate was just beyond the two glass doors directly in front of the elevator, occupying the entire tenth floor and the third floor.

"Natalie here yet?" Joe asked, observing the empty chair beside me. His shoulders were back, chest out as he paced quickly between the floor-to-ceiling windows and the doorway.

"She's on her way."

"That hippie. I bet she's still high. Did she tell you about her farm yet? Do you smoke pot too?"

"No," I answered, as though in front of a judge.

"I don't care if you do, just don't show up high—we have shit to do."

Clap-clap, swing—out he went and through the glass doors into Corporate. Just as they latched shut behind him, I heard, *"Paul!"* He'd gone looking for our CEO.

I had returned to scanning my inbox by the time he came back.

"So did she—did she tell you about the farm she's leaving me for?" he continued, as though he never left. "She's fuckin' nuts—never going to make any money. Have you seen Paul? Call down to the third floor—see if he's here."

I reached for the phone, but he shook his head. "Never mind—I'll call him myself later. When is Natalie getting here?" My eyes darted from the phone, to Joe, back to the phone. I took a deep breath.

"I'll call her. Can I help in the meantime? She's been really great, by the way. Helping me settle in."

"What would be really great is if she wasn't leaving."

I adjusted myself in my chair. "Uh . . . well, that wouldn't be very good for me," I muttered.

He reversed quickly, his pitch rising. "You'll be great, too."

Either Joe liked Natalie a lot more than he let on, or he didn't like me, and I knew the latter couldn't be true. Just that morning, I got an email from his wife, Alice, which read, *I hear we are very lucky to have someone like you*, and she could have only heard this from him. I wondered if it was this jarring abruptness that made all the men who worked at Babbo groan and give a subtle eye roll when George snapped down the phone at the podium, whirled around, and announced to the room, "Joe is on his way in."

"Sorry I'm late." Natalie slid through the doorway, bike helmet in hand and with a bulging tote bag on each shoulder. She looked like a hippie in her rumpled jeans and T-shirt, her long, thick chestnut hair tousled from the ride over the Brooklyn Bridge.

She might have appeared casual, but Natalie was all business—militant, even—and extremely organized. As we sat side-by-side going through her inbox, most of which was requests—people wanting something from Joe—it was our job to find a diplomatic way to refuse. She even kept a folder of Word templates labeled *politely decline.*

"I've come up with a million different ways to blow people off," she said, raising her eyebrows. "When I inherited this office, I got a paper Rolodex and Joe. Those were my resources. I will *not* do that to you," she told me, her brown eyes serious.

Ping . . . a calendar alert appeared on the screen.

"Parking tickets!" she exclaimed. "Checking nyc.gov on a weekly basis to scan for Joe's unpaid parking tickets is paramount. He ended up in jail a couple of years ago on New Year's the last time his assistant forgot to pay one, but it wasn't on my watch. Sometimes he'll toss them on the desk, but sometimes he'll forget to give them to you, so you have to check. When the alert pops up, stop what you're doing and check."

Jesus. I'd heard about Joe missing the opening of Otto because he was in jail. I didn't know at that time that it was possibly his assistant's fault.

"How many does he get?"

"A few per week. He paid over eight thousand dollars in parking tickets last year."

We were interrupted by the *clap-clap* of Joe's sleek dress shoes against the floor. "That's less than the seven-fifty a month I'd have to pay a parking garage outright—which is nine thousand a year. I'd rather take my chances with the meter maids." He set down his empty porcelain cup on the desk in front of us.

Natalie looked at my black pumps. "Tomorrow, bring a pair of sneakers and keep them here."

I peeked at the floor and noticed several pairs of worn shoes with muddy laces sticking out from under the desk.

Joe glanced at me with a smirk before heading back out the door. "I don't know why she keeps all those shoes here."

It's because she never leaves, I thought, eyeing the coffee cup he'd left behind.

We barely paused the entire day. Natalie seemed to get an email every five minutes and messengers popped in with packages for Joe. We'd open them immediately, then sweep the packing peanuts off the floor. The phone on her desk never stopped ringing. She was always on the move—heading into Paul's office or HR. Joe bounced in and out of Corporate and, while he was there, in and out of our office. We spent half the time he was in Corporate poking our heads into every office looking for him. She kept a running list of questions in a Word doc at all times, titled *Ask Joe*. It was at least four pages long. Each time we slashed through a question, another took its place. No wonder Joe was hard to find.

Our first meeting with Joe—if you could call it that—was to sort out the travel for his upcoming trip to Vinitaly in two months. Vinitaly was a massive Italian wine fair in Verona, and anyone who made Italian wine had a booth there. Joe attended every year and brought along a few of the New York–based chefs from the group.

"You should come with us," he said to Natalie.

Isn't she quitting? I thought.

"Um . . . I've got too much to do with the farm."

"Why not? You'll be out of here by then. You'll have all the time you need," Joe continued.

Natalie kept politely declining before I finally interjected, "You should go; are you kidding? I'll go!"

She raised her eyebrows, then continued running the flight details and prices by Joe.

When Joe *clap-clapped* out of the office, I turned to her. "What's the matter with you? That's a free trip to Italy."

She rose from her chair and peered out into the hallway, checking if the coast was clear. "Joe's a bit of carrot dangler," she said, looking uncomfortable. "I don't think he'll ever pay for that flight. You gotta watch for that. Get him to say things in writing, and then book your travel or whatever else he OK'd immediately, before he backpedals."

I deflated. "Why?"

"He means it in the moment, but then his cheapness gets the better of him."

By the end of the week, Natalie and I decided the best way for Joe to get used to me was for her to stop coming in and to let me manage him on my own, but she agreed to make herself available. She fully expected me to call her multiple times a day and was somewhat alarmed when I didn't, as though she'd somehow been gaslit into thinking the job was hard. When I finally did reach out to her, she conveyed as much to me, half-joking and half-curious as to the state of my sanity.

But I had something that Natalie didn't: an army of colleagues who'd come through Babbo over the years, each of whom spoke in varying degrees the almost indecipherable language of Joe. Babbo was the hardest restaurant to work in, hands down. The absurdly cut-up space, the crowds, the pickle. So often within the group, people were farmed out of Babbo to other restaurants. I didn't need to bother Natalie because I had plenty of resources to pull from when managing the daily onslaught of grunts, incomplete phrases, and fragmented thoughts that came out of Joe as he was walking away from me.

Every restaurant was like a dysfunctional family, with the head partners like the parents, and I'd always thought Joe to be the more passive of the pair, between him and Mario. The parent you didn't fear. I thought Joe malleable, to some extent. I was wrong.

Office Joe was very different from Babbo Joe. I didn't recognize the guy who stormed into the office wearing a sleek black suit during week two of my new role, cut me off when I spoke, and moved at an unnecessarily fast speed. Everyone at Babbo said "fat Joe" was nicer, but I had yet to notice any distinction between pre- and post-weight-loss Joe.

Joe barely spoke at Babbo, and when he did, his speech was slow and instructive. Here at Corporate, he didn't slow down. He didn't repeat. He didn't even give me the courtesy of delivering his orders in person, should my eyes be faster than my ears, but instead relayed them via a muffled call from his cell phone in the middle of deafening traffic, frequently beginning with: "ARE YOU READY—ARE YOU READY??" It felt like he was prepping me for the second coming of Christ. He'd send texts with one word: *Call*. He usually reserved these texts for working hours, between 8:00 a.m. and 6:00 p.m., but if I went sixty seconds without responding during this window, I'd get another, followed by another. Everything seemed to be cloaked in a kind of unnecessary coarseness and urgency. He barely finished forming one word before starting on the next, as though his latest idea would slip from his consciousness as quickly as it had come. Sometimes he called me, and after a deep sigh and a long pause, he said, with real devastation in his voice, "I forgot why I was calling you."

It felt to me as if he were manic: abnormal jumpiness; wired, unusual talkativeness; racing thoughts; distractibility. I'd seen plenty of clients during my social work days in that state and worse, but I'd never relied on a client to sign my paycheck. It was never my responsibility to get clients to do whatever they were supposed to. One of the golden rules of the practice was to "be where the client is at." But the office was teeming with people in a constant state of wanting something from Joe—Paul, our CEO; Fran, our CFO; every restaurant manager and wine director; random business partners on side projects I never knew he had; his mother, Lidia; employees from the winery in Italy. Joe insisted they spoke English, but they really didn't.

"It's like you traded fifty clients for one big client," he joked the day I was introduced to Maury, his longtime CPA. Maury was a seventy-year-old Long Island native with a year-round tan from weekending in *Flah-rida*. He smelled like cigarettes, began almost every sentence with "Now listen to me," and he called Joe *Joseph*, which I thought nobody did except for Lidia.

Lidia was how Joe ended up with Maury as his accountant—Maury had been keeping the Bastianich family books since the 1980s, when Lidia opened her first restaurant on the Upper East Side.

"I know what you put up with, I know what goes on in this office—I've known Joseph since he was a little boy," he offered once, as I tried my best to explain diplomatically why I wasn't able to set their next meeting.

More often than not, what everyone wanted from Joe was his time, and that was the one thing he made crystal clear that I was never to give. Under no circumstances was I to put anything on his calendar without running it by him, no matter who was asking, even if he'd told that person to their face that he'd make time for a meeting.

Helping Joe avoid committing to an appointment with people he actually needed to see was a big part of my job. I was never to box him in—never commit him to a meeting or call—and under no circumstances was I to confirm or deny whether he was in town. He frequently said, exasperated, "We don't need a fucking meeting— why do they always think we need a meeting?" When he did agree to one, he'd spend three minutes extracting information from the attendees, and then he would get up and unceremoniously walk away.

Joe watched every minute of his time closer than he watched his pennies, which was really saying something, but I was already beginning to see the advantages. I was in awe of the amount of work we got through in one day. Decisions were made in an instant and stuck to. Done was better than perfect. Few explanations were given. The work we completed in one day would take three in social services.

I acted a little manic myself, just trying to keep up with him. I was worried everyone might think I was crazy, but no one seemed to bat an eyelash as I traipsed behind Joe, struggling to balance a notebook, pen, phone, and cup of coffee. He yelled my name from one end of the office to the other to summon me instantly. He called it out in short, thundering bursts from the conference table in the middle of the tenth floor, where he held court with the restaurant GMs. His shout had enough force to travel across the room, through the set of glass doors, and into our office. He drew in a long, deep breath, tilted back his head, and paused briefly before slingshotting my name into the air.

One day, Paul pulled me aside and said the best way to get Joe to stop doing that was to pretend I couldn't hear him. But I couldn't do that. Why would I want to do that? Up and off my chair, through the glass doors I'd go, pen and notebook in hand, scampering out toward them. I was needed. I belonged. There seemed to be an unspoken understanding between me, the staff at Corporate, and the restaurant

GMs that we'd all climbed into the same wobbly boat, and I was the one stuck holding the oar.

"When is Joseph available? I'll be in Flah-rida next week and I need to see him before. I know he doesn't want to, but we have to go over his returns," Maury said.

"Ah . . . probably the best thing is to email them to—"

"He won't read them," Maury interjected.

I sighed, promised to try.

That afternoon, Joe was in a good mood.

"You want a coffee, Kim?" he offered as he headed through the glass doors. A few minutes later, he clapped back through the doorway and set an espresso cup next to me. Gazing out the window, he asked, "So whatta we got, whatta we working on?"

"Maury is asking for an appoint—"

"You can't let them do this to you!" Joe barked, his voice jumping decibels. "I don't need to see Maury. Why? Why does he need to see me?"

Caught off guard and stammering now, I whimpered, "It's about your taxes . . . he said it's important—"

"This is how it's gonna go: Maury emails you whatever the fuck forms he wants me to sign. You print 'em. I sign 'em. That's it!" It was as if I were suggesting that Maury give Joe a root canal. "Don't let them infect you with their kind of thinking." He stood over me in silence for a few seconds, rubbing his hand over his head.

I looked away. Anywhere but at him. I didn't want Joe to see how nervous he made me.

"Fine. A phone call. I don't want him and half his office showing up here."

I exhaled. Nodded. We moved on.

"You're a good girl," Maury told me afterward.

Joe wanted something from his employees, too: their unwavering allegiance on whatever cockamamie scheme he'd just thought up, which usually fell out of the scope of business as usual and included such things as last-minute private dinners, an impromptu party for the launch of someone's book, and his various art projects. One day, he decided to create a sculpture of a bunch of grapes, like the alabaster ones popular in the seventies, using old bowling balls. He had me call around to bowling alleys all afternoon until I found one way out in Queens that agreed to sell us their old balls for ten dollars apiece. More tasks piled onto my plate as the days went on, but I couldn't help feeling grateful to be there, working on oddball tasks for this kooky, albeit jarring version of Joe I'd never known existed.

Joe had a name for those who did not immediately concede to his often time-consuming ideas: *obstructionists.* Here in the world of Joe, this was the worst thing a person could be.

Truthfully, I liked Joe's ideas because they put me in contact with people who normally I'd never get a chance to know.

"Call Ben and see what the guys want."

Ben managed the Foo Fighters. He had texted Joe about planning a small party for the band at one of our restaurants after their upcoming show, which was in just a few days.

"Are you going to text him back first, or should I—"

"*No*—this is for you to do. Just run the details by me; let me approve. Offer the Piemonte room at Del Posto if it fits."

I took calls from folks like this at Babbo but usually had no clue who I was speaking to until it was time to collect a name for the reservation. This was different. I wasn't a nameless reservationist they'd never remember. Now I was in charge of planning a party for famous rock stars; their manager was eagerly anticipating my call. This was what I left social services for.

When Ben said Del Posto would be perfect, I thought the hard part was out of the way. But Casper, the GM of Del Posto, pushed back on the last-minute reservation. I could tell by the way Joe looked at Casper that he was riding the edge. I always thought Casper made a lot of sense, but I kept my mouth shut.

"Where do you expect us to put the ten of them—at the bottom of the stairs? There is no place for them," Casper protested.

"Figure it out," Joe snapped. "That's what real restaurant managers do, Casper."

I felt guilty for the way Joe treated Casper. I too wanted Casper to figure it out. I wanted to call Ben with triumphant news, maybe go to Del Posto on the night of their reservation and greet them as they strode through the front door. I wanted to be like Meredith.

When Joe clapped out and left us alone, I said, "I'm sorry, Casper. I know you're stuck between a rock and a hard place."

He sighed and shrugged. "I'm like a cockroach, Kim. That's where I live."

There was a group of nine or ten Italian guys in the office. They were there because of Eataly. Initially, they'd stopped into Corporate sporadically, but now they seemed present every day. They pitched camp at the long wooden conference table in the middle of the tenth floor and remained for a good part of the day, their shoulders hunched over their laptops. They kept to themselves and spoke only in Italian. There was only one woman among them. She had long black hair, and always looked up and said *"Ciao"* quietly as I passed.

The only one I'd been introduced to was Eataly's founder, Oscar Farinetti. During my first week, he came in fresh off a flight from Italy and situated himself in our yellow office in the big leather armchair positioned kitty-corner to my desk. His suitcase was beat up, the four corners covered with several thick pieces of duct tape, all matted together and rolling up at the ends. He wore a plain navy sweater, dad jeans, and simple brown moccasins, and sat quiet and still while waiting for Mario and Joe to arrive. Oscar didn't look or act like a man who had sold his electronics company for five hundred million euros just a few years prior.

Joe told me that in the 1980s, Oscar was Italy's version of "Crazy Eddie," the electronics retailer who put out wacky TV commercials promising "insane" low prices on home stereos and who spoke faster than a coked-out auctioneer. Oscar owned a company that made household products like washing machines and managed to put one in every Italian household. He decided to invest his newfound wealth into his real passion—food.

Oscar created the first Eataly in an abandoned warehouse on Torino's outskirts. He filled it with the best Italian food products from every region and added several different restaurants, each devoted to a food group. Italians went nuts over it. He opened a few smaller outposts in Japan, and the Japanese loved it too. At some point, he set his sights on bringing the concept to the United States and found a willing partner in the group with Mario, Lidia, and Joe's strong ties to Italy. They rented a massive fifty-thousand-square-foot space in the old toy building on 23rd Street. It seemed like someone from the press called about it daily, each asking for an exclusive first look before the official opening—and not just Eater and the other food blogs, but the *New York Times* and the *Wall Street Journal*. Joe just told them, "It's going to be a game-changer!" and this fulfilled their need for a quote. A market full of hard-to-find Italian products, right here in New York City, where you could pause from your shopping, sit down and have a meal, or push your cart through the aisles of dried pasta, Mulino Bianco cookies, and jars of Sicilian tuna fish while sipping on a glass of *fah-lahn-ghee-nah*. There was nothing else like it.

Along for the American leg of Eataly's journey were Oscar's sons: Roberto, Michele, and Flavio, and a few ride-or-die employees from the flagship store in Torino. They showed up to the office in jeans, old sneakers, and worn-out T-shirts pilling and dotted with little holes. They seemed nothing like the slick, aristocratic Italian men in crisp Armani suits featured in *Vogue* and *Tatler*. Joe referred to them as the *Alba mafia*.

"Them Farinetti boys look rough," an Otto employee joked one day when he swung by my office. I stood up from my desk and looked out toward the conference table. One of the sons sat alone— the middle one, Michele, who was practically mute. He glared back in my direction over his laptop, but something about his expression read more shy and uncertain than "rough."

Edo, one of the ride-or-die Torino employees, was the first to find his way into my office. He was from Bra, which he said was like Hoboken to Alba's Manhattan. Tall and lanky, he looked like he barely ate, even though he was in charge of buying all the imported Italian food we'd carry in the store. He wore his curly brown hair about two inches longer than the men did in New York—they all did, actually. Each one sported a mop of wild, untamed curls.

The other Italians kept their distance, but Edo was slowly becoming a friend. He popped in to say hello; asked where Joe was. He seemed happy to be in New York City and eager to meet everyone. I liked him.

The Segal brothers, Aaron and Ari, two young Americans born and raised in Manhattan, were another sort entirely. I met them on my second day in the office. They'd just flown back from Italy and came straight from the airport. Blurry-eyed but revved up, they walked out of the elevator and stood gripping the straps of their backpacks in the entryway, looking around. They caught Natalie's eye, and she beckoned them in.

I have no idea what I said to Aaron as I shook his hand; all I thought was, *That was fast.* Any hesitancy I had about going after a Mario and Joe yes-man vanished on the spot. He was handsome in a smart, nerdy way and hung back in the corner of my office as we tried to make conversation. Although warm, his gaze alternated between the floor and me. I could tell right away that Ari was older by the way he controlled the conversation, but he did so in such a way as to not overshadow his brother; in fact, it seemed as though he was carrying him. Ari didn't stop talking the entire time and was completely enamored that I'd worked at Babbo for so long. When Ari explained that they were managing partners, both brothers smiled broadly. I was confused because they seemed way too green to be on equal footing with Mario and Joe in the venture. I assumed they'd signed on as the workhorses in exchange for a minuscule share of the earnings, like the profit-sharing deal extended to some restaurant managers in the group. It wasn't a bad deal, but I always felt like those guys were sort of owned. I wanted to warn the Segals of the rigors that came with working for Mario and Joe, but I didn't know how without being disloyal to the group.

In the days that followed, I thought about the Segal brothers a lot, hoping they'd come to the office more, and also worried about them. Turned out, "They have very rich parents," as Joe put it one day, and they really were managing partners.

Joe took the lead, corralling the operation with the same curt force he did everything else. Once the Italians started coming in daily, so did the Segals. Ari and Aaron always wore light blue dress shirts with jeans. The Italians got the memo pretty quick, and soon the whole lot of them showed up every day in baby blue button-downs, which by 10:00 a.m. were soaked with sweat under the arms. This was the Eataly boys' uniform. It wasn't long before the Italians also started cutting their hair.

One night, I ended up alone in the office with Michele. I was heading out for the day when I spotted him at the conference table, looking as though he was trying to work out the right words in English to make his presence known. He didn't have keys to lock up and didn't know how to set the alarm, so he was forced to pack up his things and head out with me.

We got in the elevator. Alone in the small space together as the elevator slowly crawled down from the tenth floor, what had been a constant but subtle undercurrent became a riptide. There was a feeling of something so tangible that I could not help but turn my head to look at him, as if he had actually said something that needed to be acknowledged. His face was hopeful, eyes dancing. And I relaxed.

Our elevator ride sufficed for a proper introduction and seemed to unleash Michele's excitable nature. He visited my office frequently, sometimes just to say "*Ciao*." He spoke decisively in a gleeful, raspy voice full of exaggerated inflections. I was not alone in my affinity for him. The rest of the boys rallied around him; aside from Joe, he was the natural leader. It had nothing to do with being the founder's son. When he was quiet, he was almost plain-looking, with a rather nondescript face, blue eyes, a stocky build. But as soon as he focused his attention on you, Michele suddenly became the most charismatic man alive. He was electric.

Months passed, and the tenth-floor conference table could no longer hold their growing numbers, so Ari decided to lease the floor directly below as Eataly USA's headquarters. The elevator being what it was, it made sense to keep the door to the stairwell open. All who came and went between the floors had to pass my door. I found this extremely useful.

Up the stairs Michele came, bounding into my office like a little bull, and always with some assembly of the boys in tow. They traveled in packs of no less than three and ushered in an air of nervous energy, like young brothers on Christmas morning. Michele would position himself between me and whoever he had come in with, a subtle claim of which he was totally unaware. I always had a hard time concentrating on what he was saying. I was too busy looking past him to the doorway, wondering if Aaron was going to come inside. He rarely did. When he stepped in, it seemed only to serve as a nonverbal cue to hurry Michele along.

Aaron would occasionally pop into my office when the boys wanted something from Joe—usually time. Sometimes he would plead with me not to cancel yet another already thrice-rescheduled meeting. I held zero sway over Joe but let Aaron go on anyway because I loved being around him so much.

"Please don't let him cancel again," Aaron implored. He took a seat on the ugly orange couch next to my desk, which was purchased to match Mario's crocs.

"Lavazza is technically one of our partners at the store. Joe canceled with no notice last week. They got mad." I tried not to smirk when Aaron slumped deeper into the couch, legs splayed and feet planted on the floor.

Though not as outwardly inquisitive as his brother, Aaron too wanted to hear all about the restaurants and seemed to like my stories about the crazy things guests had done over the years. He told me Del Posto was his favorite. I confessed I'd never eaten there. Aaron rolled his head to the side so he could see me, looking cautious. "I'll take you to Del Posto," he said.

I couldn't respond. I looked away, down, anywhere but his face, as if meeting his eyes would burn mine out of my skull. I wanted, but I never seemed to be able to just say "Okay."

The next day at the office, Ari came by to ask me to make a reservation for Aaron and his girlfriend at Babbo. "Aaron *really* wants to take her there," Ari said.

I froze. Whenever Aaron wanted a reservation, he just asked me himself. Now I had to set up dinner for him and a girlfriend I hadn't even known existed, at what was essentially *my house*?

I felt desperately sad, as if I'd lost something that had actually belonged to me. I felt like a fool. I made the reservation, and later that day when Aaron and I crossed paths, I smiled coldly.

I was two months into the role and it seemed as though Joe was getting used to me, as evidenced by his recent use of the word *we*. Up until now, I'd been *you*. An individual. Not part of the gang, which was what I had to become if I was going to last. In the office, being scooped up into *we* was something you wanted, even if *we* were in serious trouble.

"We forgot to include Giacomo Conterno! How could we do it, Kim?" Joe circled the small room, bewildered, clapping down on the floor harder than usual.

"Who writes a book about Italy's finest wines and fucking forgets to include Giacomo Conterno?" He retreated to the desk and cradled his face in his hands.

Who's Giacomo Conterno? I wanted to ask, but kept quiet. I didn't want to ask anything that could possibly turn me back into a *you*.

Cillian never said anything about Giacomo Conterno, but judging by Joe's long face, this was a major blunder. I felt called to action— helping people get out of a tight spot, especially not one I caused, was where I was most comfortable. I'd show him. I wasn't going back to social work. I wasn't going back to Clifton Park. I was no obstructionist. I was going to ride out this budding comradery as long as possible.

"I can call Jane!" I practically shouted, as giddy as Mr. Smee bringing Captain Hook his tea and slippers. His literary agent would be able to sway his publisher, I was sure.

"NO!" he bellowed. "Do not call Jane. We're too late. It's done."

My mind raced, but there was nothing I could do to solve this.

There was the occasional setback on the way to morphing into Joe's right hand.

A writer from *People* requested an interview with Joe about his weight loss. The *New York Times* had done a feature story on Joe's transformation—how he took up running and now ran the New York City Marathon every year. Running also enabled him to continue eating pasta—and in the month I'd been his executive assistant, we had a dozen requests from the press wanting to do a piece about Joe's recipe for staying fit—running fueled by eating pasta.

"*People* wants to do a before-and-after story on your weight loss," I told him during our next phone call.

"What do they want?" A car horn blared in the background, making Joe almost indecipherable.

Raising my voice so he could hear me through the traffic, I said, "When you were big—when you were heavy—they want to ask you about—"

"Don't insult me," he growled.

I gasped out loud, my breath caught in my throat. "I didn't mean . . . I'm sorry, I . . . "

After a few seconds of dead air, he said, "I'm kidding!" His words were so upbeat, it was like a different person on the other end of the line.

I hung up shaken. Which was the true Joe? How could I do my job well if I wasn't sure?

Ten minutes later, I heard the familiar *ding, clap-clap*, followed by a *whoosh* of something whizzing through the air, and then an ear-splitting *whack* against the hardwood floor. I peered over the edge of my desk. A bag of Hershey's miniatures lay on the floor in the middle of our office. Joe had thrust his arm through the doorway, tossing the bag clean through the air in my general direction without so much as pausing as he continued through the glass doors into Corporate. These little tokens of remorse would later expand to cups of Mudd coffee from the truck around the corner and whole pizzas from Eataly, once the store opened.

"You want to come take a beer with us?"

Michele stood half-in, half-out of my doorway. I could've used seven beers after that afternoon's candy-throwing incident.

At 6:00 p.m. we took off walking along 17th Street toward Rye Bar. It was known for its craft beers, which the guys loved. Edo and Aaron were a few paces ahead.

"*Diciotto*," Michele was saying to me, earnest, "is our fake number. When you say to someone, 'I call you a million times, but you never call me back.' We Italians use *diciotto*."

"Eighteen!" I beamed proudly.

"*Brava*, Kim. How long you been studying Italian?"

Michele had walked in on me early that morning, around 7:45 a.m., wearing a headset and staring at an image of a smiling train conductor on my computer as I butchered the words *stazione ferroviaria*— "train station."

"I bought Rosetta Stone Levels 1–5 last week. I think it's going to take me six months," I said.

"Eh, Italian is not so easy for U.S. people to learn, Kim," he warned gently. "English is much easier for us to learn, and besides, we have this in school. . . . I think this will take you a lot longer."

It was still light outside, but the inside of Rye Bar was as dark as night and swarming with people and chatter. It smelled like beer. Our group jostled through the crowd and found a nook between the front and back rooms. Edo returned from the bar and handed me an amber-colored beer in a small glass with a stem that looked like it was used to serve cognac. The guys were all speaking Italian, even Aaron, who sounded just like them. They caught themselves every few minutes and apologized. I told them I didn't mind; I wanted to get used to hearing it so I could learn faster.

"It helps if you drink," Michele said. "You understand more."

"The real way to learn is to get an Italian boyfriend—is the best way, Kim," added Edo.

I would not have minded that either but couldn't think of a witty reply fast enough. Or maybe it was that I knew I couldn't really follow through when someone flirted with me. So I just nodded in agreement.

I drank the beer quickly, as I always did when I was nervous or excited and didn't know what to do with my hands. Half was gone after just a few minutes. I was already feeling the alcohol, which reminded me that I hadn't eaten anything that day except for some of the Hershey's minis. We were all hungry, so we decided to walk to Aaron's apartment on 19th Street, a few blocks away, and he'd cook us all dinner.

I walked into Aaron's apartment last. A young woman I assumed was his girlfriend, probably the one he'd taken to Babbo, stood in the living room. She caught sight of me and grew flustered, saying something quickly in Italian while waving her hands in front of herself, before turning around and walking out of the room.

I stood there with my hand still out. The guys looked annoyed.

"Typical Italian girl," Edo offered, shaking his head.

"She's just changing, that's all," Aaron quickly added.

She was back inside of a minute, all smiles, wearing a black cotton dress and speaking rapidly in Italian to no one in particular, heading straight for me.

"I'm Eva," she said warmly, as she took my hand.

We all stood around drinking while Aaron got to work preparing steak in the kitchen.

I asked where the bathroom was, and Eva enthusiastically volunteered to show me. She made a left into a corridor just before the front door, then continued straight into the bathroom. It seemed odd, but I followed her inside.

Eva stepped all the way in, then turned to face me. I hung back, hugging the sink to give her enough room to pass out the door. She took me in with her hazel eyes for a moment.

"I have heard them talk about you," she said in a low voice, before slipping her lithe body past me, eyes down.

I was speechless. I stood in the bathroom, staring at the spot where Eva had been seconds before. Her cryptic tone and downcast eyes were a stark contrast to her warmth up until that point, as if she didn't like whatever she'd heard. But I felt like I was on fire.

It was enough to be around all of them. Sitting at Aaron's kitchen table, eating the steak and salad that he and Eva made for us, I was drunker than I liked to be, but too happy to care. This was what happened when I didn't spend my nights in an old basement. When I was within sight of other people, I got invited to dinner. This was what it felt like to have friends who didn't have babies yet and didn't work until 1:00 a.m. I would have taken this job just to be near them—Aaron, Edo, Michele—had I known they existed. I sat there with young men my age, who did things I desperately wanted to do, like speak a second language and fly off to Europe every few months like it was no big deal.

I lay in bed wide awake that night, waiting for the beer and wine to wear off so I could fall asleep. I relived the encounter with Eva over and over again, searching her words and face for some clue. I had to know what the boys had said.

"Foot up!" Ari's wife Julie commanded with such force that I immediately complied, lifting my throbbing foot onto the plastic chair. *This comes naturally to her*, I thought. To be bossy. It was instinctive.

"I'm not a doctor," she said, "but everyone in my family is."

Julie was pretty. She and Ari looked alike in the face. There was something similar in how their eyes squinted when they smiled, which was often, and the authoritative way they held their chins up. I liked her just as much as I liked him and was glad someone was taking charge of the situation.

"Did you see Aaron run up those stairs?" I thought I heard her say. I was in a lot of pain and still wrapping my head around how quickly the situation had turned. Something was crouched on the ground in the entryway and sliding slowly from one end to the other. I blinked, and it was Michele, on his hands and knees, wiping up the trail of my blood that was hardly visible against the dark wood floor.

The wound was small, no more than a quarter inch, a perfectly straight slice just below the second and third toes on my right foot. It was really beginning to hurt. So much pain for something so small, but then again, the knife fell from about four feet off the ground.

Earlier that day, we'd received samples of buffalo mozzarella and a few other kinds of cheese at Corporate, overnighted from somewhere in Italy. It was May 2010, and the store was set to open in a few months, which meant a lot of food products were coming into the office. Ari mentioned while we were all hacking into the samples that his wife would be coming to Corporate tonight and that he'd like me to finally meet her.

"We can eat the rest of the cheese," I suggested, "and maybe open up some of the leftover *Today Show* wines collecting dust on the floor of my office."

I really wanted to meet Julie. I was down to one good girlfriend who hadn't decamped to the suburbs of New Jersey or Connecticut, but she'd had a daughter the year prior and wasn't around like she used to be. My colleagues at Heights and Boerum Council and the law firm were mostly middle-aged women in a completely different stage of life. They grew up in places like Sheepshead Bay at the end of Brooklyn, and Staten Island, and were content to live there forever. That wasn't the New York I left Clifton Park for. I didn't have any true-blue peers in social work, and I was desperately hoping to get some new friends out of this job. But just like dating, I soon learned that I wasn't great at making friends.

"It gets harder as you get older," my mother said, after she and my dad moved the family from southwest Florida to Clifton Park when she was forty-two. I should have been good at the overtures; we moved four times before I was twelve. Down in Florida, I ended up going to different schools three years in a row. I never had to put effort in to make friends, not then or in high school, during college or grad school. Some group of girls always adopted me. But adulthood was another story.

At 7:00 p.m., I went into the fridge on the tenth floor and plated the rest of the cheese, setting a knife on top. The two bottles of wine, the Biltmore rosé and the Dr. Konstantin Frank Riesling, were cold—I'd put them in the fridge a few hours earlier. I poured a glass of each, grabbed one with my right hand, then balanced the cheese plate on my forearm and pulled it into my ribs the way they did at Babbo, before grabbing the other glass with my left hand.

As I took my first step down the stairs to the ninth floor, I watched the knife slip off the plate, and I braced for the expected clang against the concrete. Instead, I felt a surge of pain as if someone had hit the top of my foot with a hammer. The blood came immediately, warm and flowing. I'd been stabbed. I'd stabbed myself. The knife had swan-dived top first into my foot. I felt it go in, a creepy, invasive kind of hurt. That was what it felt like to be stabbed. And then I felt nothing.

I hadn't dropped the glasses or the plate. I set them down on the steps and walked back into the entryway. The blood was coming in a steady stream. I thought about walking to the bathroom at the other end of the floor but phoned for help instead. Edo twice. Then the newly hired PR director who always worked late. When she picked up, I said, "I stabbed myself—by accident. A knife fell on my foot."

Now they were all up here. This was not how I'd pictured the night going. Ari's wife led me through the glass doors of Corporate toward one of the conference room chairs, telling me to sit down and put my foot up. I spared a second to wonder where my shoe had gone. The knife must have pierced right through the leather strap of my sandal. The lot of us debated whether I should go to the ER for stitches, but Julie decided, "I can take care of it." She took me in a cab to her and Ari's apartment on Hudson Street and cleaned out the wound in their bathtub. I'd never seen anyone so eager to tend to someone else's dirty, bloody foot, but I didn't mind. It wasn't so much that I trusted her; I just wanted to be her friend. I was still pretty poor and glad to be spared the hospital emergency room copay. It was also nice to have someone take care of me for a change.

"Sounds like alcohol was involved to me," Joe declared the following day.

I shook my head, exasperated. "No—I hadn't even touched the wine yet. It was an accident."

"You expect me to believe that you worked at Babbo for however long, and you don't know *not* to walk around with a knife hanging off the edge of a plate?" he said, before losing himself in laughter. "Didn't Natalie hurt her foot last year? What is it with this office and getting foot injuries while being inebriated?"

Suddenly, being happy came easy. I longed for Monday the way most people did Friday. Nothing could sour it, not the eleven-hour days, garbled instructions, a stab wound, or the exhaustion of fulfilling Joe's crazy but fun ideas. Joe could fling anything he wanted to at me—I wasn't going back. I'd left those sad, lonely days behind me—the days of watching dementia rob my clients of their memories, cats and rats and the bedbugs, the bloody aching feet swelling out of my cheap shoes. I had traded it all for booming *KIM*s, bowling balls, and the Eataly boys. All I had to do was listen for the sound of their sneakers squeaking against the concrete as they pounded up the stairwell, a chorus of endless *ciao*s, and for shades of baby blue to flicker past my door.

four

LITTLE LIEUTENANT

"You don't need to go to this shitshow," Joe said. I could tell he was already at the store by the way his cell phone kept cutting in and out.

My mind raced as I sputtered, "But . . . won't you need me to . . . I'm sure there will be . . . " It sounded like incoherent begging. *This shitshow* was the grand opening of the Eataly Flatiron store.

"Why do you want to go? Fine. But there won't be anything for you to do."

I slammed down my headset and rushed out of Corporate. The press tour and ribbon-cutting ceremony with Mayor Bloomberg wasn't happening for another two hours, but I wanted to get over there and plant myself somewhere before Joe changed his mind. Why did I want to go? Was he crazy? Every person in this city wanted to attend. Everyone I'd befriended in the food industry over the last ten years was there—or wanted to be—plus the mayor and every major press outlet. Not just food blogs. This was why we'd all been stressing, sweating, and working well past 9:00 p.m. every night for months, and he thought I'd miss it?

I stepped into the Lavazza café entrance to a sea of Italian men in suits—our invite-only VIP guests. Most were producers and representatives from Lavazza, Grana Padano, Illy, and other major Italian food and beverage brands and consortiums. I spied Joe and Mario standing next to each other at the Lavazza coffee bar with serious faces. It was odd to see them nervous. The staff, each wearing a pair of orange Crocs, also seemed nervous. Aaron, Ari, and Michele paced back and forth through the store, their faces flushed and glistening with sweat, as if on a mission to save to the world.

Ten of the Italian men in suits posed side-by-side for a photo, holding signs to their chest that read *Bra*—Edo's hometown. They beamed like they were at the Oscar *Vanity Fair* after party. Edo shuffled between them making introductions, many of them to me.

The Italians all wanted to meet Joe. They assumed I spoke Italian and launched into rapid conversation before they'd finished kissing both my cheeks. All my mornings spent practicing Rosetta Stone weren't enough to help. I ushered at least a dozen Italians over to Joe at Edo's request in a period of thirty minutes. Joe was right—in between the introductions, I had nothing to do, and this added to my frenetic state. I felt like if I didn't find some way to be useful or add value, I'd be kicked out—tossed out of my dream.

Aaron's girlfriend Eva was there, looking perfect in a crop top that showed off her toned, twenty-two-year-old abs. She caught my eye from across the café, waved, and smiled warmly. I hated her again.

Edo introduced me to Aaron and Ari's chatty mother. I saw Aaron's face in hers. She leaned in close. "Oh, you're Kim! The boys have told me all about you."

My heart swelled.

Despite the whirl of activity, time passed slowly as we waited for the arrival of Mayor Bloomberg—who we were told could possibly cancel right up until the last minute. If he did show, the plan was for him to enter through the Lavazza café doors and shake hands with the partners as the media snapped away, before escorting him to the Piazza, where he'd give a speech. Eataly had created seven hundred new jobs in New York City, so the mayor was eager to cut the ribbon made of pasta for the cameras. Afterward, Oscar and Joe would give him a tour of the store, the media recording their every step.

I approached Joe a few times, attempting to discuss the steady flow of work unrelated to the store opening that I could see trickling into my inbox every time I checked my phone. The third time, he took me by the arm, pulled me aside, and said, "Go pour yourself a glass of prosecco and sit down somewhere."

Soon after, Mayor Bloomberg showed. The plan went off like clockwork. Before I knew it, we'd slipped into late afternoon. The press was mostly gone. Croc-wearing staffers were getting the store ready to open to the public, who'd formed a line that wrapped around 23rd Street and down Fifth Avenue.

"It is just a store," Michele had said to me a few days earlier, shrugging his shoulders as if preparing for the possibility of failure. That no one would care. None of us were prepared for what transpired that day, or what was to come.

"The wines!"

I'd been trying to reach Joe all morning. He was due to appear live on *The Today Show* at 7:00 a.m. the following day to promote the new book that didn't include Giacomo Conterno, but he hadn't tasted the wines he'd be presenting yet.

Over the phone he said, "Come now to Eataly with the wines and bring a wine key. Quick-quick like a bunny."

I stuffed the three bottles into a dusty tote bag I pulled out of the bottom of Joe's desk drawer and set off clinking across 20th Street, then up Fifth Avenue.

The store had opened two months ago, and just like on opening day, every morning there was a line to get inside Eataly that put any I'd seen at Babbo to shame. On the weekends it stretched halfway across 23rd Street, almost reaching Sixth Avenue. The security guards knew me, but die-hard visitors clamoring for gelato, Neapolitan pizza, or fresh mozzarella became visibly perturbed when I walked up to the door, slipped inside, and then closed it in their faces. Some would try to follow me in, so I usually entered through the loading dock on 24th Street.

I slowed my pace as I stepped on the slippery cement of the loading dock, straining over boulder-sized black bags of garbage. A few more careful paces and I pushed through the double doors and into the store, merging with the hordes of tourists snapping pictures—many of whom were proud Italians—and neighborhood folks knocking their shopping baskets into one another as they sifted through packages of presliced salumi and held wedges of Grana Padano or Taleggio cheese wrapped in cellophane up to their noses. Michele whizzed by, zigzagging through the crowd and flanked by two cameramen from Rai, Italy's national TV network. The crowd was thick up ahead, so I cut through the Piazza—the center of the store, fashioned to look like a real Italian piazza—but was stopped by a nervous-looking Vittorio. Vittorio was from Alba and worked in Eataly's wine shop. He had given me Italian lessons early in the morning before the store opened, when it became clear Rosetta Stone just wasn't going to cut it.

"Is Joe coming today?" he blurted, without so much as a *ciao*. "Can you ask him—no, tell him I need to know which Tignanello he asked me to order because he was not clear—"

"Vittorio, I will never remember this," I interjected. "Can you write me an email or shoot me a text and I'll ask him? He's sitting in Pizza Pasta—I'm on my way to meet him right now."

Vittorio's eyes widened with relief. "Okay!" Then he paused. "Eh, Kim . . . in Italiano?"

Rolling my eyes playfully, I called back as I continued through the store, "*Puoi scrivimi un email!*"

I reached the back of the line to enter Pizza Pasta, Eataly's busiest restaurant. It served *only* pizza and pasta and was tucked in the back, but it was unmissable. There was always a line, even fifteen minutes before we opened at 10:45 a.m. The gold dome atop the wood-fired oven made it pretty visible too.

I snuck in through the back of the restaurant, dashing along the adjacent aisle of dried pasta and canned tomato sauce—a trick learned from Jeffrey, the longtime food writer for *Vogue*. He'd position himself against the cans of San Marzano tomatoes, waiting for guests to rise from their chairs, then he'd swoop in and sit down amid their rumpled napkins and plates with pizza crusts. Other guests used this tactic but would usually acquiesce when the staff pleaded with them to get up. Jeffrey wouldn't budge. He'd holler for Joe, and the staff would call me.

"Jesus," Joe would say, rubbing his bare head. "Tell 'em to let Jeffrey do whatever the fuck he wants. He's so old, hasn't he earned it?"

I spotted Joe's black suit jacket and the back of his head at a table in the middle of the restaurant, the servers quickly setting the tables around him with paper placemats and rolls of silver.

"All right, what do we got?" He rubbed his hands together. "Let's do this."

Joe managed to pull a bottle from the bag as I was setting it down on the table. He looked to a passing server and asked her to bring over three wineglasses and a second wine key as I struggled to slice the thick foil covering the top of the Chianti.

"Come on, come on, come on." He flapped his fingers back and forth. "Give it to me—I'll do it."

"I've almost got it," I protested, still out of breath from the walk over from Corporate. My hands lacked the muscle memory he didn't realize he had. My wine opener at home was that one from Bed Bath & Beyond with two long handles on each side that, when you pressed down, yanked the cork out for you, breaking the foil in the process. I wasn't used to opening bottles with the simple wine key that the somms used on the floor.

It was November 2010. Since opening day, we'd begun doing everything at Eataly—at the store. I set up every meeting, every quick coffee and phone call, there. Every job interview with prospective GMs or wine directors, every time Joe needed to sign something he swore he'd read but hadn't, I ran over from Corporate and searched for him within the always-at-capacity space.

In between calls and meetings, Joe would pull a plastic container of cut honeydew off the shelf of the ready-to-eat section like he was going through his own refrigerator, eating it with his hands as he walked around, watching the staff interact with guests. I was told that sometimes he gave polite, helpful instruction, like Babbo Joe. The staff were always eager to relay this to me, their eyes lighting up as they quoted him verbatim. Other times, he frightened the shit out of people with his curt speech and blank stares. Whether they were afraid of him or not, most people came to me first, and Joe seemed to like the arrangement as much as I did—"Ask Kim" replaced "Make it happen" and "Get it done" as his most uttered catchphrase. He couldn't have wished for a more willing gatekeeper. The more reasons I had to be here, the better.

Joe loved the store because all of this, in a sense, was his "game-changer"—he was right about that. I loved the store because it was where the boys spent most of their time.

"Why are you always here?" a manager at Pizza Pasta asked me one day. He was on to me.

I answered as honestly as I could: "I come looking for friends."

The boys were constantly introducing me to some prominent Italian who'd flown in from Torino or Milan or Rome: employees, partners, or contacts of Oscar; prominent Italian chefs he flew over to do events—"the Oscar show," Joe called them.

There was Sebastiano, a partner of Oscar's who was descended from an old line of Italian nobility that could be traced back over one thousand years. According to Ari, Sebastiano supposedly had thirteen names, but the past April, Ari had also told me that Eataly was chosen exclusively to feed Italy's space program during their next launch, and I believed him for a full five minutes.

Sebastiano married a textile heiress from one of Italy's richest families, and they lived on the edge of Alba in a castle that was built for the son of the first king of Italy.

"You work here with us, Kim; you need to understand where we come from. You have to go to Alba. When you go, you can stay at my house," Sebastiano said the third time I spoke to him, his hand clapping down on my shoulder like I was an old friend.

I rarely saw Lidia's or Mario's assistants here. Meredith and her team worked out of an office in Otto's basement. Lidia's assistants worked uptown, out of Felidia. Joe and I were the only ones from the group who were at Eataly every day, so the boys shuffled all guests to me when they needed reservations at Babbo or someone else's impossible-to-get-into place.

From the Eataly side, it was Edo who unofficially shepherded the visiting Italians. Overall, he was making much better use of the store and its constant flow of new people than I was.

"It is so easy to meet people in New York, Kim. Last week in the store, I meet this mother with her daughter who is home from college. And you know, I go around to the different counters with them, I help them with all the products and what to buy. They love me; they love Eataly! And then—I fuck her that same night."

"The mother or the daughter?" I quipped. Like the rest of the Italians, Edo was always misusing the word *fuck*. They mistakenly believed it to be on the same level of offensiveness as *cazzo*, their equivalent, which was much more acceptable in polite conversation.

Establishing real intimacy with strangers seemed effortless for Edo. His slender, classically good-looking face only aided his pursuits, and I suspected made up for his vehement gesticulating, which was excessive even for an Italian. Sometimes I was afraid he'd accidentally hit me in the face. He didn't try to hide how he felt about anyone or anything—everything was expressed. All of the Italians were like this. If they liked you, you knew it. If they thought you were attractive, it was reflected in the widening of their eyes, and how without hesitation they'd lean close to you when speaking, until they were only a few inches from your face. They didn't try to conceal their feelings, whether platonic or romantic, as American men of their age so often did. They were not at all afraid. They were not at all like me. I could talk to anyone, but usually it was as part of my job, as if I needed the role to give me a reason.

Edo knew this. His nickname for me revealed it—*Little Kim* he called me, as though I were fragile.

I envied his ability to connect on that level with strangers, or anyone, for that matter. The thought of not being Edo's friend was terrifying.

Their acceptance of me—Edo, Michele, and all the Italians, Aaron and Ari—their constant, genuine happiness to see me, the way their eyes lit up each time I walked into the room or around the corner, had become like a drug. I ached for it. And even though Joe only sent me running to the store once or twice a day, I showed up there roughly double that because I wanted to be near them. I wanted to be near all of it.

I didn't know who Aaron wanted, but it wasn't me. He no longer went out of his way to talk to me, like I could have sworn he used to before the store opened. But there was something I'd noticed for a while now—a series of gestures that occurred between Ari and Aaron whenever I approached in the store. It drove me a little nuts. Ari would do any number of things to Aaron: elbow him, place a hand on his shoulder, an outright tap to his forearm. He would turn his body all the way toward his brother, lean toward him, and stare into his face until Aaron looked up from his phone and, after a quick beat, looked in my general direction and let out a slightly forced but warm "Hi, Kim."

Sometimes I'd watch Ari to see if he did it when someone else approached—a tap, a nod, lean in—but he didn't. I'd only seen him do it for me.

Perhaps Aaron was the same kind of screwed up as I was, and his brother was trying to nudge him into action. Or maybe Ari knew; maybe it was all over my face and I wasn't fooling anybody, hiding my heart away. Maybe Ari knew how disappointing it was when

Aaron ignored me and felt sorry. I wished I hadn't been cold to him after learning about Eva. Or that I could forget about him entirely. But every time I witnessed the bizarre interaction between the two brothers I felt panicked all over again, and couldn't stop thinking about him.

The forecast called for heavy snow. When George phoned, I agreed to help out on coat check at Babbo until 10:00 p.m. I was determined once I hit my one-year mark with Joe, just a couple of months away, to get enough of a raise out of him to cover what I was making at Babbo in one year, and then I'd quit working at Babbo for good. Until then, I thought I might as well make some money, since for once I wasn't on Joe duty. Natalie had said the week between Christmas and New Year's was the only break I'd get. Joe had flown off with the family to spend Christmas at the winery in Friuli. My plan was to make some cash and head home before the subways and streets turned into a mess.

I pulled back the doors and saw the Christmas tree still atop the center table, decorated with the usual sparkling pink and green pear-shaped ornaments. At least five drunken guests would ask to take one home every night. Since it was only two days after Christmas, I anticipated a slow night and judging by the half-empty pickle, that was what I was going to get. Jimmy Day was behind the bar. This was a good night to be back working on the floor.

Coat check shifts were usually grueling. An ill-managed coat check situation could bring the whole charade to a screeching halt; we played a significant role in keeping the conveyer belt of guests moving through the restaurant. I had to be organized and fast. If I couldn't find a coat or a package within sixty seconds, a bottleneck would start to form. That was why it was so important that the guest held on to the little orange ticket we gave them in exchange for their coat because without it, it'd be near impossible to find their item.

We had only a tiny closet in front of the stairs that led into the basement. To add more space for coats, we ran a cord against the wall of the narrow stairwell. We used a thick, plastic-coated wire with small loops every six inches, and placed the hangers so they wouldn't slide down the line. We packed that hallway six hangers deep, some of which held four or five coats each and were so heavy—especially if the coats were soaked from the rain—that they were quite hard to lift. This left little space to get down the stairs and was torture for the somms who needed access in and out of the wine cellar, sometimes with a two-thousand-dollar bottle of wine in hand. They squeezed their shoulders together, stretched out their arms, and made their way through the thick brush of pea coats, trenches, and parkas.

One night in the middle of the second seating, the cord snapped. Cillian's face was a mask of horror as he swung open the door to find me standing halfway down the staircase, dumbstruck with fear and knee-deep in a mountain of coats, each one abandoned by its little orange tag, which were now scattered all over everything like confetti. They might as well have been shards of broken glass.

Just as I was finishing my post-Christmas shift, I caught Jimmy Day's face cracking open into a huge smile and heard him call out, "There he is." I looked up to see Gareth walk in and take a seat at the bar.

Gareth was Jesse's best friend from college and a frequent visitor to the Babbo bar during Jesse's tenure as floor manager. He lived a few blocks away on 10th Street. On the rare occasion that I went out with the Babbo gang after hours, Gareth was usually there. Seeing him come in made me realize I hadn't talked to people outside of the job in months.

"What are you doing here?" I asked as we hugged.

He pulled back to study me, blue eyes bright. "What are *you* doing here? Didn't you quit Babbo when you started working for Joe?"

I laughed. "I'm still plotting my way out, but I'm almost there."

I hung up Gareth's coat and walked over to the service station at the other end of the bar, waiting while Jimmy Day counted my singles before exchanging them for two twenties and a ten. "That's the guy you should've gone for, Kimba," he said, as he held the bills out for me to grab, eyebrows raised.

I didn't realize how much I missed Gareth until I saw him sitting there, dark hair damp from snowfall. I hadn't seen him since the incident.

In May, we'd learned that Jesse was accused of stealing between thirty and forty thousand dollars from Joe and Mario while working as Otto's GM. I saw the email in Joe's inbox from our CFO, Fran. It was oddly sparse, as if she knew I'd be reading it even though it came into Joe's personal AOL account. Ever since he'd missed a major meeting with Mario, I'd had to start checking it. The subject line read *Missing Money*. Fran wrote that the assistant district attorney assigned to the case was on his way to pick Jesse up and bring him to the station, along with Fran, and Joe was to meet them there.

My stomach dropped. I read the email over and over again, as if I'd gain more information. I had a million emails to answer but couldn't concentrate on anything else. I had to know what was going on. I couldn't eat to save my life but was supposed to head down to the Village for the opening of Anfora—the latest venture from Toby, the former Babbo somm—which happened to be a few blocks from Gareth's apartment. If anyone had heard Jesse's version of events, it was Gareth.

When I arrived at Anfora, Toby's business partner offered me a glass of white wine. I downed it in minutes and headed to the corner of the crowded room to text Gareth.

Are you with Jesse right now, by chance? I texted.

Come over, he responded.

According to Gareth, Jesse was claiming innocence. My heart told me that Jesse was guilty but could not accept it and was certainly not ready to say it out loud. I hoped Gareth knew something or had some piece of information that would settle it in my mind one way or another. Instead, I ended up doing that for him.

I told Gareth about the email from Fran. He was quiet after hearing it, then asked me when the email had come in. A few moments later, he excused himself, saying he needed to follow up with the lawyer his father had arranged for Jesse.

I knew from Gareth's gray face as he apologetically ushered me out the door that it was true.

A few days later, I learned from Joe's AOL account that Jesse had met Joe at Del Posto and confessed. Allegedly, he'd gotten into trouble with gambling. He thought he could replace the money before anyone noticed it was gone. But the harder he tried, the deeper he got into debt. He must have been so scared.

I didn't really eat for days. My heart raced each time the HR director popped into my office looking for Joe. "I need to talk to him *about Jesse,*" she'd whisper. I was afraid to talk about it, afraid my voice would crack, that I'd lose my composure and all the feelings I unknowingly still had for him would come barreling out for all to see.

I'd heard through food blogs that Joe went to the judge and asked for leniency, advocating that Jesse not be given jail time and that the charges be dropped. A member of Jesse's family allegedly paid Mario and Joe back. But Joe didn't discuss that with me. I'd never known anyone who'd been in trouble like that, except some of my former clients. I was desperate to know exactly what happened, what was true.

When I brought it up the following day to Joe, he snapped, "I don't want to ever hear his name again."

It would have passed for his usual growl to someone who didn't hear it every day, but there was something off with his voice. It sounded hollow. Weak. It seemed to me that Jesse had hurt Joe badly. He'd never admit it, but Joe loved Jesse as much as I did. Before the alleged theft, Jesse had become his protégé; as soon as a GM role opened up at Tarry Lodge, Joe and Mario's Westchester outpost, Joe maneuvered him into it, even helping him find an apartment and lending him his sleek black Vespa to commute.

Once the shock wore off, everyone who was friendly with Jesse from the group started checking in on him. How much trouble had he been in? Some of his former girls weren't so forgiving, and even though I had genuine concern for him, I understood their lack of sympathy. The GM of Casa Mono, Jamie, helped him with his résumé. I texted him a few times the first month or two afterward, and I was careful not to let Joe find out that I was still in touch. It seemed like the kind of thing that would anger him, like something an obstructionist would do. But eventually, I stopped thinking about Jesse.

Now here was Gareth, months later, in Babbo. It was the first time we'd seen each other since the conversation in his apartment.

Since it was Jimmy Day's fiftieth birthday, he suggested Gareth and I join him and his boyfriend Peter for drinks after his shift ended around midnight. Gareth and I headed over to the bar at Otto to kill time, and he filled me in on how Jesse was doing.

I was glad to hear they were still friends. Gareth was a happy person who only dwelt on happy things and had a way of ensuring that whoever was with him did the same. He'd worked a few coat check shifts with me at Babbo after he'd dropped out of medical school and needed to pick up some cash. Coat check was more anxiety-inducing than carrying trays, but it didn't feel like that when I worked with Gareth. His cheerful demeanor, not to mention his strong hands and arms that could carry three times as many heavy coats up and down the stairs as I could, made the shifts fun.

"I'm supposed to meet up with Jesse later," Gareth said, holding my gaze for a moment. There was something complicated in his expression.

"I don't mind if he comes," I said. "He just can't come here to Otto—that would be the end of my job!"

Gareth pulled out his phone and sent a quick text. He told me that he'd moved down to DC recently and was back home for Christmas. He was dating three women, but no one seriously. He liked his job, and in a few days, he was flying to the Galapagos Islands with friends, where he'd spend the New Year.

"I want to go somewhere like that," I said wistfully.

"Come with me!" he said.

"I don't have a passport."

Gareth gaped. "Kim, you need to get a passport. How can you not have a passport? What if Joe wants to send you to Italy at the last minute? How would you feel if you had to say no because of something like a passport?"

He was right. I told him that I'd get a passport with my next paycheck.

Aside from those few coat check shifts and that night in Gareth's apartment when Jesse's fate hung in the balance, I hadn't spent much time alone with Gareth. Without Jesse present to overshadow him, I realized how attractive he was. Ruggedly handsome with strong features—not pretty, like Jesse. It felt good to sit next to him. Like whatever your troubles were, he'd take care of them. I liked this quality about him for Jesse. I liked it for me, too.

"What about guys, are you seeing anyone?" he asked.

It had been so long since I'd dated anyone seriously that I immediately tensed up. Hemmed and hawed. I told him there were a lot of young guys at the store, guys I was interested in, but no, I wasn't dating anyone. I hoped he didn't keep probing. I didn't want him to realize the last person I'd slept with was Jesse, over a year ago.

"I don't always know how to make things happen," I admitted. "I'm a little closed off."

Gareth turned his body toward me and rolled his eyes fondly. "A little? Kim, you're a clam."

I wished more people talked to me like that.

We emerged from Otto into a full-blown snowstorm. The ground was covered and glowed white against the dark sky as we made our way the few blocks back to Babbo to pick up Jimmy Day and Peter. We had one drink there and then set off for the Blind Tiger, known for its craft beers, where Jesse was waiting for us.

Soaked through from the fast-falling snow, we piled into the Blind Tiger and were met with a blast of heat, as though standing in front of a campfire. Jesse gave me a hug, further chilling me from the melting snow on his coat. He looked good but seemed humbled. It felt strange to look at his gorgeous face and not feel consumed by it. I hated that Jesse had stolen from Joe, but the theft set me free from him. It took something that severe to cause my feelings to evaporate. I don't think anything else could've done it. This was a man who I'd developed stronger feelings for than for Liam, who I almost married. But that night, as he stood in front of me, I saw only a kid who was slowly re-building his life, and a friend who I held absolutely no torch for.

Gareth and I moved to the wooden bar. We settled in with crisp pilsners and whiskey shots. He continued to prod about the new job, how much I was working. "Joe expects too much from all of you."

Gareth was no fan of Mario and Joe, and not because of the situation with Jesse. Aside from those few coat check shifts, Gareth had never worked in the restaurant industry. He thought we were all insane, the way we scrambled to answer the phone when Joe called, even on days off. "You should be going on vacation with friends too. You need to be getting out more—you need to do things like this."

"Kimba and Gareth, get over here!" called Jimmy Day. "I want a picture for my birthday!"

I stood up and realized how drunk I was—silly-stage drunk, fun drunk. The five of us huddled together, falling over each other, laughing as a stranger took a blurry photograph. We ordered more pilsner until the barman told us it was time to go home.

By then the landscape was unrecognizable. The snow reached above my knees, making it hard to walk, but we had no choice. It was fun, having the city streets all to ourselves. Gareth told Jesse and me that we could stay at his place. It didn't seem as though the subway was running, and trekking over to the East Side to catch the 6 train would have amounted to an arctic expedition. We parted ways with Jimmy Day and Peter and headed north.

We came upon Fifth Avenue. There were no tire tracks and not a car in sight. There was the kind of silence that came only with snow. All we heard was the crunching of our steps and our laughter as we threw one another down, hard, onto three feet of dense snow in the middle of the empty avenue. It looked like a vast meadow in the middle of nowhere.

I didn't realize until then that Gareth and I were going to sleep together, but I think Gareth knew as far back into the night as Otto.

In the doorway of his family's apartment, we peeled off our icy boots and socks. Gareth gathered up dry clothes for Jesse and me to sleep in, and I changed in the bathroom. My eyes and cheeks were pink from the whipping wind and the alcohol. Then I headed into Gareth's room.

"These shorts fit like underwear. I can't sleep in these," I said, yanking down the terry cloth hem. I leaned against his bed. He was already tucked in, gaze heavy.

I tracked his bare shoulders above the blanket, swallowing hard. "Where am I sleeping?" I asked, with a knowing smile. Maybe it was the beer and the whiskey, or maybe because Gareth was Gareth, but being this close to him didn't scare me at all.

"Here," he said, and pulled me into his warm bed with one arm.

We forgot all about Jesse in the living room until he opened Gareth's bedroom door, half a question tumbling out of his mouth before cutting off abruptly.

I didn't see Jesse's face; I was firmly underneath Gareth. But I saw Gareth's tight expression.

Jesse closed the door, and we immediately forgot about him again. A few minutes later, the front door slammed.

I didn't remember falling asleep, but suddenly the sun was up and I had the anxious urge to get up and get out. I had to get to work. It was Monday. Where was my phone? My phone was dead. Joe was in Italy and already had a six-hour start on me. I forgot all about what Natalie said about this being the week I'd get a break. I had to get back to Corporate where I could collect myself, have some breakfast, put on dry shoes, check the inboxes, and figure out how I felt about last night. Part of me couldn't wait to bolt out the door and work gave me a perfect excuse, but part of me didn't want to leave Gareth. I tried to get out of bed, but he pulled me back to his warm body.

After a minute, though, my anxiety won out and I told him it was time for me to go. He gave me a pair of his old jeans, a belt, and an ugly lime green button-down, and I bolted. In wet, cold boots, I trudged up Fifth Avenue toward Corporate.

Gareth called later that morning.

"I spoke to Jesse. I told him he has no right to be mad at you. Me, yes, but not you."

"Why would he be mad at you? He never even really liked me—" As soon as I spoke the words, I realized they weren't true. I barely had time to process that Jesse probably did, after all his crap, have feelings for me, because that wasn't everything Gareth called to tell me.

"I think you should take Plan B."

"There's no way I'm pregnant," I informed him, "and we used a condom."

"I don't think we did after the first time," he corrected wryly. "There's no evidence in my room that we did."

And then I thought about it. I had no idea where I was in my cycle. Why would I? It had been forever since I'd had sex. My breasts weren't the slightest bit sore, which meant I was at least ten days away from my next period. This meant it was possible I was ovulating.

I hung up on Gareth and called the one college friend I had left in the city. "Well, technically you could be," she agreed.

All I heard from my married friends was what a chore it was for them to get pregnant. For months they tried and tried. I didn't feel intuitively that I was or that I had anything to worry about there. But it seemed to make Gareth feel better, and on the off chance, I took Plan B. The instructions stated it could make you up to five days late, and if you still hadn't gotten your period after six days, to call your doctor.

The fourth day of being late, I started to get a little nervous.

I scrolled through Facebook while lying in bed. Pictures of Gareth came up. He looked like he was in paradise, on a trip with just one friend—a woman named Marta. I looked at the other people tagged in her photos. They had the same last name. They all looked like her. This was her family.

Gareth went to the Galapagos Islands with a woman over New Year's to meet her family.

She's not my girlfriend, Gareth texted. *Not yet. I don't know what's going to happen with her. I didn't lie to you, Kim.*

You kept telling me to come with you—why would you even say that? I texted back. I was enraged.

I don't know why I said that, he texted back. *I was happy to see you again, and I meant it—you need to do things for yourself like that.*

I curled up in bed, more scared than angry. It killed me that he had misled me about his trip, but what bothered me the most was how the thought of having a baby with Gareth didn't scare me at all. Not until I found out about Marta.

Pangs in my abdomen woke me a few hours later. I felt damp and sticky between my legs. I had gotten my period.

One Saturday when I was still working the day phone shift at Babbo, Joe came roaring in at about 2:00 p.m.

"Eric is coming," he said.

I put down the phone.

"I don't have it on the calendar—do you have it on the calendar? Did Eric ever get back to you about this?"

About a month earlier, Joe's friend Eric had emailed us about securing a date for his birthday party in the cantina, the small, bricked room in the basement. He gave me a few dates to check but never got back to confirm one.

The room was free; that wasn't why Joe was pacing. It was a strain on the kitchen and the floor when we hosted parties, even for only eight people like this one. We usually brought two extra servers in to handle a party downstairs. But on this short notice, we wouldn't be able to find anybody.

I saw the wheels turning in Joe's brain as he darted between the empty pickle and the dining room, past table one where I'd set up my arsenal. I took a slow, deep breath, rechecked my inbox and sent mail for anything from Eric. Nothing. *It wasn't my fault.*

"We can do it!" Joe exclaimed. "We can be the waiters, bring the food down, and serve the wine. What do you think? How long are you supposed to be on the phones for? He's bringing some cool people—it'll be fun."

Eric was a big TV and film critic. He'd been coming to Babbo for years. He usually brought in interesting people like Dr. Cornel West—I *definitely* wanted to go to his party. I had no idea how I was going to pull off carrying plates of food down the stairs, but I was too excited to worry about that for the moment. I was still a *we*, and we were going to a party.

I reminded Joe that the Robin Hood Foundation had given him four tickets to the Sheryl Crow benefit concert at Irving Plaza that night.

He didn't hesitate. "That's tonight? Okay, we'll do that first."

I was packing up the reservation book at 5:30 p.m. when Joe told me to meet him and his friend Owen, a big mountain of a man with rosy cheeks like a cherub and wild curly hair, back at Babbo in one hour and we'd all go to the benefit together. Owen was a singer-songwriter Joe picked up God knows where. They had been playing guitar together the past few weeks.

We stayed at the show long enough to hear Sheryl sing a few songs and have one glass of wine. I didn't know what I was supposed to be doing—was I working, or just hanging out? Not that I minded. Joe always seemed happy after he knocked back a few.

On the taxi ride back to Babbo, I learned that Owen was just as thrilled to be going to Eric's party as I was, but for a very different reason. Jim Carrey was on the reservation book tonight with a four-top at 8:15 p.m. Apparently he and Owen were once close friends but had had some kind of falling-out years ago, and Owen hadn't seen him since.

"Are you gonna go up to him?" Joe inquired, eyes wide in anticipation. A mischievous smile spread across his face. "Just leave me out of it."

We shimmied single file through the pickle and I recognized Eric's long black dreadlocks and familiar blazer that I'd hung up in the coat closet many times over the years. He turned to Joe with a huge smile, wisps of gray hair lining his face.

"You didn't remember I was coming?" he teased.

Joe steered us downstairs into the basement. Parties in the cantina started with champagne in the wine cellar. Its temperature was kept at sixty degrees Fahrenheit, and combined with its twelve-foot ceilings and dim lighting, it felt like we were drinking in some secret cavern. It wasn't until Joe asked me to hand a champagne flute to the gentleman on my right that I noticed I was standing next to Quentin Tarantino.

Still confused about whether I was working or crashing the party, I asked Joe if we needed to check in with the kitchen. "Nah—don't worry about it," he said.

We headed into the dimly lit, amber cantina to take our seats at the small, ten-person table that took up the majority of the room, and I wound up seated between Owen and Tarantino. Joe stood up and gave a quick speech, made fun of Eric for not telling us they were coming, and then introduced Owen and me as his friends. I texted him under the table to make sure he didn't need me to help him run in the food and wine. It wasn't until twenty minutes later that I realized he was not going to make me help him work the party, and that we were definitely crashing.

I was happy to have sat next to Owen. A few of his wiry hairs scratched my cheek as he leaned in to say, "I'm going to check it out upstairs." The more wine he drank, the more he ventured up the stairs to "casually" walk by Jim Carrey's table, egged on by Joe and me. "Uh-oh, there he goes!" Joe jeered, as Owen rose from the table for the third time.

Eric's guests were all in the movie business. I had no idea what any of them were talking about, but I didn't feel anxious because while everyone was kind, no one paid much attention to me. I felt like I was in the Twilight Zone, but also like I belonged—or at least wasn't out of place. It didn't matter that I didn't have much to contribute to the conversation. The introduction from Joe was all I needed—I was in. I had a seat at the table—literally.

At one point, the man seated across from Tarantino broke into a story about Bonnie and Clyde and how after they were killed, their bodies were carted through the street heaped on an uncovered wagon. He said the townspeople had sliced off chunks of their fingers as a kind of memorabilia.

Tarantino turned to me. "I don't believe it. The fingers would've ended up in jars of formaldehyde for sale on eBay by now."

I left shortly after they whipped out cigars. As I stood to head back upstairs, Joe flapped his hand back and forth, calling me to his end of the table. He motioned for me to lean in and said in my ear, "I think Quentin Tarantino looks like a duck," before taking a big inhale from his cigar and blowing the smoke toward the door he'd propped open with a chair.

I'd proved myself a worthy sidekick that night, marking the beginning of Joe really including me. I soon became his second-in-command, a full-fledged member of every "crew." I felt like a confidant, a trusted ally. Firmly part of the inner circle. I felt like a friend.

Joe had an old Ford Expedition he convinced a mechanic to rig so it would run on used cooking oil instead of gasoline. When he got low on fuel, he had me call ahead to the porters at Del Posto, where he filled up outside the restaurant's loading dock. There was only one place he could bring "the truck" come inspection time—to some mechanic in the Bronx, which thank God he didn't ask me to do. The truck made a *glug-glug* sound when he stepped on the gas, and when he slowed down or came to a stop, the whole interior of the truck—what felt like its bowels—rocked back and forth, like if you stopped short while running and felt your internal organs bouncing around inside your skeleton.

A few months after my night with Gareth, Joe and I were driving down Fifth Avenue from Corporate, heading to Babbo. He pulled up out front and we wobbled back and forth for a few seconds.

"Are you out of here yet?" he asked, indicating the restaurant with a jerk of his head.

I had just gotten my raise and didn't have to work at Babbo on Saturdays anymore or pick up hostessing shifts.

The day I'd finally pinned Joe down and pressed the issue, palms sweating and heart in my throat, he said, "You shouldn't have to work two jobs, and you're doing such a great job here."

I almost fell off my chair. Natalie had warned me that getting so much as a "good job" or "nice work" out of Joe occurred as frequently as a solar eclipse, but there it was. To be free of a second job for the first time in ten years felt like I'd won the lottery. Even though I'd be taking home the same amount of money each month, I didn't have to spend every Saturday at Babbo to do it.

I had yet to give my notice at Babbo. As desperate as I was to leave, to finally be that person who made enough to only work one job, I was afraid. I'd started working at Babbo four months after moving to New York, and in the ten years since, it'd become my home. I could walk in any time and find almost anything I needed—a bathroom, free coffee, sliced bread from the Sullivan Street Bakery, Cillian, Jimmy Day, Gina, George. When I was still at NYU, if I hadn't called home in a while, my parents would ring the employee line looking for me. Even if I wasn't working that night, somebody always knew where I was.

I told Joe as much. "I'm afraid one day I'll walk in and I won't know a soul in the place."

He turned to me with a look to kill others. "Life goes the fuck on, Kim."

Joe got out of the truck and left me sitting there alone. It wasn't his words that filled me with shame but the way he said them: the flicker of disgust on his face, as if what he meant was, *Which way are you going? Are you going with me, with Eataly, with all these new things we've got going on, or do you want to stay small down here in the basement?*

I walked in and found the hospitality manager. I told her not to give me any more shifts.

five

THE RESERVATION RACKET

I hated the way I'd left things with Gareth. But so much had happened at Corporate that it made the last year fly by like ten days.

Last May, Joe had been cast as one of the hosts on *MasterChef*, with Gordon Ramsay. Now he had a gaggle of agents at CAA—Creative Artists Agency, one of the three big talent agencies in Hollywood—who pitched him for more TV shows, speaking gigs, and license deals. Even though this was his first shot at being a series regular—a complete newcomer, the low end of the totem pole by Hollywood standards—Joe was treated like an A-list star. This was partly due to the restaurants, but mostly because he was one of the owners of Eataly. That was its power.

I thought my days might slow down with him based in California for three months of the year, but all it did was kick The Joe Show into high gear. We learned I could run the operation alone from Corporate. Joe calling from L.A. was no different than him calling me from Becco or Babbo or from somewhere inside the store.

Someone from CAA called me at least once a day asking for a reservation at one of our restaurants, or if we could arrange for the director of *Weeds* or the executive producer of some soon-to-air HBO show to have a private tour of the store, and Joe always said yes.

When Joe found out Italy was producing their own *MasterChef* series, he pushed to be cast as one of their judges. The casting director and head writer of what would become the Italian version of the show visited the USA production to gauge the operation. There, the casting director told Joe, "You don't *really* speak Italian," but Joe got his act together, worked on his language skills, and ended up getting cast. This meant he'd have to spend an additional few months of the year shooting in Milan and brought an onslaught of new names, numbers, and titles to our universe. A relatively normal person would have cried uncle at the towering, almost impossible-to-manage mountain of projects, but any fear I had was outweighed by excitement. Who didn't want to be in contact with influential TV executives, agents, and writers?

Hollywood wasn't Joe's only source for new friends. He made a new one every day, wherever he was in the world. He liked to collect people, and he always seemed to cross paths with someone who had just the piece he needed for one of his big ideas. He weaved them into his days like he did all the other resources we pulled from. It was my job to know these people and help Joe make use of them.

There was Donna, a globe-trotting wealthy Australian married to a big guy in the jewelry market. Joe crossed paths with her while competing in the Kona Ironman World Championship triathlon in Hawaii. When Donna wasn't visiting her daughter in Tel Aviv, she hopped between Sydney, Los Angeles, New York, and parts of Europe, and we set her up at the hard-to-get restaurants in each city.

As if we had nothing else to do, Joe decided to explore some writing projects. No one was kidding themselves that he actually had time to sit down and write, so his literary agent introduced him to Sharky.

"He writes porn" was how Joe initially had described him to me. Sharky wrote *about* porn, had served as the editor of a marijuana aficionados' magazine, and nurtured a first-rate hatred for Hugh Hefner. Sharky's voice was full of gravel, he had a cat named Jeepster, and he always wore a black fedora. He was the only person who could get Joe to concentrate on one thing for hours at a time. He'd send in his work for Joe to review that once I'd opened would cost me a good forty-five minutes; I couldn't put them down. They'd spend the afternoon at Corporate—I blocked off chunks on the calendar named *Writing sessions with Sharky*, which often turned into guitar-playing sessions and opening a few beers, while I was four feet away from them, banging out emails. But there were worse ways to spend an afternoon at work.

At the end of these meetings, Joe always tried to get Sharky to leave with something, a parting gift. It was how I knew how much Joe liked him. Usually Joe offered wine, as the office was littered with sample bottles left over from *Today Show* segments and a few good ones that someone had sent in, which sat on the floor getting ruined by the sun that poured through our shadeless windows.

Liza had been a longtime Del Posto regular who'd morphed into an Eataly regular. She ran her own company: the ALTZ Group represented all the makeup artists, hair geniuses, and stylists, the people who got the Nicole Kidmans and Angelina Jolies of the world ready for their *Vogue* cover shoots. Liza was tall and slim, with a wavy blond bob that hovered just above her shoulders; her skin and makeup were always perfect. She was the woman you moved to New York to become.

"She's crazy rich," Joe said once. She looked like it; she looked like she belonged on a red carpet even when wearing leather pants and a plain gray T-shirt.

When introducing me to his latest find, Joe would say, "Here's Kim, my assistant who I was telling you about," and then he'd say something to the effect that I had such and such in common with this person, or something he thought might make me seem interesting. His delivery never wavered, as if he truly believed what he said to be the truth, but it bit him in the ass the day I met Liza.

The look of confusion on her face when I approached her and Joe seated at Manzo's best table—Eataly's fancy, white-tablecloth restaurant tucked behind a towering wall of olive oil—told me that Joe had probably told her I was "into fashion, too." She smelled expensive. Her perfume wafted over as she extended her baby-soft hand covered in gold rings.

I asked her months later what kind of perfume she wore. She just shook her head, looked away, and said, "Oh, a little of this and that." Women like Liza didn't give away their secrets.

That day, I was wearing a cheap white parka from American Eagle with a coffee stain on the front, flare jeans I'd never had shortened, and snow boots with fake fur that looked like roadkill. It'd been a long day. My hair was stringy. This was how I met the chicest woman alive. I could've killed him.

Liza's best friend was a guy named Sven who was the president of one of the top modeling agencies in the world, whose headquarters happened to be across the street from the store. After Liza introduced Sven to Joe, he was in Eataly all the time. He and his husband loved

Joe's family wines. Sven ordered them by the caseload—which Joe sold him at wholesale—much to the dismay of the guys who ran the Eataly wine shop.

"Why is he doing this? We don't make any money off those cases," Vittorio would lament.

Sven was none the wiser. He was just tickled to have an "in" at the store.

"I love my red table wine!" he'd exclaim, tossing his head back, eyes squeezed shut.

There was a high that came with having an inside connection to whatever was "hot" and "new," and Liza and Sven understood this—perhaps better than Joe and I did. The fashion and hospitality industries had this in common: both worked in trade, using favors, gifts, and even introductions to the right people as currency. What really turned people on was getting something that no one else could. An eight-top at Babbo, because Babbo didn't seat parties larger than six people. A private olive oil tasting in the back of the store with Eataly's chief oleologist, Edgar, where they'd sip just-pressed, peppery, neon-green oils Edgar had brought back from Tuscany in tiny bottles. An 8:00 p.m. table at Eleven Madison Park during fashion week. Running this racket from our side quickly became my highest priority. Joe was happy because he had someone—me—essentially working a side gig managing his relationships; I was happy because it made me important to these people.

"Call Sven and see what he wants," Joe commanded, as he stepped off the elevator and into our office.

I'd seen the email come into Joe's inbox from Sven and was already on it.

"He wants to bring a few executives to Manzo for a meeting today at noon. No eating. Just coffee. He said Kate Upton might join them toward the end."

He nodded once, already moving on. "Make it happen—tell whoever's at Manzo I said it's fine."

I grimaced, waving him back. "The GM of Manzo says Ari and Aaron are saying no; they are overbooked for lunch and they can't spare a table just for coff—"

"Dipshits from Dalton," he snapped. Dalton was the elite private school the Segals had attended on the Upper East Side. "Tell them it's for Kate-fucking-Upton. Can you explain this to them, please? Don't they know that we want people like that in the store?"

"But Kate Upton might not—"

"*Kim.* I don't care. She'll come next time. Or next time he'll bring Giselle or whoever else he reps. Make sure they understand this."

Some people might have hated being in the middle like this, but I didn't; I loved having an excuse to talk to everyone. I loved knowing everything that was going on. I preferred to know more than Joe. That way, he was always dependent on me. I was always needed.

Joe never stopped hustling to keep influential people in his restaurants. It was more than the money; I got the impression that he wanted these people to like him. I wanted them to like me too.

I was also compensated, unofficially, for my role in running this racket.

Donna breezed through town and left a tiny, fuchsia-colored square box with the word *Buccellati* stamped in gold across the top. Inside was a chunky sterling silver cocktail ring shaped like a gardenia.

Glossy white shopping bags bearing the ALTZ Group logo were dropped onto the office floor by a messenger. I'd pry myself away from my desk and paw through tubes of Tom Ford lipstick, Sisley Black Rose face oil, NARS blush and eye shadow compacts, four different shades of Giorgio Armani Luminous Silk foundation ("So you can mix and match!" Liza said), and a fistful of Givenchy eyeliner pencils. There was a small glass vial of what looked like gold glitter paint, which was called Chanel Sublimage L'Extrait Intensive Restoring Treatment. A Google search showed it selling at Bergdorf's for six hundred dollars a bottle.

When I asked her about it later, she said, "I have a special relationship with Chanel," shrugging like she'd just swung by my office and brought me a coffee. The paper insert said to use "one pump per week," but I slathered it on twice a day, and after a few days, Paul stopped me at Corporate and asked if I was getting more sleep. But I wasn't well-rested; it was just Liza's six-hundred-dollar face serum. I was still a workaholic lunatic.

That Christmas, Liza gave me my first Chanel bag. I remember placing the stiff black box on the ugly orange couch, pulling off the lid, and staring at it while running my fingers over the heavy chain-link strap.

Jay, a famous American novelist and longtime Babbo regular, always sent chocolate chip cookies and a bottle of Dom Perignon at Christmas.

Once I returned from the bathroom to find a nondescript box on my desk. Peeling back the white tissue paper revealed a velvety brown suede jacket—I could smell the leather before I saw it—from a Del Posto regular with a card that read *My boyfriend owns VINCE*. I treasured these luxuries I couldn't afford, but the real prize was being important to these people. They depended on me.

I became a one-stop shop for all Joe's contacts. Instead of them having to keep track of the different GMs at our restaurants and Eataly, which by then numbered thirty worldwide, they called me for whatever they needed, and I *made it happen*.

My favorite gift was an eighty percent discount on a shiny black Moncler parka, the French luxury outerwear brand. Joe and the

North American president of Moncler met God knows where and decided, for a month, that they were BFFs.

I splurged on a new pair of Tory Burch block heels—only two inches, so I could still chase after Joe—and cut my hair into a short bob just past my chin.

"This is a good look for you Kim, this jacket. . . . You look nice," Edo remarked in approval as I approached him and a manager at Pizza Pasta inside the store.

"And those are great shoes," the manager added.

Suddenly, Michele was squeezing himself in between them to get a good look.

"She's got a new coat and new shoes, and a short new haircut," he sang, playfully tugging on the ends of my hair.

"I like it. It's sexy!"

"*Michele,*" the manager gasped, even as I grinned and basked in their appreciation.

"What? What'd I say?" he added before spinning on his heel and heading back in the direction he came.

That April, Joe tasked me with delivering Liza's birthday gift in person. "Make sure she knows what she's drinking."

"I didn't realize he was sending *you,*" Liza said, when I arrived at her apartment on the West Side. She tossed her wavy hair back and forth and motioned for me to follow her in.

"It's too delicate to give to a messenger," I explained.

I placed the bag on the black marble island in her kitchen. Her apartment smelled just like her—a rich blend of vanilla, cedarwood, and patchouli. I wanted to look around but didn't want her to see me taking the place in.

"You have to decant this. Do you know how to do that?" I asked, as she gently pulled the bottle of 1978 Chateau Rayas Chateauneuf-du-Pape from the bag and folded back the gold tissue paper I'd wrapped it in. The label was brown, oxidized, and ripped, which lessened its value in the wine world but to me, and I suspect to Liza, made it all the more precious.

"Joe said to call us when you're ready to open it and we'll walk you through it."

She turned to face me. "Thanks for walking it over. I want you to know how much Sven and I appreciate all your help with reservations. I know Joe tells you to do it, but it feels like you care."

"I do!" I exclaimed, maybe a little too enthusiastically.

Liza smiled warmly. "You want a splash of Vespa Bianco?"

I left Liza's fancy apartment twenty minutes later, trotting back across 19th Street to Corporate feeling like we were real friends.

I was flying high from my new influential connections and swag, grateful to be around people who I wanted to be like, but couldn't help but notice that everyone was going somewhere but me.

Gareth was officially in a relationship with Marta from the Galapagos Islands. She worked out of DC, ran a fashion blog, and spoke Spanish, French, and German, and her job took her whizzing all over the world. I had a hard time picturing Gareth as a willing Instagram husband, dutifully photographing her in various travel-inspired outfits, but his chocolate Lab, Pablo, showed up in half the photos.

We lost Michele to the Eataly Rome store. Oscar sent him to prepare for its big opening, slated that summer in July. "Is not forever," he said, sheepishly, while looking at the ground whenever anyone brought it up.

There was less life in the store after he departed. Upon entry, instinctively I scanned the store for two things: Joe's shiny head—my actual reason for showing up—and a huddle of blue shirts. I could catch one of the boys out of the corner of my eye from across the entire store. It didn't matter what situation I was about to walk into with Joe. If I spotted just one of them, I felt better. Stronger. Protected. Especially if I saw Michele. He was the only one who could snap me out of the work zone. His eyes always held a look of care, happy to see me no matter what storm was brewing. I wondered if he knew how good it felt to be looked at that way. He served as a buffer to the insanity of the job, an antidote to Joe's roughness.

Everyone was talking about flying to Rome for the opening—Edo, the Segals, some of the managers. I was dying to go but I had no reason to; with my mediocre Italian, I brought no value. There was no way Joe would spare the expense to send me.

But there were new faces flying in too. Not long after Michele's departure, I headed down to the ninth floor looking for Edo and found a stranger at his desk. His name was Alessandro. He'd flown in with Oscar's business partner, the thirteen-names, you-must-come-stay-at-my-castle Sebastiano, for no reason at all. Just for a chance to see New York for two days with an old college buddy.

"Oh. Where's Edo?" I asked, as I hurled myself through the doorway, stopping short.

"Sorry to disappoint," he said, smiling. I would've known he was an Italian even if I hadn't heard him speak. His deep tan skin looked out of place against his pale blue eyes. All the Italians let themselves get tan. I didn't feel particularly strongly for him, but he was attractive, dressed well, was around my age, and wasn't wearing a ring. The lack of a ring, in particular, was becoming an increasing rarity on men in their midthirties. I felt like I was getting left behind.

Alessandro invited me out to lunch, so I said I'd go. I didn't do this enough: go out with someone, get to know them, and see what developed. It was spur of the moment, and I was a little bit proud of myself.

"You have to be dating *somebody*, Kim," Joe had remarked a few months earlier, unprompted. Even the spirited seventy-something executive producer of Joe's Ironman special, who was there at the time, agreed. Taking me aside by the crook of my arm, he said, "He's worried about you." I stared in disbelief. My own boss, and this guy, playing yenta? The producer's watery, kelly green eyes framed in bushy white eyebrows looked as though he was ready to fight me on this. Looking back, I understood his resolute expression. I thought I had plenty of time, but this old man knew better.

These two discussing my nonexistent love life was embarrassing but illuminating. I wondered who else noticed the fact that I was always alone. Were people at the store talking about it behind my back, and Joe was the only one blunt enough to blurt it out?

So I took Alessandro to lunch. It wasn't like I'd have to see him after tomorrow anyway. He was only in town for three days. I ordered tap water, but he sent it back and asked for a bottle of mineral water.

"Your New York water smells like a swimming pool," he laughed.

I stuck my nose in my glass. It did.

He headed back to Milan the next day with Sebastiano. It took a month of flirty, noncommittal texting before he asked if I wanted to go to Rio with him for a few days.

My brain screeched to a halt. No way was I flying to Rio with him; I could barely show up for a second date. But since he was so far away, across the Atlantic in Milan and thus totally within my control to avoid if things got weird, I said, "Maybe." We even swapped hotel suggestions for the trip because it was fun to entertain the thought.

As we sent increasingly extravagant and unrealistic options back and forth, I realized Alessandro had no intention of going either. But it reminded me that I still had yet to get my passport. And then Alessandro pointed out what should have been glaringly obvious: "Why don't you accompany Joe to Milan for the summer? I'll introduce you to all my friends."

I'd hoped for a reason to ask Joe to send me to Milan for a week or so while he was out there shooting *MasterChef Italia*, but it hadn't occurred to me to push for the whole summer.

I went to the post office on 23rd Street and filled out my application. Two weeks later, I was thumbing through the blank pages of the small navy and gold passport booklet, ripe with possibility.

It didn't take much coaxing for Joe to agree to let me accompany him to Milan for the summer. The third time I'd mustered enough spine to bring it up, suddenly his big eyes popped and a lightbulb went off.

"You can help when guests come over. I wanna do a lot of entertaining this year."

Everyone helped me. Liza assigned a junior stylist to take me shopping, helping stretch my minuscule clothing budget over a few pieces at J. Crew and Zara. Sharky called me a few days before my flight, saying he had a gift for me.

"Use it for cookin' or killin'," he said, as he slid a shiny, bright red Swiss Army knife across my desk. Something tender in Sharky's gruff voice made me think he was genuinely worried. Should *I* be worried about me?

I packed up the knife along with Donna's ring, the black Chanel bag, and a black silk sundress the junior stylist and I had found on a sale rack. I rolled the suitcase I borrowed from my father into the elevator and waited downstairs for a Dial 7 car to bring me to the

JFK international terminal. These were the only people in my life; the only people I spoke to regularly. The ones who needed to know I would be operating out of a different time zone. Except for my parents, there wasn't anyone else outside of work who would notice I was gone.

six

BITS OF CASING
AND LEMON PEEL

"What you gotta do is go around to all of the happy hour places come *aperitivo* time and find the ones with the best spread. I'm not talking about that oily, crap bruschetta they serve at Isola. Some places have full-on buffets—they put out pasta trays, pizza, salads 'n' shit. The idea is, you buy one or two glasses of wine. They charge a little more for it at this hour, but then you can eat as much as you want. Just do that for dinner every night."

Joe and I were in Milan at a time when the euro was much higher than the dollar, and this really irked him. He sounded like he was giving a homily when he talked about saving money. His enthusiasm made me feel as though we were in this together; like we were real friends. He liked having someone to be cheap with, someone who could actually benefit from these discoveries.

We continued walking down Corso Garibaldi toward the Duomo. Luxury boutiques; uncrowded, well-kept restaurants; and the occasional hardware store no bigger than a broom closet made up the ivory, neoclassical façade. Trim Milanese dressed in fitted suits and flowing, knee-length skirts sailed down the middle of the street on identical yellow BikeMi bicycles, Milan's bike share program, not a one wearing a helmet. I soon joined them, biking to each end of this small city, always arriving at my destination a sweaty mess but feeling good in my silk sundress with my Chanel chain strap across my chest.

Joe and I passed an old brick church set back from the road— allegedly built by St. Ambrose in the third century. Gazing up at this relic while Vespas streaked by snapped me into reality: I was finally in Europe.

Joe waved his hands back and forth rapidly along the sides of his head, abruptly flustered. "You have to recycle here—they expect you to wash a can of beans! Last year I said *fuck it* and just put everything in the garbage, and the psycho who runs my building went through my trash—she picked through my garbage. There was nothing identifiable in there; I don't know how she knew it was me, but *she knew*. So now I just take a little baggie out with me when I leave the house every morning and toss it into the cans on the street. But you can't get caught; they'll fine you."

I told him that was what we had to do in Manhattan too. He made a noise of disbelief.

A few days later, Joe told me that he'd made us a composting spot out on the balcony off the kitchen, which was really just a large ceramic planter filled with dull-looking soil left behind by a previous tenant. He put in a few rib bones, a lemon peel, the skin of a yellow onion, and the bits of the outer casing pulled off a small roll of cured meat.

I cleaned it out every few days until he lost interest.

I had the apartment all to myself my first night in Italy. The Bastianich family wasn't coming out for a few weeks, and Joe was traveling with the cast and crew of *MasterChef Italia* to some little town up north for an *esterna*—an offsite challenge.

I'd been in charge of finding Joe a place to live that summer, which allowed me to get to know the city quite well for never having been. I was careful to show him only options that would make it convenient for me to join, before I'd worked up the courage to ask him to take me along. The apartment he ended up choosing was also my first choice. There was a bathroom and a small bedroom with a pullout sofa bed immediately to the left of the front door; the other three bedrooms and two bathrooms were on the opposite side of the massive eighteen-hundred-square-foot space. The apartment took up the entire corner of Via Guercino and Viale Montello in the *quartiere cinese*, Milan's Chinatown. This place was slightly bigger than the home my family had lived in down in Florida.

"It's old-school Park Avenue, Kim!" Joe had exclaimed, as we sat in the office clicking through my curated rental options for the summer. One look at the high ceilings, built-in bookshelves, Juliet balcony, intricate crown molding, and classic décor and furnishings in that regal old building, and I too got caught up in the allure of something I didn't have in childhood.

The only caveat was that it didn't have air conditioning. "We don't need air conditioning, right, Kim?"

"No, we don't!"

I took the little bedroom with the pullout sofa. It'd be horrible to sleep on for two months under normal circumstances, but I'd have pitched a cot in the kitchen if that was what it took to get me to Milan. The ceilings were eleven feet high. One wall in my room had eight individual floor-to-ceiling closets, four stacked on top of four. The shower in my bathroom wasn't a real shower after all, but a mini tub with a removable shower head that you'd use to wash the family dog, so I would have to share a bathroom with Joe's kids when they arrived. But so what? I was finally here. Having this space all to myself was unbelievable—having a real kitchen again, a full-sized dining room table, felt incredible. None of the apartments I'd lived in in New York had dishwashers.

"Won't it be weird living under the same roof as Joe?" one of the Corporate employees asked. She eyeballed me like I was crazy. *She* was the one who was crazy if she thought I was going to miss my shot at living abroad in an apartment that I could never afford, with an Italian celebrity who'd given me fair warning that he planned to "host a lot of people and have parties," and that it would be part of my job to help orchestrate them.

My student loans hadn't really moved. After thirteen years, I'd paid off little more than the interest. I didn't have an extra thousand dollars a month to save toward a vacation; tagging along with Joe was the only chance I had to do something like this.

The fridge was stocked with the line of Bastianich family wine— "Help yourself," Joe told me. So I poured myself a big glass of Friulano and walked around the apartment, sitting for a few minutes inside every room. I grabbed a chair from the dining room table and wedged the front legs onto the Juliet balcony facing the street, and listened to people speaking Italian as they passed underneath me. There was no doubt that I was in Europe—the buildings across the street looked like ones I'd seen in movies set in Paris or Prague. I even thrilled at the ambulance sirens and the carabinieri, the Italian federal police, as they screeched by. Two and a half years after taking the executive assistant job, I was finally here.

I closed the balcony doors only after realizing I was getting bitten by mosquitoes. I pulled out my sofa bed, which smelled like mildew, and passed right out.

***

Either Joe went out at night or he invited people over to the apartment for wine, and he always included me in both. I knew he wanted someone to play host with, but I think that he also just liked having me around. He would not have said yes to me coming here had he felt otherwise.

Truthfully, I loved *and* hated these outings. I couldn't understand what everyone was saying. They all spoke way too fast. I had studied enough of the language to recognize many of the words but couldn't put them together quickly enough to keep up with the conversation. After a few hours of this, plus two or three glasses of wine, I was mentally shot and often couldn't process even the most straightforward email when I got back to the apartment. Late-evening email was crucial: last-minute reservation requests from the folks in New York and L.A.

These evenings came on the heels of me working from the dining room table for nine or ten hours straight, so at that point I was dying to get out and experience the city, regardless of how exhausted I felt. Most of my work was done in English. When I did work in Italian, it was written—I WhatsApped Joe's driver to confirm his morning pickup, I read the latest press clippings sent by his PR rep. Having to practice speaking Italian in front of your boss, who'd said more than once, "I want to see some results," felt like being set up to fail. But there was no way I'd miss the nightly excursions, especially after being alone in the apartment all day. They just weren't entirely social for me; they still felt like work.

Joe's friends from the *MasterChef Italia* set were either famous themselves or had worked in the TV industry long enough that they weren't fazed by celebrity or my proximity to it, and therefore every one of them seemed genuine. I liked the show's head writer Serena, who was the one who'd told Joe when he was campaigning for the show that he didn't really speak Italian. She gave Joe a lot of flak, just like his wife Alice did, and he took it. Her constant smoking kept the mosquitoes away while we sat outside Cantina Isola on milk crates and overturned plastic buckets.

Isola, as we called it, was a low-key bar—a neighborhood *aperitivo* spot located a few blocks from the apartment. Joe started going there last year during his first year filming *MasterChef Italia*. He'd been trying to get the owner to carry his family wines. Isola poured good wine during *aperitivo*—the oily bruschetta they put out was not so good—but it was the busiest place on Via Paolo Sarpi; people spilled outside it every single night. It was basically a small wine shop with sixty square feet of standing room inside. There was a covered wooden gazebo right outside, but that filled up by 6:00 p.m., and by 7:00 or 7:30, there was a crowd of people drinking in the street. If we didn't know where to go, we'd roll a few blocks over to Isola and try to scare up some seats.

"Remember last summer, Joe, when you called Kim in New York and asked her to make us a dinner reservation at Fingers here in Milano, in thirty minutes? You were in Milano, but you called someone in New York who doesn't even speak Italian to call a restaurant in Milano," Serena chided, accentuating the deep lines in her bronzed face.

Joe shrugged. "Well, that's what she does."

Joe's Italian friends didn't seem familiar with someone who operated like he did and how much work he drummed up. They couldn't believe that I was still working—answering emails and taking calls from both my American and Italian cells. I didn't dare leave the apartment without both phones and a charger and an adapter—all while downing glasses of wine and crushing mosquitoes on my leg alongside them at Isola. Serena joked that perhaps I'd not learned how to speak better Italian because I was lazy, and I felt a rage swell up in me. Never in my life had I wanted to hit a person in the face like I did then.

It didn't help that this was the time of day—evening in Milan—when L.A. got cracking. People from inside the reservation racket would reach out with an urgent need for a last-minute reservation in one of the three restaurants that we had in California—Osteria Mozza, Pizzeria Mozza, and Chi Spacca. They were three of the toughest doors on the West Coast. I couldn't miss a WhatsApp from one of Joe's agents, should they need to put the head writer of *Modern Family* in for lunch at Pizzeria Mozza in three hours, or ignore that email from Jim Brooks, creator of *The Simpsons*, who needed a four-top at Osteria, or the head of the *MasterChef USA* production company who emailed me from the podium at Pizzeria, hoping I could find him a five-top, *right now.*

The team in California had a different sensibility than those of us on the East Coast who worked under Mario and Joe. They worked under chef Nancy Silverton, who ran a more low-key operation. Back in 2001, she'd sold her beloved La Brea Bakery for fifty-five million dollars, but all these years later she still tied on an apron and worked the line at her own restaurants.

Once, an L.A. reservationist took me to task for calling "in the middle of service on a Friday night" to put in a last-minute reservation on behalf of Joe. This reservationist did not understand that part of the reason she had a job was to stand by that phone and wait for Meredith or me to call with some ridiculously disruptive last-minute request, and happily do it. We represented her boss.

Erica, Nancy's right hand, spoke the East Coast language. "Ugh, they *don't know*," she'd lament, when I'd be forced to call her and rat out my fellow reservationist.

I felt a sense of personal failure if I missed a call or a text from a member of the racket or failed to negotiate what I thought was a reasonable ask. Like if I did, they'd stop calling me and start calling Meredith instead.

I'd forgotten to let Jay the novelist know I'd be living in Milan, and a few weeks after my arrival, I received an email from him. We normally communicated by text only, to which there was not an "out-of-country" auto-reply.

"I've been texting you," he wrote. "I thought you weren't helping anymore."

Words from hell.

It was much easier to manage the nightly wave coming from the West Coast from the subway on my way home or while having a glass of wine in my apartment, as opposed to trying to follow a conversation I'd no real hope of following, avoiding embarrassing or disappointing my boss, all the while not drunk but not exactly sober. I was careful not to look anybody in the eye so they didn't suddenly say something to me that I couldn't reply to.

The details of these magical reservation transactions, with all parties, always needed to be in writing. That was key. It was my insurance policy. We couldn't have the Foo Fighters show up at Del Posto with ten people and the restaurant not know they were coming because the reservationist I spoke to on the phone put it in on the wrong night. I caught my own mistakes just before they exploded this way too. I probably made ten of these calls a day, and they all needed to be approved by Joe first.

These were not always straightforward requests. Sven wanted a table at Del Posto but they weren't going to eat; a friend of Joe's from high school wanted to bring in his own wine into Babbo. And if they knew how to reach me, then they were of discernable weight to someone in the group. Keeping everything straight as I juggled a borrowed iPhone in and out of Wi-Fi, from a milk crate, while it was openly suggested that I was lazy, sometimes made me question why I was there. George at Babbo didn't want to put it in the book. Casper at Del Posto didn't want to put it in the book. I had to *make them* put it in and accomplish two things simultaneously: Don't make them hate me. Don't make them quit.

George took no care to hide his deep sighs, which always signaled the start of a battle.

"*Kim.* . . . Patricia Bader has a five-top at 5:30 p.m. tonight. How did this happen?"

Patricia Bader was a woman Joe knew from his days in finance, right after he'd graduated college. She'd book a five- or six-top at Babbo, show up thirty minutes late, not place her order for another hour, and hunker down until 10:00 or 10:30 p.m. We were supposed to have stopped giving her first-seating reservations.

George's irritation was valid. We lost a full turn on one of our largest tables on the nights she came in. A six-top could easily bring in two grand. This, Joe understood. But he wanted to appear hospitable. He didn't want to have the uncomfortable conversation because it was "in the gray," but this murky area he left for George and me to wade through. Joe wanted us to *make her* get up and leave by 8:30 p.m.

One night, Joe found his own way to deal with Patricia Bader. She'd booked a private party in the cantina and was entertaining of bunch of Wall Street heavyweights when Joe walked into the tiny brick-walled room. He sat quietly among them for a few minutes, then pulled a pen and scrap of paper from inside his jacket and began writing. He then launched into a limerick about "Five-hour Patricia who doesn't know when to get up from her table." He never said a word about it to me, but she called me the next day. I couldn't stop laughing.

"You'll be standing around doing nothing. Don't go."

Joe did not want me attending the opening of Eataly Rome. He'd discouraged me from going to Eataly Flatiron's opening too, and now he was giving me a hard time about going to Rome. I brought it up because if I went and ended up working the whole time, I wanted the company to pay for my train ticket and hotel. Otherwise, I would have just told him at the last minute that I'd be there too, assuming he wouldn't care what I did so long as I was available if he needed me.

"Why do you want to go so badly? There won't be anything for you to do. Everyone you know will be busy running around and working. It's an opening—one big Oscar show."

I wanted to snap out of my pleasing assistant mode and argue with him, tell him that I wouldn't be a bother. I wanted to yell, *Don't you understand this is what I came for? Why I put up with the mildewy mattress, the bits of food in the balcony planter, and workdays that end only when my head hits my pillow each night?*

"Do you even have someone to go with, or are you just showing up by yourself?"

I emailed a few people I knew would be around—Edo, Ari, Aaron, and Vito, who worked out of the Flatiron store and whose family owned a big Neapolitan pizza chain that Eataly partnered with. Vito was the only one who wrote me back. He sent me the name of the hotel. He asked how I was liking his country, what other cities I'd be going to, and how I was surviving sharing an apartment with Joe.

But I heard nothing from anyone else, even though I followed up a few times. I wanted to go so badly and be part of what I knew everyone would be talking about later, all the spontaneous gatherings that these significant events gave birth to. They'd all spoken to me about Italy, told me about their adventures. I wanted to be in Italy with the Eataly boys.

But maybe Joe was right. Perhaps I'd be standing around by myself.

I decided to stay home and was devastated. They all headed to Capri afterward and spent a few days in the sun. Maybe I'd have been there too if I'd gone.

I made my own friends in Milan independent of Joe and the *Master-Chef Italia* crew. Funnily enough, I had one-date, do-you-want-to-go-to-Rio Alessandro to thank for it: he threw a party for one hundred people at his home in Forte dei Marmi and I was on the guest list, as promised. Most of the people I met there didn't have kids and were not married; we lived the same lifestyle.

Alessandro was entirely right about me needing my own friends while living in Italy. He was entirely full of shit when he presented himself as single.

My first weekend in Milan, Alessandro said he'd pick me up in the early evening the night before the big party, and we'd drive down to Forte dei Marmi together with a few of his friends. Most guests would be staying in nearby hotels, but he set aside one of the bedrooms of his home for me.

Technically, Alessandro didn't owe me anything. We hung out in the New York office, we had a lunch date, exchanged some flirty messages on Facebook, and made quasi-faux plans to go to Rio—a trip that we both knew we weren't going to take. But I thought at the very least there was potential. We'd spend some time together in Italy, and we'd see. I thought, at a minimum, the woman sitting in the passenger seat of his car when he picked me up would not have been his live-in girlfriend for the last seven years.

I was in the car with them, driving down the highway, and all I could think was *This fuck*. And she knew: she'd been making exaggerated displays of affection since I'd gotten in the car—rubbing the back of his neck or his leg. Her eyes were like a scared rabbit's when she turned to greet me as I climbed into the back seat. I bet he did this to her all the time.

As a single woman in my early thirties who was a bit of a loner, I was no stranger to married men or men knee-deep in a relationship hitting on me. How I loathed them. When they made a pass at me, it was as if they were saying, *You're cheap. I'm willing to bet you'll let me use you.*

What could I do at that point? Tell him to turn around? We'd left the city. In the back seat with me was another woman named Isobel, and I soon learned that she would be my roommate at the house. I would focus on meeting people—hopefully, all of his friends were not like him. I'd make friends. I'd wait until the weekend was over to tell Alessandro what a sleaze I thought he was.

We hit a stretch of the road where lush green hills towered over us on both sides, but it was hard to enjoy them because Alessandro wanted to make better time and was speeding to the point where his girlfriend Camilla, Isobel, and I were begging him to slow down. He finally did after a harrowing five minutes, laughing all the while.

Our first stop once we exited the *autostrada* was a restaurant where we were joined by fifteen people. We were led to a long table outside. It was pitch-black around us, but I could hear the faint sound of the sea.

During our introductions, everyone was incredibly warm and eager to speak English with the American who worked for "Joe on *MasterChef*," but once we started taking seats around the table,

Around midnight, a group of jovial chain-smoking women each wearing sky-high heels invited me to join them at La Capannina di Franceschi, an iconic nightclub built in the 1920s. What could I do but say yes?

As I crawled into the twin bed in the upper spare bedroom of Alessandro's gray beach house, careful not to wake Isobel, I'd almost forgotten about his trickery. I had friends in Italy.

When we returned to Milan after the weekend, Santos and Monica reached out first and drew me into their world. Santos zipped around town in a hot little hunter green sports car. He told me with a bashful smile that only fifty in the world were made.

Another friend of theirs, Ignazio, owned a bar behind the Duomo, and several times a week they all hung out there. Since the party, someone had always called to invite me.

One night Santos drove me home from Ignazio's, and while we were stopped at a red light, two people jumped in front of us and started taking pictures of the car.

"Come on, guys," Santos said quietly to himself. "Germans," he said to me, shaking his head. His car might have been showy, but he was not. His kind brown eyes and round face suited his personality.

Santos and I went out for drinks another night, and he took me home on the back of his bicycle. We passed the Duomo, which was deserted. Its white marble spires glowed against the black sky. We wrapped around the Castello Sforzesco, which like the Duomo, was silent and almost completely devoid of people. There were no skyscrapers in Milan; nothing competed with their ancient majesty.

I looked up as Santos pedaled and panted his way toward Via Guercino. By the time we arrived in front of the two wooden doors to my building, his back was damp and hot. He kissed me at the door.

Santos didn't seem like the kind of guy who'd cheat on Monica, so maybe they weren't together, but I was hesitant to get any more involved with him after Alessandro's shenanigans. I broke away from him sooner than I'd have liked, but I didn't want to get in the middle of some weird thing. I could barely figure out Americans, let alone Europeans and their wiggly sense of fidelity. I headed upstairs to the apartment.

As soon as I'd gotten home from the party, I'd called Alessandro out.

"Eh, I try to be serious," he said, "but also, I try to be free."

One night I saw Alessandro and Camilla through the smoke at Ignazio's bar. It was crowded, and I recognized a lot of people from the weekend in Forte dei Marmi. At some point, I spotted Alessandro with his arm around the waist of some random woman, and Camilla was across the room. Who knew what their deal was, but that was not for me.

A few days after my midnight bike ride with Santos, Joe decided to throw a party at the apartment. Lidia was in town to film a guest spot on *MasterChef Italia* and was staying with us. I invited Santos and Monica, and traditional Dante.

I was hit with a twinge of guilt when Santos and Monica entered side-by-side. I was reminded how famous Joe was here by the admiration on their faces, and how Monica nervously flipped her hair behind her ears as Joe cut across them in the entryway and extended his hand.

"My car is just outside. Do you think Joe would like to see it later?" Santos asked earnestly as Joe abruptly headed for the kitchen. More people from the set piled into the apartment, their booming Italian echoing off the walls, as thundering as the barroom at Otto on a Saturday night. One by one, I took in the kind, unfamiliar faces of people I'd had an email relationship with for the last year.

Joe invited a tabloid journalist he'd met on Twitter. I supposed it would be my job to watch her. I reluctantly introduced myself when she arrived. Later, when Joe took a swipe at my Italian, she cut him off and turned to me. "I think your Italian is beautiful, Kim."

"We need more food," Joe said testily, motioning me to follow him into the kitchen. Lidia was there in her silk pantsuit and full stage makeup, busily unpacking the boxes brought over from the set, pulling out bags of crushed ice, shellfish, arborio rice, and stainless-steel pots and pans.

Joe reached into a box and pulled out two rock-hard tubes of cured salumi. "Can you slice this up, fleck some Grana on the board, and bring it out?"

I grabbed a wedge of Grana Padano from the fridge and a wooden serving board from atop the microwave. Our old-school Park Avenue apartment didn't come with a full set of cutlery. There was only one sharp knife, which Lidia was using.

I went to my suitcase, retrieved Sharky's pocketknife, flipped open a blade, gave it a good wash, and got to work but couldn't break through the slick, tough meat.

"You don't know how to do this?" Joe suddenly cried out.

His expression morphed from annoyance to sympathy as he switched to dad mode. "Watch. Take the tip of the knife and wedge it under the casing, like this. Make a tear. Then you just grab the end of the skin and pull it—it'll peel off like a ribbon. Now you can slice the meat easy."

Finally, I got to meet Marigold—a friend of Joe's. She looked every bit the part of a young American writer who dabbled in the art scene and was living in Paris with her longtime, much-older boyfriend—who happened to be one of France's most famous actors. Her blond hair was short and chic. She wore a black and red dress in a rich, thick fabric. I was willing to bet it was by legendary dressmaker Azzedine

Alaïa. Marigold showed up with her mother, who looked just as elegant. Dante found them and the trio hit it right off.

I couldn't stop pressing my hands down the front of my black skirt when I met Marigold. I had on one that I used to wear while hostessing at Babbo, now so faded that I only wore it at night. I rubbed with my thumb against my Buccellati cocktail ring from Donna—grateful that at least I had on something nice.

When night fell, we learned not only was it stupid to rent an apartment with no air conditioning, it was also a bad idea to rent one without window screens. We usually closed our big beautiful windows well before dark, but that night, no one paid attention and as soon as the sun set, it seemed every mosquito in Milan descended upon us. Joe and Alice's no-smoking policy was quickly scrapped to counter the pests, and one by one our Milanese guests whipped bottles of bug spray out of their handbags. But the smoke and the spray didn't do much good, and every few minutes I was slapping one down on my arm, leg, or ankle. Even so, nobody thought to clear out—everyone was getting drunk and having too good a time.

I couldn't shake the feeling that Monica wanted something from me. She had this pleading look on her face. Whenever I found myself alone for a minute, setting a dirty plate into the kitchen sink, pulling a bottle of Calabrone from the back bedroom Joe's boys shared, or retreating into a corner before attempting my next conversation in Italian, suddenly she was there, as if hoping to get me alone. I worried that Santos had told her about our kiss. Their English was good, but there was still a slight language barrier. Enough that I didn't know how to subtly find out if they were romantically involved. They were both so kind and got along with all the people Joe invited to the apartment. I didn't know how to break that barrier, even with female friends. Cross that line of intimacy. I was afraid of what they'd say. Afraid of the confrontation. Afraid of those gray little moments that were so easy for me to handle for Joe. For my former clients. But never for myself.

I'd had so much Vespa Bianco that my mouth was saturated with an oily, peachy-pear taste. I needed water but wanted the drunk feeling to continue, so I kept sipping from my wineglass. I noticed Joe across the room. It looked like he'd fallen asleep standing up. His eyes were fluttering, his head bobbed up off his chin. *I'd better get over there before he goes down*, I thought. I tried to stand, but my brain was slow to get the message to my legs, and I remembered what Joe always said about how people drink when put in a room with unlimited high-quality booze—*They behave like animals, Kim.* He was going to topple, and I couldn't get there in time. Everyone was pressed close, and the acoustics amplified the yelling, screaming, and drunken laughter. I was failing the cardinal rule of Kim in Italy: have fun, but always be working.

Suddenly out of another corner came Lidia.

"JOSEPH!"

She beat me to him. Her words snapped him awake. He caught himself and came to.

The last thing I remembered was talking to Lidia, saying as little as possible because I knew I was slurring my words.

She eyed me cautiously. "I think you should go to bed, Kim."

seven

NIGHT DOGS AND DAY DOGS

I woke up still drunk at 5:45 a.m. I had thirty minutes to catch my train to Rome. Pain pulsed through my skull every few seconds. I had sleep apnea; I wasn't supposed to binge-drink and then pass out like I used to in college, and the combination of this and inhaling everyone's smoke made it impossible to fully expand my lungs, as though there were a twenty-pound weight strapped to my chest.

My hair stank—the whole apartment stank like cigarettes—but I had no time to shower. I changed into green cargo pants and a sleeveless pink silk blouse, put on my ring from Donna, threw pajama pants and an extra T-shirt into my bag, double-checked that I had both my phones, my passport, keys, wallet, charger, and adapter, and bolted out the door. At least my trip got me out of having to help the family clean up the place.

I didn't have time to grab a coffee before getting on the train to Rome—that was how close I came to missing it. But there was no line for the guy selling large, cold bottles of Acqua Panna mineral water. I got on the train, sat down, and drained the water in less than ten minutes.

My phone vibrated with a text from a former Corporate intern who had eventually returned to Italy: Massimo. He was somewhere on the train, and on a mission to be helpful. When we found each other on the platform in Ostiense, standing under the merciless sun, he told me his mother told him, "You will be her guide to Rome." Massimo quoting his mom reminded me of that old stereotype about Italian men—they lived with their mothers well into adulthood, until they got married, even if that didn't happen until they were fifty. He couldn't have been more than twenty-two.

When Massimo learned from Facebook that I'd be in Italy for the summer, he wrote with an offer to show me whatever part of his country I wanted to see. He didn't seem to like the idea of a woman traveling alone.

Massimo seemed to have taken his mother's words literally because he had the next two and a half days planned out for us. He reiterated it was "not enough time to see Rome, Kim!" but this was the most I could spare with so much happening. Joe had recently agreed to do some event for the wines in Sardinia, which was proving to be a nightmare to organize. He'd be filming a guest appearance on an episode of *MasterChef Poland* at the end of the summer, which I'd successfully negotiated myself. And, after learning that Joe was in

Europe, a producer from *The Today Show* reached out to ask if he'd fly to London and do a wine segment with the hosts, who were there for the Summer Olympics. It meant more to me not to have to work at all during my short time in Rome, rather than extend my trip and end up working all day. I'd be back at the dining room table in two days. I loathed the idea of taking vacation days when we were busy, but with only two weeks left in Italy, I didn't have a choice.

I had arranged for Massimo and me to stay with a family friend of the Bastianiches. Luca, the father, operated a trattoria close to Joe's family winery in Friuli and also made his own wine. He and Joe were close friends. Everyone knew Luca; he'd been coming to Babbo for longer than I could remember. He'd spend a month or so in New York every year to sell his wines. Fabrizio, Luca's son, was in Rome for university. He'd spent the last few summers working as a busboy at Otto, so I knew him too. Fabrizio was known in our group as being a dead ringer for Jesse.

As I planned my trip to Rome, Joe kept telling me to "call Luca and ask if you can stay at Fabrizio's place," but since I knew Fabrizio, I wrote him directly. He kept politely putting me off, without explicitly saying no. When Joe asked, I told him as much, and he lost it.

"Does Luca know this? Luca and Fabrizio *live* in the Babbo apartment when they stay in New York. Bullshit, Kim—call Luca!"

I felt awkward forcing the issue with Fabrizio; he must have had a good reason for not wanting to host us. I began researching hostels and cheap hotels instead. I was poor but could swing two nights in a cheap Roman B&B—on my Visa card.

The next thing I knew, Fabrizio wrote to tell me that Massimo and I were welcome anytime, which meant Joe had called Luca.

Massimo and I hopped into a cab and rolled down the windows to let the warm breeze in as we whipped along Rome's rusty-orange infrastructure—it was blazing hot that day, and sweat was already gathering under my arms. Having drunk my weight in Vespa Bianco and Sven's "red table wine" the night before, and having not showered that morning, I was glad to be traveling with Massimo, the young, plain-faced, traditional former intern, and not a guy I was dating.

I couldn't understand anything the chatty cabdriver said. He sounded completely different than the Italians I knew, who, in that moment, I realized were all from the north. *We're definitely in the south*, I thought, as I listened to the cabdriver's words roll slowly into one another.

When we arrived at Fabrizio's place, I learned the reason for his hesitation.

"Try not to leave this room while you're here because one of my roommates is crazy," Fabrizio said, as he ushered us into his small bedroom. It was student housing, a three-bedroom he shared with two other students.

Massimo, brimming with gratitude, explained that we had a packed itinerary and would barely be there.

"Good, because she is really insane. Don't talk to her if you run into her. We got in a big fight and I don't want her going crazy and kicking you out."

"Would she really make us leave?" I asked.

Massimo's eyes widened. "I don't know. She just screams at me sometimes. Call me if she tries to."

The bedroom had a twin bed and really was quite small. Fabrizio showed us a sliver of a room in the front of the apartment with a small daybed connected to the wall and no door, and Massimo looked relieved and said he'd sleep there.

Fabrizio was supposed to go to Cividale for the next few days to visit his parents. It dawned on me that perhaps he was making the trip so that there would be room for Luca and me, and I felt guilty as hell.

"I could stay tonight, if you want," Fabrizio offered. He handed me a hanger from his closet for my spare shirt as I started to unpack. I felt the heat coming off his arm. He leaned in closer to my face. "I can show you both around the city tomorrow. I don't have to go home tonight."

Something about Fabrizio's offer, his sly, Jesse-like smile, and how he looked in his tight T-shirt, made me think that this big fight between him and his female roommate—the rage he attributed to her—was about sex. Them having it or not having it. Yet another pairing I was not about to get in the middle of. Besides, the Bastianich family would never let me live it down if I slept with Fabrizio, who was like one of their kids.

When I rejected his offer a second time, Fabrizio settled for joining us for lunch. The three of us set off for the new Eataly Rome store. We had each already been inside at least one Eataly. This one was no different except it was three times the size of the one in New York—like an airport of Italian food. But I wanted to see Michele again.

Michele found us shortly after we secured a spot at the fish counter and were already slinging back sparkling rosé. He let me hug him long and hard even though I stank like last night's alcohol and sweat. I held on as long as I could. He looked bewildered, and said he was busy as usual, but stayed to make small talk. I had almost forgotten how prominent Michele and his family were in Italy until I watched Massimo's and Fabrizio's faces as they hopped off their stools to greet him. They shook his hand like he was someone important. Someone older.

"When are you coming home?" I tried to keep the whine out of my voice.

Michele tilted his head back and adjusted his footing. He looked exhausted, but his blue eyes still glittered with energy.

"Who cares about me—you are in Italia. *Finalmente!*"

We polished off the bottle of rosé and a tower of oysters and shrimp. Massimo and I bid goodbye to a reluctant Fabrizio and set off to tackle our list of sites. Massimo hadn't been to Rome in six years and seemed just as eager as I was to be there. He took me to the Spanish Steps, the Trevi Fountain, the Pantheon—which left me dumbstruck—and the church of St. Lucy, who was one of my mother's favorite saints. When the sun began to set and we could feel the air against our skin, I was ready to head to Campo de' Fiori to find a spot for dinner, but Massimo reminded me of the last stop on our itinerary: the Colosseum. How could I have forgotten?

We made our way on foot through the cool evening air. Out of habit, I pulled my phone from my bag and opened my email, which I hadn't checked in at least three hours.

This proved to be really stupid.

There must have been thirty emails of significance. I couldn't stop scrolling. There were a few back-to-back ones from Joe—*Call* (really?), the producer from *The Today Show* wanted to change the date of Joe's London segment and had needed an answer two hours ago, and Jay the novelist wrote with a last-minute request for a lunch res at Pizzeria *in forty minutes*.

There was a bench just outside the Colosseum. "Go ahead," I told Massimo. "I need to make a few calls; I'll be right there."

We were too late to access most of the inside, but Massimo found a way in and came running back, his backpack swinging from side to side.

"Come on, Kim!" he called, but I was in the middle of battling it out with a newly hired Pizzeria Mozza reservationist who clearly *didn't know*. By the time I unglued myself from my phone, Massimo was sitting next to me and it was totally dark.

Feeling defeated, we headed back toward Campo de' Fiori and chose a little outdoor restaurant tucked into the edge of the piazza, one Joe recommended to everyone.

Massimo did not make fun of me when I ordered Rome's staple pasta dish—*cacio e pepe*—made only with pepper and Pecorino Romano cheese. It hit me how spoiled I was when I realized it tasted just like the *cacio e pepe* I'd had a million times at Lupa, another of the group's sister restaurants in New York. I was grateful to have a kind friend who asked nothing about work—the only time he brought up Joe was "Tell Joe I said hello!" Such a sweet, good-hearted kid.

I'd successfully spent most of the day off my phone, and while I missed the Colosseum, no one died. I tucked into Fabrizio's twin bed that night after Massimo and I snuck into the apartment undetected by the so-called crazy roommate. I thought only about what he had planned for us the next day. We were getting up at 5:00 a.m. to try to beat the line into St. Peter's Basilica. I didn't check my email before bed.

The next morning, I had several messages from Joe's American PR lead, Carla. "Just checking on the status of tomorrow's blog," the first one read. The rest increased in panic as the deadline loomed.

Shit. Joe wrote a blog, meaning *I* wrote a blog for Joe for each week's episode of *MasterChef USA*. It was due to Carla the same day the episode aired, which was yesterday, because it had to post to People.com the day after—*today*.

"I thought it wasn't airing this week," I wrote back to Carla in disbelief.

California was nine hours behind, so she answered almost immediately. "That's next week. Next week is a rerun. Tonight was a new episode."

I was always embarrassed with the writing of these blogs, but I couldn't devote the proper time it took to edit and rewrite. I had to watch the entire episode, which was actually two one-hour episodes aired back-to-back, then I had to draft a 350-word post on Joe's behind-the-scenes insights, which I made up because I am not Joe and I was not behind the scenes. So figure two hours to watch it, two hours to write it, and then forty minutes to an hour of nagging Joe to approve it. He finally would say, "Yes, I read it, it's fine." He'd done no such thing, but I didn't care; I just needed to get him to say he did. Before sending, I reread and usually deleted a couple of lines that came off too mean. Joe and the show's producers liked to push this aspect of his personality. He was hired because he was not afraid to make Gordon Ramsay look nice. But I always caved at the last minute, softened a few things I considered low blows. "You lack the killer instinct," Joe told me one day. He didn't mean it as a compliment, but I took it as one.

Each time I went through this process, it added about five hours of additional work to my week to produce a first crappy draft, which everyone said they loved, and then it would post to Yahoo.com or People.com, and the fact that I'd fail miserably as a copyeditor was online for all to see. In spite of this, Joe received frequent compliments on them. "Kim, you're funny—people always tell me they love what I wrote—*good job.*" The elusive *good job.*

I stayed inside Fabrizio's dark apartment for the next five hours and banged it out, missing a good portion of one of my two days in Rome.

Massimo texted me around the time I finished and told me to come meet him and two of his friends from university, and there was a part of me that was so defeated, I considered for a moment not leaving the room. I smelled bad. Had to risk a run-in with Fabrizio's disgruntled roommate to get to the bathroom. What was I doing in Italy if I wasn't really experiencing Italy? I sat on the edge of Fabrizio's little bed, in his dark and bleak student-housing bedroom, and thought seriously of quitting when I got back to New York. But none of that changed my current moment, so I got up, snuck in and out of the bathroom, then went to meet Massimo and his friends.

They chose Open Baladin for dinner—Teo Musso's place just outside of Campo de' Fiori, which was famous for their American burger. Burgers were all the rage in Italy. Teo Musso made the craft beer Baladin. I knew him—sort of; Joe knew him. He had partnered with Oscar to make beer for the opening of Eataly Flatiron. Joe described him as a "big hippie."

Massimo and his friends apologized for the choice of restaurant; being an American, they thought I ate like this all the time. But back in New York, dinner was usually something from Eataly: raw green vegetables slathered in pricey olive oil that I scored free out of Edo's office, and *carne cruda*, which is chopped Piedmontese beef that is sushi grade—served raw, with olive oil and kosher salt. I hadn't had a good American burger in the last year.

Francesco, one of Massimo's friends, was in Rome studying music. He played the cello. The other, Lorenzo, was celebrating a new job at Fendi in their finance department. They were friendly, like Massimo, and were interested in my work for Joe, and in hearing about Massimo's and my adventures helping to open the Eataly store in New York.

Lorenzo looked like he'd work in finance at Fendi. He was a sharp dresser in his blazer and jeans. Toned body, like the older European men who visited Babbo when I was a hostess. But his deep brown eyes were warm. His demeanor was calm and confident as he listened to me bitch about the blog, Joe, every single person in L.A. We were halfway through dinner when the thought struck me: why was he being so nice? I'd have run fast in the other direction if I were him. That was not my best moment. But his interest didn't wane.

Lorenzo offered to take us around the city after dinner, and none of us were ready for the night to end. Rome was dark at night. It felt like we were walking along a secluded street in Brooklyn Heights or Greenwich Village, where the only sources of light were the old-fashioned lanterns outside brownstones. The moon was only half full that night but like the Duomo and the Castello Sforzesco in Milan, without any competition it shone in the sky as if I'd never seen it before.

We moved on foot in the dark to the Jewish ghetto and the Portico di Ottavia. My effort to shake off the day spent working begrudgingly from Fabrizio's bedroom failed. It should have been easy to snap out of my funk with these three, but I couldn't stop complaining about work while simultaneously checking my phone and *doing* work. Even when walking in this beautiful city with a man who I suddenly realized was pretty great.

Francesco and Massimo were ahead of us now, but Lorenzo remained at my side throughout my tirade, listening thoughtfully. "You should get another job when you get home," he said quietly.

I scoffed, even though I'd had the same thought just hours earlier. Where else could I get a job that offered me moments like these? It was worth it, right?

I woke up the next day thinking about Lorenzo. I really was a slow learner. It boggled my mind that I would pass up a night walking under the moonlight with a man like Lorenzo in a city like Rome because I was too frazzled from work, too out of touch with the current moment, and too worried about what shape I'd be in for more work tomorrow—but I'd go to Portofino and sleep with a guy like Alessandro. Which, a few weeks earlier, I had.

MasterChef Italia was due to film an offsite challenge in Portofino. "You should bring a friend and come with Alice and me," Joe had said. But I didn't have anyone to bring.

And then I heard from Alessandro. He too had heard about the shoot. Portofino was like a small gossipy town, and Alessandro was a partner with Sebastiano in a local company that produced olive oil and jams there. He'd be in Portofino during the filming, he said. "Come and stay with me at Sebastiano's house."

The only type of romance I'd had during my trip was that one kiss with Santos. Alessandro was "free but not free." Feeling like I was back in his car while he careened dangerously around the curves in the road, I said yes.

At the end of the day, we all ate outside at one long table—Sebastiano, Alessandro, the family that owned the restaurant, Joe and Alice, Sebastiano's neighbor, me. The restaurant overlooked the marina. Just five feet behind me was shimmering aqua water and more white yachts and sailboats than I could take in. No one seemed to bat an eye that Alessandro had brought me, and that we were both staying together in Sebastiano's house overlooking the sea. No one wondered about Camilla.

"Be careful, Kim," said Edo, when I took his call from the dinner table and quietly told him where I was and who I was with. As if he knew I didn't really want to be there, didn't want to be with a guy like Alessandro.

The only thing that was appealing about sleeping with Alessandro was I'd never have to see him again. I didn't have to worry about the emotionally awkward aftermath of trying to date him. He didn't work with us; I'd only have to deal with him again if I wanted to. I thought back to the last guy I'd slept with, Gareth, who now lived in DC. I feared a pattern emerging.

I'd had a friend in high school who always ended up sleeping with men she really didn't want because it would have been awkward for her to back out. I was horrified the first time she nonchalantly explained this to me. But that night in Portofino, I understood her completely. That was exactly what I did. I was already there.

"Don't worry about where you'll spend the last few days of the summer. You will meet someone who will invite you somewhere. It's like that here," Joe said to me during my first week in the apartment. He was right. Our lease on Via Guercino was up the next day. I'd arranged for Joe to fly to Krakow for his appearance on *MasterChef Poland*, and the rest of the family would head to the winery in Friuli on the border of Slovenia.

"You're not coming to Poland anymore?" Joe demanded. "Why?"

Because I'll stab you and leave you to die on the streets of Krakow, covered in your composting bits of lemon rind and salumi casing, I wanted to clap back, after surviving the summer with him. But I didn't.

"There's too much to do," I told him. "I have to get home and get things in order, plan the *Today Show* segment—this is a big one, Joe. You can't fudge it—"

"So what am I going to do in Krakow now?" he said out loud, to no one in particular. "What's your mom going to say?"

Part of me wanted to go—my mother's side was Polish, and it was an opportunity to see another city for free. I should have tried to maneuver myself into the London trip as well, but it was all becoming too much. Joe's mind never slowed. And I could feel mine—both my mind and my body—breaking down.

We weren't any busier than usual. Last-minute schedule changes, flights and speaking gigs in some city Joe had never been to before, the constant barrage of press, the reservation racket, and whatever cockamamie idea Joe cooked up in the last hour. It was that I couldn't handle much outside the job, and after two months of navigating a new city, new language, the fuckery that was dating here, I was shot. Something would happen to me if I didn't slow down. *I* would be the one to die—of exhaustion—like a dog on the streets of Krakow if I went. I never thought I'd say it, but I needed to go home. Who would have thought I'd be dreaming of getting back to New York in order to find peace and stillness?

I was sitting at the dining room table, waiting for Sebastiano to pick me up and take me to Piemonte. With our lease up but my flight still a few days away, he arranged for me to stay at the winery he and Oscar owned, Fontanafredda, on the outskirts of Alba. I told him I didn't need anything, just a room, and I'd figure out meals and whatever else on my own. Michele told me there was a garden near the estate's restaurant I could work from if the weather was nice. I was looking forward to seeing the place my Italian friends loved so much, and where most of them had come from, but also happy I had zero plans during my stay in Alba and that Joe would be occupied for a good part of the time I was there. He was stuck on a soundstage in Poland—I was home free.

A little more than an hour later, we exited the *autostrada* and the road became dark. Sebastiano had his friend Alberto, some guy helping with the plans for the soon-to-be Eataly Milan, riding shotgun, so I was in the back seat and couldn't see the headlights on the road ahead. It looked like we were driving in total blackness. The engine purred as we climbed a steep incline, and then suddenly, the car stopped. A strange-looking animal with tall, skinny legs, moving like a wounded dog, trotted across our path.

"What was that?" I gasped.

"Pumbaa," Sebastiano replied. He meant a wild boar—*cinghiale*.

We reached the top of the hill. This was Sebastiano's home: the castle, not the winery.

"Is too late tonight, Kim. You'll stay here and I bring you in the morning."

We got out of the car, and two large dogs came charging. They were Sebastiano's large fox-haired terriers. They didn't approach with wagging tails, offering licks. They nuzzled Sebastiano but otherwise were here to sniff Alberto and me out. They smelled pungent, the way I imagined a bear would.

"These are the night dogs, Kim. They sleep during the day. We have to put them away in the morning because they will attack the day dogs."

I looked up but couldn't discern the outline of the castle against the black sky. Sebastiano led me through a door and to an elevator just inside the entrance. We took it up to the third floor. It was dark inside too, the cement floors hard as our shoes slapped lightly against them. But I could see that the space was grand. High ceilings, slate walls. It looked sparse, like a museum.

Sebastiano continued down a long hallway, passing a number of closed wooden doors. We came to the end, and he walked me into the last room and said, "Now in the morning, you go down to the kitchen, and the girls will prepare for you aaaaaanything you want!"

"The girls?"

Smiling widely and nodding, he replied, "Yes, yes, the girls. The ones who take care of the house."

It dawned on me then that Sebastiano had live-in servants.

"*Buonanotte*, Kim, you are finally in Piemonte!" he exclaimed, as he made his way out. Pausing for a second in the doorway, he turned back and pointed to the far wall of the room. "As soon as you wake up, look out that window. You never see anything like it in your life. It is the first thing you do tomorrow morning."

I woke up the next morning to total, blessed silence. Folding back the ivory-painted wooden shutters, I pushed open the glass windowpanes. There were no screens. A few curious wasps bobbed inches from my eyes and forehead, but even my lifelong fear of all flying things that buzzed could not pull me back from that window. Out before me was the start of Barolo, and I was looking down on it from the top floor of a castle that had been built for the son of the first king of Italy. Endless slopes of vines stretched out for what looked like miles. There was a large swimming pool two stories directly below. The air smelled like every red wine I'd ever drunk with Michele and Edo, or at Babbo since taking over as Joe's executive assistant. It smelled like dirt, and what Joe's youngest son once described as "a wet dog coming in from the rain."

The sleek, gray marble bathroom inside my room was impressive but odd. The toilet was set in the corner of a room the size of a large bedroom. I felt weirdly exposed to be naked in a room this size, one I would not ordinarily have to myself, like I was naked in the middle of a stranger's family room and the occupants could walk in on me at any time.

Sebastiano said I should work from their home until about noon, when he'd be back to pick me up and take me to the winery. I was in no hurry. After the girls helped me with breakfast—they would not even allow me to make a Moka pot of coffee myself—I took my laptop and phone out to a small iron table on the front porch, and almost immediately a black Lab came right for me, wagging his tail. This was one of the day dogs, Ugo. He was unrelenting with his affection. He'd been nosing around in the soft earth and was smearing it—from his muzzle—all over my bare leg. He smelled just like the night dogs but was much more loving. He had some kind of problem with his hip, and his back end swung sharply to the side when he walked, but he still managed to knock me off my chair and onto the cement and plant himself on top of me. I almost had to take my laptop back inside and finish work from the dining room, but eventually Ugo contented himself with lying across my feet.

The sun was shining, there was a good dog at my feet, and I sat for a few minutes sipping my coffee, staring out at the grounds and thinking about nothing, when suddenly I remembered the back porch of the house on McCarroll Street, before I was even a social worker in New York.

"You got your coffee, Kim? I got mine, too."

Sheryl walked out of the sliding glass door, coffee mug in hand, and pulled out the chair across from me at the patio table.

Sheryl lived in a "community residence"—a small group home for adults with disabilities. This was where I worked as a residence counselor for three years during college. Whenever a staff member took a cigarette or coffee break out on the back porch, Sheryl usually followed. I mistook her for a fellow counselor on my first day. It wasn't until another counselor, Heidi, told her that it was time to start prepping for lunch, that today it was her turn, that I realized she was a client.

I had wanted to work in retail at Macy's or Abercrombie & Fitch so I could get the employee discount, but I knew this job would impress the admissions committee of the undergraduate social work program at Siena, where I went to school (the social work program was hard-core—you had to apply to get into it even after you were accepted as a general student), and it paid $6.75 an hour, a little more than retail. I lucked out when I was placed at McCarroll Street, a small house in the suburbs of Schenectady inhabited by four women.

The ladies all worked part-time at an assembly factory a few towns away. One had experienced brain damage in utero; another was born with Down syndrome. Sheryl's demeanor was childlike.

The other ladies needed verbal prompting to complete activities of daily living like showering and brushing their teeth, but Sheryl did not. They were prone to emotional outbursts, tears, and frustration. Arguments would break out. But Sheryl was very independent.

It was up to the staff to help our clients manage their meals, but I felt uncomfortable doing so. Eating was a source of pleasure for them. Meals were a big deal in the house, especially dessert. The ladies didn't make much at the factory and were all on social security disability, so their food allowance was only thirty-five dollars a week each.

Sheryl was in her late thirties when we met. She was told when to wake up in the morning and where she was allowed to get a job. She was told whether she could have an extra dessert. Whether she could go to the mall or the library or the bowling alley. She was told that her boyfriend could not sleep over, and that she was not allowed to sleep at his. They were not to try to have sex. She was told that they were allowed to be engaged, but that they would never be allowed to marry. Despite these restrictions, Sheryl woke up every day like she was going to Disney World.

I couldn't help but think how much Sheryl would love Piemonte—Pumbaa crossing our path, the night dogs and Ugo, the sprawling, green grounds, the elevator inside the castle, the bathroom in my bedroom that was bigger than the McCarroll Street kitchen. The perfect porch for sipping coffee. When I first met her, she'd been only a little older than I was now. That good heart of hers would not have cheated herself out of what she deserved. Good men like Lorenzo, instead sleeping with a guy like Alessandro, because I didn't really want him anyway and there was no chance of getting hurt. What would Sheryl have done with all of this? What would she have done with my life? My pretty face. My summer in Italy. My night in Rome, and everything else that came to me, which I'd mismanaged.

Instead of dropping me off down the road at Fontanafredda, Sebastianio and his wife, Federica, invited me to join them for dinner and stay in their home/castle one more night. Sebastiano's three eldest sons worked up a sweat as they darted around the dining room at breakneck speed, hurling the ten-month-old baby Matteo around in some kind of wheeled contraption with a basket that sat three or four feet off the ground. I was scared for the baby, who looked like he was having the time of his life as he jutted from one side of his little basket to the other. I glanced over at Sebastiano's wife, Federica, to try and gauge the situation, but she was not alarmed.

"Over it" was how Joe described her. "She's over life. When you have that much money—billions of dollars—what do you have to look forward to? You can go anywhere, buy anything."

She'd been nothing but kind to me. She was certainly less animated than her husband, but it wasn't hard to be.

The boys were sent off somewhere else in the castle to have their supper; the dining room was for adults only. The household staff brought a few small family-style plates to the table. Sebastiano surveyed them for a moment—they were simple dishes, typical of everything in Piemonte—simple, but of the highest quality. Elegant. There was whole roasted branzino, glistening under the bright chandelier; couscous; and a simple salad of tomatoes. Also a bottle of Gavi, a common white produced in the region.

Sebastiano suddenly broke into a wide smile. "Kim, you can have aaaaaanything you want!" he exclaimed again in his singsong way.

I suppressed a smile.

Federica turned to Sebastiano and rolled her eyes. "She's not a baby, Sebastiano. She is more than thirty years old. She knows she can have anything she wants." We couldn't help but laugh at him.

It was nice to be welcomed into their home. Sebastiano didn't treat me like the help, like Joe's executive assistant—none of the Italians did. They treated me like a friend.

Sebastiano and Federica had promised the boys that if they were good, they could join us for dessert. As the meal wound down, I heard whispers in the back corner of the room. Peeking into the dining room, wearing matching pajamas, were the four boys. Sebastiano gave them the high sign, and they proceeded toward us, single file and carrying themselves much more gingerly than they had earlier, their eyes shining. The second oldest was carrying baby Matteo. They might have been the richest little boys in Italy, but they still got excited when company came over.

Since we hadn't made it the day before, I assumed Sebastiano would take me to Fontanafredda first thing in the morning, but he and Federica seemed in no hurry. Their slow pace, their way of letting life unfold moment to moment, was in great contrast to how I spent my days. Just like while walking with Lorenzo, I became aware of how fast and frenetic my own mind was.

We had lunch by their pool, Italian style, which meant it lasted three hours. The outdoor pool was one floor down from my room and provided the same view. Stretched out before us were rows of hazelnuts, followed by the beginning of the Barolo DOC or Denominazione di Origine Controllata, a designation granted by the Italian government that regulated winemaking regions. Off in the distance was La Morra, another region, though not as prestigious as Barolo, that produced wines from the Nebbiolo grape.

Sebastiano and Federica gave me a tour of the grounds and the castle. It had its own chapel. Federica told me that before they decided to buy the place, there was a lot of interest from foreign buyers—Russians. People in the town didn't like the idea of outsiders having such a precious landmark, owned by someone with no ties to Alba.

We creaked up a winding, wooden staircase single file to the top of the tower, up to the roof, and I swear you could see all of Italy.

Sebastiano and I departed for Fontanafredda after 5:00 p.m. The winery had its own inn, and this was where I'd spend my final two nights in Italy.

Sebastiano assigned one of his employees to take me all around Alba. She brought me to a festival in a little town called Piozzo, just down the road on the grounds of the Baladin beer headquarters. A barefoot Teo Musso was there, and within five minutes he asked us if we wanted to taste the beers he'd been working on.

We followed him out of the festival and up a steep, quiet road dotted with small, simple houses. We came to one that was across from a sun-washed red barn. It was the barn we were headed for; this was where Teo was rumored to be aging his craft beers in old Barolo and Aglianico wine barrels. I'd also heard he had re-created his childhood bedroom somewhere inside the barn, down to every last piece of furniture and toy. But he continued toward the house until he was pressing his face right up to the window.

"*Mio padre,*" he said, as he waved us closer to have a look. Through the window, sprawled out across an old recliner, legs outstretched, was an ancient man in a cardigan and brown pants, dead asleep.

We crossed over to the barn. There were rows and rows of large barrels. He must have brought us twenty small glasses of his beers, some tinged a rusty maroon color from sitting in the wine-stained wooden barrels. The childhood bedroom was indeed there—a small, simple room with a twin bed, nightstand, and a few items including an old clock. I couldn't help wondering if this was his actual home now, where he slept each night among his boyhood things and his barrels of beer.

Sebastiano had also arranged for the Fontanafredda groundskeeper, Ivan, to drive me to Malpensa to catch my flight back to New York. I had wanted to avoid this because it required poor Ivan to wake up before 5:00 a.m.

Before leaving Milan for Alba, Monica had kindly offered to host me at her apartment, so I had texted to see if I could stay with her on my last night.

You are always welcome, of course! she wrote. *But there is one thing. I hope you don't mind. Tomorrow night Alessandro will be staying here with me too. He usually stays with me one or two nights per week—jaja:)*

I had stared at the phone in disbelief, then let out a snort. Now it all made sense. How could I have been so stupid? Her pleading looks, her whispers to softhearted Santos, waving to their end of the table and asking me how I managed to meet Alessandro in New York that first night we'd met. Monica too was one of Alessandro's girls. Just like Camilla, she saw me coming the night of the party when he introduced me to everyone. One look at me and she knew Alessandro was up to his usual shit.

I politely declined, told her I'd changed my mind. Ivan and I would be up at 5:00 a.m.

I woke up the next morning in my room at Fontanafredda, my last day in Italy, to someone banging on my door. It was Ivan; I had overslept.

Ivan got me to Malpensa in record time, and I made my flight by some miracle, rushing through the airport. When I landed, I took a car from the airport straight to Corporate, wheeled my suitcase into my little yellow office, and worked from 1:00 p.m. until 7:00 p.m. like I'd never left at all.

eight

GROUPIE

"Eh, Kim, do you know what happened to Joe? He is happy all of the time now."

Edo didn't like to commit to an opinion or take sides and rarely admitted to having an interest in things, so he had to be really curious.

Vittorio had asked me the same question last week in the store, stopping me as I streaked past Manzo. "Do you know what is happening with Joe? Why is he so happy and so nice these days? Don't you think it's weird?" He moved his face closer to mine, pulling on his bottom lip as if I were about to unearth some secret.

"I don't know," I said, but closer to the truth was *I'm too busy to think about it.*

They were right, though—there had been a long, uninterrupted stretch of days featuring *Fun Joe.*

"*Hell*-o," Joe would say, as he exited the elevator and *clap-clapped* slowly into our office, before gazing out the window as if strolling around on a beautiful spring day. This happened even in the morning, before wine could've been a contributing factor. I had a feeling it was because of the Wild Ramsons.

Joe had formed a band with a few of the guys who worked at the store. They'd been lugging their gear—guitars, a drum set, a steel pedal—into La Scuola, the cooking school in the back of Eataly, on the nights it was empty, and one night Joe walked in on them mid-jam session. Things moved fast from there.

Joe used to join the servers at Babbo for karaoke on occasion, and he'd tried busking on the streets of Milan during his first summer there, but after their accidental meeting, he and the guys got serious quickly. Sharky was added to the mix, and Joe got them a gig out in Las Vegas. Now that Joe was back stateside, the group practiced in the Babbo apartment above the restaurant several times a week.

Music and the Wild Ramsons hijacked priority over all Joe's affairs, but you wouldn't hear any complaints out of me. Dad was happy, and I didn't care why. Joe going full-throttle into music might have created more work for me, but if it weren't this, it would be God knows what else.

Except for Joe, the Wild Ramsons members were all younger than I was. Joe didn't want to kill the vibe, so when I was with them, he didn't give me a lot of work to do, even when things he was hot on— things I knew he wanted an answer on ten minutes ago—came up.

His rapid-fire instructions were few and far between when among the Wild Ramsons, and when he did shoot something out, he frequently changed gears midsentence: "We'll talk about this tomorrow—remind me."

When he wasn't practicing with the band, writing songs with the lead guitarist, buying bags of candy for the confused staff at Corporate, bringing me cups of coffee from the Mudd truck, or otherwise being inexplicably nice to people, he was going to every local music show he could, working that circuit hard and collecting friends.

"Did you see that email from Rita Houston come in? You know who she is, right?"

I did not.

"She's a DJ for WFUV. We're putting on a benefit at Del Posto for the radio station. Rita's gonna emcee, the show will air live, and she's getting all these acts to play for free. You gotta fly people in from L.A.—call her now. Find out what we need to do."

The only night we could do the benefit was the same day as the New York City Marathon, which Joe was running again, but this did not deter him. A normal person would not host and perform in a music show after running twenty-six-point-two miles, possibly in freezing weather, but I was no obstructionist, so I got to work sorting out the details with Rita Houston and the team at Del Posto.

When I returned from Milan that past summer, I had moved down to Murray Hill and onto my friend Jamie's couch while looking for a new apartment. Jamie had been the general manager at Casa Mono for close to a decade, and she was a rock star. Rumor had it she was dining solo at the Babbo bar while Mario and Joe were plotting out the concept for Casa Mono, and she proceeded to order every single *secondi* on the menu. She was five foot six. Joe was intrigued and offered her the job running their soon-to-open lone Spanish project days later.

She ran that place as though it were her own, meaning she stopped just short of telling people to fuck right off if the situation called for it. But you needed to be an unyielding force to work that door, which was second in calamity only to Babbo.

In real life, Jamie was one of the funniest people I knew. Joe had tried to set her up with Jimmy Fallon years ago. She'd been one of Jesse's girls at the same time as I was, but by the time we realized, we were both finished with him and didn't care.

Jamie had a one-bedroom apartment in the East Thirties, and she frequently put people up on her couch—chefs, servers, whoever was in need. She let them stay for months at a time without asking for a cent in return. She was stocked with good wine and the location allowed me to get to Corporate even earlier. It was a comfortable spot until Hurricane Sandy came.

The night of the storm, Jamie and I were binge-watching *Downton Abbey*. When the power went out, I went to bed, but Jamie suited up in rain boots and her winter coat.

"There's no power over at NYU Hospital. I want to see what's going on," she said, pulling on the hood of her beige parka, her eyes wide.

I snapped my head off the pillow and pushed off my pile of blankets. "What the hell can you do about it?" I imagined Jamie treading along the sidewalk toward First Avenue, gripping her hood as the seventy-miles-an-hour wind blasted through the streets. The news reported that air conditioners were being ripped out of windows and plummeting to the ground—if she got hit with one of those, she'd be dead.

Jamie didn't come back for an hour. She stood outside the hospital and watched as the nurses and doctors ran out of NYU Hospital with babies in their arms—they were evacuating the NICU into ambulances. No one had power.

It was the cold that woke me early the next morning. Manhattan was mostly without power, as were the outer boroughs. Our restaurants were closed. Members of the Eataly staff got to the store to salvage what they could from the refrigerated and frozen sections and rescue the mother yeast we used to make all the bread. It had been alive years before the store was created.

Manhattan was like a ghost town. I didn't have much cash, and all the ATMs were down. I walked down Third Avenue and found one deli open and selling coffee, and that warm cup felt so good as I held it to my nose.

Jamie's apartment grew colder every day we went without heat and electricity. There was no hot water. Her friend offered us his apartment in Park Slope, one of the few neighborhoods that never lost power. Jamie went, but I stayed behind so I could be ready to get to Corporate or the store if needed. I couldn't be stuck out in Park Slope if Joe or someone else wanted me, and the subways weren't running regularly. I wore three pairs of socks to bed, layered on my warmest sweaters, and huddled under several blankets—covering my head completely helped trap the warm in—but the cold still woke me every few hours. Showers were fast and painful. The only bit of relief was standing by the gas stove as water boiled for tea or making coffee in a Moka pot. I turned the oven on for a couple hours at a time in desperation, a trick learned from Ms. Keller.

Lidia's restaurant Felidia allegedly had heat, but it was only slightly less freezing there than in Jamie's apartment, even with a space heater blasting underneath my workspace. I walked up to Felidia on 58th Street the next couple of mornings, miserable and lethargic but grateful to have somewhere to go and people to see. Prolonged exposure to the cold with no relief wore me down. I was fine on Tuesday, but then it was Thursday and I couldn't think straight. My gums above my two front teeth were so cold, they ached. I was tired from the moment I woke up and had no patience for those around me.

There was always some story on the local news about a shoddy landlord whose tenants had been without heat for months—it happened every year, and it was always in a poor neighborhood—people who didn't have gas-burning fireplaces, summer homes to escape to, or even an extra sixty dollars to pick up a space heater. I showed up to Felidia in tears because of a few uncomfortable days, but there were people who lived in the cold every day, kids who went to school like this.

Friday came. Power had been restored to much of the city but hadn't reached us yet in Murray Hill. New York, in general, was a mess. The mayor canceled the marathon in the early evening, just as Sebastiano, who'd flown in to run the race like hundreds of other foreign runners, landed at JFK. Power generators heated the race tents for the organizers and press in Central Park, but there weren't enough generators for hospitals still without power.

Whether or not we could continue with the benefit was touch-and-go for a while, but finally we decided to move ahead on Saturday.

We got power back at Jamie's on Sunday. I took a hot shower, finally able to stay under the water long enough to get really clean. I blow-dried my hair for the first time in a week. Scalding water dripped and steam hissed from Jamie's old radiator, and standing close to it felt like heaven. Having to head out into the damp cold was almost torture.

I volunteered to work the wine table at the benefit. I got anxious sitting around with nothing to do at these parties. It also let me meet and talk to everyone.

I shivered past the doorman at Del Posto, slipped down the marble staircase, and headed to the Piemonte room. I wanted to find Noah, one of the musicians we'd flown in from L.A. We'd been emailing and I'd meant to Google him but completely forgot in all the chaos. I had no idea what he looked like.

"You know who his father is, right?" Joe had said a few weeks earlier when I ran the price of Noah's flight by him. Noah's dad was part of a legendary folk-rock band from the '70s: a music icon.

I scanned the faces of the four or five guys standing among the guitar cases and cables covering the floor, looking for a trace of his famous father, when suddenly Noah found me. He had a wide-set face with a square jaw. Prominent cheekbones and freckles. He did look like his dad.

This was how I wished I'd felt when meeting Santos or Dante—to like someone instantly. Like Aaron as he stood looking at the floor in my little yellow office. And honestly, in the elevator with Michele. . . . It was nothing as intense as what I was told love at first sight felt like—that had never happened to me; I'd probably die.

The show whipped by in a blur. I spent most of it just outside the room, running the makeshift bar set up at the bottom of the stairs, which was slammed from start to finish. I didn't mind; it gave me something to do, and I had a view of the musicians and could hear everything.

"We gotta do this again. Kim, tomorrow we're getting the next one on the books!" sweaty, euphoric Joe called out to me as he ushered the musicians and Rita up to the lounge. The rest of the Wild Ramsons were just as elated, as if they'd all been taken hold of by the same rush. Joe hobnobbed with all kinds of people, but this was a big deal for the Wild Ramsons, and they more than held their own.

Joe poured everyone shots of Lagavulin, and I began to understand why people partied after shows; we were keyed up, and it was impossible to do anything else. Big crowds and large concerts made me nervous, but I had friends addicted to going to shows, and tonight I got it.

Joe was pretty drunk but Alice was there, so she would get him home safe without my having to worry. I took my shot and headed to the empty chair next to Noah. I didn't grow up in a home where folk-rock was played—my parents were big Neil Diamond people. I wasn't interested in his father. I was interested in hearing about his time growing up in France with his mother, the apartment in Paris that his grandfather left him. He made it easy to lean into him. To forget we were at a drunken after party.

Noah invited the other musicians and me back to the apartment where he was staying, just a few blocks from away. The Wild Ramsons' drummer swung by our end of the bar, and I asked him if he wanted to join us. He said no, but added, out of earshot of Noah, "Take the rest of the guys with you. Don't let them miss out on that."

Noah and I ended up in the kitchen of the apartment alone after a couple hours. The others called out goodbyes as they exited the apartment. We were standing so close that leaning in to kiss me would require little movement on Noah's part, and the moment to do it came almost immediately after the door shut.

He hesitated. *He was going to make me do it.* Strangely enough, it was easy for me to do. He shifted his weight toward me, and we slid along the rim of the counter and into the corner. We stayed there for what could have been a minute or twenty.

And then I told him it was time for me to go. He looked confused. I doubted this happened to him a lot. At first, he thought I didn't mean it, even tried to pull me, playfully, by the arm into the bedroom. Poor guy had no idea he was dealing with one of the most rigid, closed-off women he'd likely ever encountered.

What if I met him in the light of day, and he was the kind of person I'd be embarrassed to have slept with? I'd rather forgo sex than struggle with that kind of morning-after baggage. I knew this spoke to my insecurity, my unwillingness to be with the wrong guy even for one night, for fear I'd get stuck with the stain of him forever. That was how I felt when I thought about having slept with Alessandro.

Not that I didn't want Noah—I just preferred to have a meal with him first. I told him to call me tomorrow, his last night in town. He looked so disappointed, I wasn't sure he would.

When I got home around 4:00 a.m., restaurant girl Jamie was wide awake and just getting in herself.

"Why the hell are you here?" she exclaimed. "I Googled him—can I go over there? What's wrong with you?"

But Noah did call me the next day, and I set us up at the bar at Casa Mono, our Spanish restaurant the size of a shoebox: it had just two seven-seat wooden bars and thirteen tiny oak tables. I tasted my first Spanish food at Mono. During my last year at Heights and Boerum Council, I'd end up alone at the bar at least once a month—nobody cared about the employee permission rule there. I couldn't afford it, but I treated what was probably my depression with plates of pink Ibérico ham, manchego, grilled razor clams, and port wine so old it bubbled up on the edge of the glass like maple syrup.

I liked to bring dates there; we could watch the chefs cook behind the bar, and it gave me something to talk about should things become awkward, and I always felt a little awkward. I also knew everyone who worked at Casa Mono, so it took the pressure off when the chef or Jamie would approach to chat during the night. The only one of our restaurants I didn't take dates to was Babbo—that would be like bringing someone home to meet my parents, even though I hadn't worked a shift there in three years.

Chef Jackson—Jax—was cooking. Shortly after we'd taken our seats at the bar, Jax swung around the end and set a plate of something he'd been working on between Noah and me. One bite confirmed what I'd long suspected, that the young chef had a crush on me—my mouth was full of garlic-laden seared beef.

Noah told me that California had just banned foie gras from restaurants, so he was thrilled to see it on the menu. He told me how his grandmother was part of the French Resistance during World War II, and that he had two little girls. I could almost picture them, how the older one sang and was practicing an Adele song for her school's talent show. He told me his father once told him, "Never get a tattoo because that's how they find you." It made me wonder what else he learned while on the road in the late '80s with his dad, things he'd not likely tell me tonight or ever. He loved hearing me recall how I wrangled Joe into letting me work in Italy the previous summer, and how I was planning impromptu music shows even though I couldn't remember the last time I went to a concert. There wasn't much else for me to talk about besides work. It was all I did. I was glad I had such a cool job, that there was something interesting about me to share.

Flames shot up from underneath the steel pans of hissing skirt steak and scallops, almost reaching the rim of Jax's baseball cap and illuminating Noah's boxy face.

We both knew we were killing time before going back to the apartment in Chelsea, but it still felt like a real date to me. Despite my anxiety, I was starting to regret that Noah didn't live in New York.

The fact that he didn't live in the same city made this easier, though. He was single, but not really available. He was a musician from L.A., traveled all over, spent half his time in Paris. I wouldn't have to put in the work required to build something with him, to try to date him. I wouldn't have to wade through the emotional uncertainty of not knowing how it would go. I could be with him tonight. I knew enough after our dinner to trust him with some of me.

When was the last time I'd allowed myself to get involved with a man I'd have to interact with the next day? Someone I knew I'd see again in everyday life?

It was Jesse, three years ago. We were repetitive, but we weren't even exclusive. To find that, I'd have to go back to Liam.

I did want someone in my life who I would see the next day, but it'd been so long that it felt overwhelming. It felt so final, the way it never had in my twenties. I couldn't miss a beat. I couldn't do anything that would throw me off-kilter; otherwise, the world I'd built would come crashing down. The only thing I controlled was work.

We took a cab across town to the apartment in Chelsea.

Noah was one of those guys who was like a portable heater. This was the warmest my body had felt in a week, even after he'd pulled off all of my clothes. He likely did this all the time. A different city, a different girl. It was effortless. The first time with a new person could be awkward, but he threw me around that warm bed as if from muscle memory. Somewhere along the line, he'd learned how to be a good lover, how to handle a woman in bed.

My mom sat me down when I was about ten. She was concerned I hadn't told her something important, though now it was lost to time. "How do you expect to get close to people, to have a husband someday, if you can't open up?" she'd asked. That question was all I remembered from the conversation, years later. As if I knew then that I'd grow up to be alone.

I had sex with Noah again that morning and left shortly after. It was already past 7:00 a.m., and like with Gareth, I felt the need to get up and get out as soon as possible. I could shower at the New York Sports Club on 23rd Street and head to Corporate.

I left Noah standing outside the bedroom, his square jaw framed in the white top sheet he'd wrapped around himself. If I had known that morning how long it would be before another man would hold me, I'd have stayed a little longer.

nine

IL CANE DI BASTIANICH

"There might an extra bonus in it for you, should something happen to Quattro on the plane to Italy this summer." It wasn't like Alice to make jokes; this was something Joe would say. I should have known she wasn't kidding.

"Won't it be nice to have a dog in the apartment? You don't mind taking him out when I'm on set, do you?" Joe had wheedled.

I loved the idea of living with a dog. I'd always had one growing up but couldn't afford it in New York, and God knows I wasn't home enough to care for an animal. When Delta couldn't change Joe's seat to accommodate his dog, I offered to take Quattro, a Jack Russell terrier, with me instead.

I'd been Joe's executive assistant for three and a half years and had learned that anything I could do to pay it forward, to fill some unexpected need that Joe had, was like banking money for a rainy day—it reinforced my safety net, added a layer of padding that would, in theory, cushion the blow should I drop a big ball, commit some drastic screw-up that could get me fired. Most people felt *more* secure the longer they remained in a role, and in some ways I did; I knew exactly how Joe felt about everything, sometimes before he did. I knew his ulterior motives for each phone call he agreed to take, each time he met someone for coffee. He could disappear for a month, and so long as he wasn't due on set, no one would even know he was gone. You didn't speak to someone ten times a day; scan their personal and work inboxes; listen in on every phone call; read almost every text, WhatsApp, tweet, and Instagram DM; sit through dinners with their mother; and not know them.

Jamie always said that Joe was "predictably unpredictable," but I no longer agreed. He just had an insane amount of patterns that corresponded to the insane amount of people, places, and ideas he was intent on amassing. She hadn't spent enough time with him to get the full spectrum, witness every act in the circus.

But there was much out of my control. The danger lay in the volume of what came in. "I'm holding things back from you, just so you know," Joe told me once.

I was certain this was true, but it did not help me. Joe's endeavors, all his big ideas, had mounted to the point of too much to manage responsibly. Every day felt like being at the craps table. I couldn't stop, even for a moment, lest I lose control of everything. Keeping up with work became an addiction. Each email I processed, each call I made on his behalf or scheduled for him, each box I ticked, each land mine I pointed out just in time for him to sidestep, brought a tremendous feeling of satisfaction and relief. I had to do it over and over again because the buzz was short-lived. I was only as good as my last task, and even if my last one was great, I didn't want to go too long without completing another, or self-doubt snuck in.

The latest big project was to build a restaurant on the Bastianich winery property in Cividale del Friuli. It was meant to be a small place with a formal dining room and casual tavern. The aim was to make it a Michelin star–worthy destination restaurant, meaning people would drive all the way out there, twenty minutes from the border of Slovenia, just to have dinner. The outskirts of the medieval town had rolling hills and rows of vines. It was simple and ancient. There was a single town square. The plan included adding a six-room bed-and-breakfast and bringing in two of our top chefs from Del Posto. I wasn't involved yet, but Joe was driving the guys at the winery crazy. He said he was going to hire someone to run it, and this person would not only act as a general manager/maître d' of sorts, but also as an assistant—"an Italian Kim," Joe said—and the thought was so tantalizing, that I'd finally be getting real help with my workload, I didn't dare believe it.

I met Alice and Quattro in the lobby of Corporate just hours before heading to the airport for my second trip to Italy. It would be the second summer in a row that I was going, and I looked forward to seeing my old friends.

"I gave him half a tranquilizer," Alice noted. "He should mellow out soon." She turned on her heel and left me to it.

Quattro panted and pulled hard on his leash. He was strong for such a small dog. We waited for the elevator as he darted in every direction, paying no attention to me or the fact that he'd just changed hands.

We got into the elevator, and he stilled. I bent down and lightly ran my fingers through his wiry, damp coat. He let me pet him for a few floors, and then out of nowhere, he bit me. Hard. Not enough to draw blood, but it hurt.

We reached the tenth floor, and the design team was in the entry-way. In unison, they cried "Aaaaww!" and extended their arms down toward him.

"Don't touch him!" I snapped, pulling the dog toward my office door. "He bites!" I shut and locked the office door behind me.

Alice said to give him another half a tranq when we got on the plane, but I didn't wait and instead immediately pressed a whole one into a soft brown dog treat that looked and felt like a Tootsie Roll. Quattro's teeth were half an inch long, freakishly big in the mouth of a twelve-pound animal.

I spent the next few hours trying to get as much work done before the flight as possible, but each time I stood up from my desk and moved toward the door to go to the printer, get a coffee, or send a fax, Quattro stood alert on his haunches, as if to say *I dare you to leave me.* I had to close the door in his face so he didn't escape.

Joe owned his own taxi medallion. He tried not to use John, the cabbie, too much, so he could pick up paying fares, but today he was bringing Quattro and me to the airport.

At 1:00 p.m. sharp, I hauled my small suitcase, a feral Quattro, and his carry-on bag to the lobby to wait for John. Twenty minutes passed. The *whoosh* of cars, horns honking, and people entering and exiting the building seemed to counteract the effect of the tranqs, and Quattro was as much a live wire as when Alice dropped him off. I kept the leash short and taut—I had to; all who passed us were fair game. It almost seemed like the dog enjoyed messing with people. He stared up at them and trotted forward—like a happy, normal dog.

Then he nuzzled his head into their welcoming hands, wiggling his back end as if soliciting affection. But once their guard was down and they were giving him a hearty rub on the back of his neck, he turned his head and clamped down.

"No no no no!" I sputtered, as one young man who worked on the twelfth floor went right in, disregarding my warning.

"It's okay, he likes me," he said, just before Quattro struck.

"Just a nip," the guy said, but he pulled back his hand as if splashed with boiling oil.

John was more than thirty minutes late. He texted twice after I sent him four messages. My left arm was tiring from Quattro's tugging. We moved against the wall to give people as much room as possible. I shouted warnings three, four, five times per minute. I walked Quattro out to hail a cab, but the first one that pulled over wouldn't take me with the dog.

John showed up almost one hour late and couldn't care less. He didn't want to take us. Likely he was late on purpose, hoping we'd give up and find another way. Joe loved him, but the guy gave me the creeps. One Saturday, he was tasked with picking me up in Brooklyn and bringing me to the Bastianich house in Greenwich, Connecticut, to retrieve a few things. He started to talk about a woman he knew, calling her "a real bitch." He must have repeated the word ten times in a matter of minutes, enunciating so hard I thought he was going to spit. "That *bitch*, she's a *bitch*, stupid *bitch*." He didn't like that I told him what to do on behalf of Joe. I finally asked him to stop saying that word, then pretended to make a phone call for the rest of the ride.

There was no grace left in me when he pulled up that day. As soon as I opened the cab's door, I yelled that he would have to pay for my nonrefundable flight if we missed it and that he had done this on purpose. I continued like this for minutes, really yelling, until I got hold of myself—I sounded like a maniac. Then I apologized.

I gave Quattro five full minutes to pee on the sidewalk outside JFK. He didn't go, and we couldn't wait.

We jogged across the lateral escalator, and suddenly he leaped high, up to my waist as if trying to get into his carry-on bag. The second tranq was kicking in. He couldn't run anymore and went right in the bag.

The seat next to me mercifully remained unoccupied after takeoff, and I set him on the floor in his bag next to my feet. What started as a soft cry became a high-pitched whimper, and people turned in my direction, annoyed, because everyone wanted to go to sleep. I unzipped the bag a few inches to stroke behind his ears—*now he liked it*. As long as I kept it up, he stayed quiet. But after two hours, my hands were cramping.

I began to feel bad that the dog hadn't peed since 10:30 a.m. The whimpers turned to yelps, so I took him to the bathroom, let him out of his bag, and put paper towels on the floor. How much could a little dog go? But he didn't go. Back in our seat, he yelped intermittently until we landed at Malpensa.

I took Quattro out the first door I saw. He finally peed—neon green—and then made like he was going to bite me, but I called his bluff and shoved him back in the bag. We had a thirty-minute ride on the Malpensa Express to endure, and I didn't know how to warn people in Italian that they might lose a finger.

Our apartment wouldn't be ready for several hours, so I took Quattro to the hotel where Joe had been staying for the last few days. Quattro went ballistic when he saw him.

"How was he?" Joe asked, fondling the terrier's ears.

"You should have told me," I said.

Joe took a good look at me while Quattro bounded with delight in circles around him. He winced. "Oh, Kim. I'm sorry. I thought it best not to say anything."

I told him about the lunging, the biting, the catfishing, the yelping, the paper towels.

"He played you," Joe says coolly. Then he shook his head. "Is the apartment ready?"

"We have two hours."

Joe must have felt very bad because he asked the front desk if there was a room available right now for me to rest in, as in, he was going to pay for an actual room for me to use for a few hours, but the hotel was booked, so Joe arranged for his friend Elisabetta to pick us up.

A black SUV pulled up to the curb a few minutes later, and out slipped Elisabetta. She wore full makeup, dangling earrings, four-inch stilettos ("*tacchi alti*"), and was very pregnant. She moved toward Quattro, who was looking up at her with his shining, deceptive eyes, and Joe and I both yelled, "Careful!"

I worried about her trotting around in those skinny heels, but she was a woman of Milan; they could run across an ice-skating rink in those things.

We got into the car, and she cracked her window even though the AC was on. "*Tuo cane puzzo*, Joe," she said, wrinkling her nose. *Your dog stinks*. Quattro smelled because he bit the shit out of anyone who tried to give him a bath.

On the drive to a café, I learned Elisabetta was a journalist. She was having her second baby, due next week. *She has a whole life*, I thought. I always considered people who hit milestones I hadn't yet as being older than I was. But I was thirty-four, and Elisabetta was actually my exact age. She was very friendly but spoke to me as though I was a kid sister.

Joe's agent at CAA used to do the same. She called me *sweetie* until I mentioned during one of our calls that I was in my thirties and had a master's, and that being an assistant was a second career. Being an assistant was considered a young woman's job, but I also gave off a vibe that encouraged the assumption. A kind of youngest sibling, subservient vibe—*little Kim*.

My first day back in Italy, and I felt just as strung out as the day I left last summer, when I scraped myself off the bed at Fontanafredda at 5:45 a.m. Why did I push to come here again? So I could tell people I was living in Milan for the summer, to create a sense that I lived a worldly, glamorous life. I was off to a good start: fifteen hours with Quattro had left me borderline psychotic, and the new blue-striped cotton jacket I wore on the plane was stained yellow under the arms. I wondered exactly who I was going to tell. I barely talked to anyone unless about some new, wild idea Joe cooked up. The people I wanted to be like, impress, or at least hold my own against didn't know I was alive, and they lived this way already—trips to Europe, weekends in Paris, meeting friends for dinner in Venice. They thought nothing of it. And they weren't here in Milan to see me. Who was I doing this for?

My ego was probably half of why I was there. But another part was that I truly loved the city. I'd dreamed of living in both Milan and New York since learning that the two places existed—that elusive, pseudo-expat life. I loved how Italians got their coffee, and the way people in Milan cared about their appearance—no one would be caught dead on the street in ill-fitting clothes, even my most down-to-earth friends and contacts. They weren't necessarily expensive, although people were known to skip out on rent to buy a Prada dress or a Tom Ford suit. But clothing and shoes fit well, were unwrinkled and clean. No one wore pajamas on the street or sloppy clothing that *looked* like pajamas on the street. I loved the old buildings and the lack of skyscrapers so you could actually see the night sky, like during my midnight ride on the back of Santos's bicycle last year. Milan was a small city. I saw the same people in the same places. I knew if I walked past the restaurant La Libera on Corso Garibaldi, I'd see the owner, an older gentleman with a curlicue gray mustache who rode his bicycle up and down the block, always wearing a seersucker suit.

The real reason I was there, even exhausted, was that I had nothing to stay home for. No life outside the job. I hadn't taken the time to build anything of my own—even friendships. Like last summer, I didn't tell anyone I was leaving except my parents and a few people in our orbit who Joe heard would be passing through town while we were there. I talked to a friend from graduate school who'd moved to New Jersey, and out of nowhere she asked, "Who do you even hang out with now? Who are your friends?" As if she knew. I had more acquaintances than I could count, but my father and sister were the emergency contacts listed with my doctor's office. There wasn't anyone in New York I felt comfortable asking.

We had a full house planned for the next month before the rest of the Bastianich family arrived, and this lifted my spirits and reminded me I was lucky to be there. It pulled me out of that angry trap of thinking this job was to blame for not having a personal life. I'd done a lousy job managing opportunities, just like I did a bad job managing my life in my twenties, allowing myself to linger working two jobs, but I was still poor.

Sharky was our first guest, spending a week before flying to Istanbul, and then back for a few days at the end of the month. "Did ya buy your ticket for the opera yet?" he'd texted me a few days earlier, when I was still in New York. Sharky and his friend who lived in Milan bought tickets to La Scala for a night at the end of July, when he would be back from Istanbul. I still had not been to the opera, though I'd been saying I'd go for years. I needed to buy my ticket while there were still cheap seats, but I worried about making plans so far in advance, Joe's schedule being what it was.

Sharky and I headed out for breakfast the morning he arrived. This year we rented an apartment on Via Londonio, just off Corso Sempione—a wide street leading straight into the Parco Sempione, Milan's largest park. We weren't far from the old place on Via Guercino and Cantina Isola, where we stopped for our second coffee. "*Caffè corretto*," Sharky told the server at the counter. "Gonna do it right this time," he added.

We watched as the owner poured out a small shot of grappa and set it next to Sharky's espresso. We dug into our pockets and snapped our coins down on the bar.

"It's 10:00 a.m.," I said.

He rolled his eyes, offering an elaborate shrug. "I'm on vacation."

There was another bar closer to the apartment, on the corner of Corso Sempione and Via Londonio, where Joe liked to stop for coffee. It was new, very bright inside with high ceilings, and had a long bar with stools so we could sit American-style and not rush right out. We befriended one of the women who worked behind the bar. She was from Istria, where Lidia's family was from.

When Joe had the energy to deal with Quattro in public, he brought him there. He figured if we got Quattro used to city living, he'd start "acting like a normal dog," but this wasn't the spot for it. The aboveground metro ran along Corso Sempione. *Ring-a-ding-ding* it went as it glided along the narrow grooves in the street. If it came by when we were out with Quattro, he lunged toward it like he was trying to commit suicide. The first time he did it, I mused that if I just let the leash slip, this would all be over. The thought startled me, and I pulled him back hard, ashamed.

He wasn't so bad in the house. "He's a good little companion," Joe said, and I was starting to see that. We'd turned a corner, Quattro and I. I could pick him up, pet him, clip his leash to his collar. He let me do it all with no coaxing. He got into my laundry once. I was at my desk when I heard snorting coming from underneath the bed. I lifted the blanket and saw Quattro having a good time with the expensive silk tank top I'd just bought but definitely could not afford. I shot my hand under the bed, grabbed his coarse fur, and pulled him out. I could have lost my hand—and the top—with one bite.

The first night in the apartment, we were alone. Joe left for another offsite challenge after we got settled. I left my bedroom door open when alone, to hear a burglar breaking in that much sooner. That night, I woke up to Quattro sprawled across my left hip and leg. Some nights I woke up to find him tangled in my hair.

Quattro was a smart dog. He grabbed his food dish between his teeth and banged it against the floor when hungry. He knew who he could depend on for care and in this house, that was me, since I was always there. At home, he was in fierce competition with Alice to be the number two to Joe and treated her like he treated me in the office—or worse, every day. He loved the kids, though. They were the ones he let give him a bath. He must have thought I was a kid too.

But Quattro just didn't do well on the street. I picked up his leash and he thought we were suiting up to raid the Duomo and taking out all the souls along the way who stretched out a hand. And there were a lot of them. Streets here were lined with people spilling out of bars and restaurants during *aperitivo* or eating at outdoor tables on the sidewalk. When the metro came, Quattro snarled and lunged like he was in the fight of his life. "*Il cane di Bastianich*," someone in the crowd would jeer, and laughter often followed.

The previous fall, Joe had been parodied on national television by the Jerry Seinfeld of Italy. The comedian did a spot-on impersonation that went viral in the country, mocking Joe and the show, calling it *BastardChef*, and turned Joe into a household name overnight. *MasterChef* shot up to number one in the ratings. Joe gained a hundred thousand Twitter followers. I couldn't understand half of what the comedian said, but he had Joe's mannerisms down pat—he even moved his eyes the same way. This year, we couldn't go anywhere without Joe being heckled. More than a few times when we were seated at some outdoor restaurant and I'd pried my face away from my phone to admire the façades of the old buildings, I saw the shutters in the windows part to make room for a camera lens. It was strange to know that I was being photographed by the paparazzi. I tended to wave.

Marigold the American writer was in town from Paris that evening, so Joe, Sharky, and I decided to take her out and make a night of it. After we were introduced at the party the previous summer, Marigold and I didn't talk much; part of me felt intimidated by her, and part of me was too preoccupied juggling Monica and making sure Joe didn't fall over.

Marigold showed up in a sleeveless ivory Prada blouse, a pink and red striped skirt, and classic red lips. First, we all swung by a bar on Corso Garibaldi for a work commitment. Joe was a spokesperson for Grana Padano, a cheese consortium that sponsored Lidia's TV show on PBS. Joe agreed to meet one of the consortium heads, who was in town only for tonight. Our liaison with Grana Padano was a pleasant but long-suffering woman named Paulina, always trying to get Joe to commit to visiting the consortium members at their headquarters in the middle of nowhere, and the factory where the cheese was made. Every year when it was time to renew his contract, she fought admirably to make the pilgrimage a contractual obligation, and every year she failed. I was very impressed with her—she wrangled more out of Joe than anyone, even Lidia. Even me.

These consortiums were old-school, run by traditional Italian men. What they wanted was for Joe to "appear" before them, the Grana Padano grandmasters, before they'd agree to continue the relationship. Joe would rather slit his throat. He genuinely liked the cheese, he ate the cheese, he'd gotten half the people at Corporate and me addicted to the cheese, he fought with Mario about the cheese because Mario favored Grana Padano's competitor, Parmigiano Reggiano. He was happy to promote it—would probably do it for free. Why did he need to tap-dance for these people?

These nights were stressful. Joe came armed with resistance and no doubt planned to leave me alone with Paulina and the Grana Padano elder, who, for all I knew, might be a lovely person but likely didn't speak English. Paulina was unafraid to call out the fact that Joe was not doing what he was supposed to, which was sitting the fuck down at this table and making small talk. And that was precisely how the first twenty minutes of the night unfolded.

Paulina encouraged me to speak Italian to the consortium head. I tried but was so plugged in to where Joe was in the room and when he was going to get his ass back here that we couldn't really keep up a conversation. Marigold spoke perfect Italian, and after a few moments of silence, she picked up with the elder where I could not.

Joe finally took a seat next to Paulina, and the three of them broke into fast chatter. I should've tried to keep up, but my brain was fried from the long day. I just had to hold on a little longer, maybe another hour, when Joe got more wine in him. Some people got mean when they drank; Joe was the complete opposite. The more he drank, the nicer he became. I'd go so far as to describe him as joyful—but most importantly, his tank emptied; he stopped talking about work. He stopped asking me things.

When will this be over? I wondered.

Marigold's soft voice cut through the chatter. "I know how hard your job is," she said, leaning toward me over the table. "I can see it."

Maybe it was because I looked up to her so much, but that little bit of encouragement breathed life into me. Just to know that someone noticed. Someone else understood that the whole of this absurd job was not equal to the sum of its parts. That I wasn't crazy; the job *was* hard.

I recalled when Natalie was training me, how surprised she'd been when I hadn't needed help. Now I understood. I wasn't special, some untiring robot assistant. I was overwhelmed, like she'd been. It'd just taken me longer to get there.

Another fifteen minutes passed and Joe felt that it had satisfied his commitment, so we headed over on foot to a restaurant owned by a new friend. Mercifully, the wine flowed. The work stopped. Marigold talked about some odd jobs she'd held—she once spent months on a sailboat off the coast of Venezuela. She'd written novels but was involved in the art scene now.

Marigold's longtime boyfriend, the French actor, had been in the tabloids lately for his friendship with Vladimir Putin. Sharky and Joe commented on it when Marigold stepped away from the table to go to the bathroom. I wanted to ask her, but she seemed private. She didn't mention her boyfriend at all. But as we all got a little drunk, Joe brought up the Putin connection. Marigold told us Putin was obsessed with his little dog, and for some reason this caused us to fall into uncontrollable drunken laughter.

We talked about music—Sharky had played in a band for many years that toured parts of Spain, and Marigold revealed that the music of Stevie Wonder had saved her life. I wished I had something to share that didn't revolve around checking Joe's inbox.

We were all pretty drunk by the time we finished dinner. We had set out back toward the city center on foot when someone suggested we go back to the apartment for a Stevie Wonder dance party.

"Kim, do we have any wine left at home?" Joe asked.

We didn't. The next shipment from the winery had not arrived yet. "Just the crusty bottle of rum that was left by the last tenant."

It was after midnight. There were no twenty-four-hour delis open like in New York. "One of these places has to sell us some beer," Joe offered. But none were open.

"What about your friend in the bar around the corner—the one from Istria?" asked Sharky.

Joe and Marigold returned to the apartment while Sharky and I rounded the corner to the new bar, where we took Quattro.

The doors were locked. The lights were off.

"Wait a minute," Sharky said. We pressed against the glass like two beady-eyed squirrels when the bird feeder was low. The woman from Istria was in the back, tying up a garbage bag. We banged on the windows. Bless her, she let us inside. She couldn't sell us beer because they'd closed up for the night but was happy to give us whatever we could carry. "You can pay tomorrow," she said.

She loaded us up with large bottles of Italian craft beers. I tucked a twelve-ounce Menabrea into my jacket pocket, and Sharky and I hobbled toward Via Londonio victorious, arms full of loot.

By the time we got into the apartment, Quattro had bitten Marigold. Joe was thrashing around in the lower kitchen cabinets looking for a first-aid kit. Marigold held up her hand. The damn dog drew blood. She looked shaken.

It was one of those nights where everyone was hopped up on each other. These people—my dancing companions—were all larger than life. We were a motley crew: a tabloid-hounded woman of Paris, a blue-collar restaurant man turned TV star in a foreign country, a writer who gave himself a nickname like Sharky. And me.

We decided to break out the rum. Joe, Sharky, and I headed to the kitchen, and Marigold took the opportunity to make amends with Quattro. I watched her bend down toward him, cooing sweet words while Quattro stared up at her, eyes shining, playing the part of a happy dog. In a flash, he leaped high and clamped down on her forearm. She bucked upright and stood there as if in shock. He jumped a second time and got her again.

"JOE!" yelled Sharky. In one fast movement, Joe scooped up the dog and sent him flying through the air into the master bedroom. Just before the door slammed shut, I watched Quattro land safely on the bed. Marigold breathed heavily, clutching her forearm as blood trickled from two deep puncture wounds from his saberlike teeth.

As fun as these nights were, they always left me wanting. I never allowed myself to completely cut loose. Joe was still my boss. I might sling back the wine like everyone else, but I was conscious that everything I said and did was a representation of Joe. This trickled down to how friendly I became with someone. What if Joe and Marigold got into a fight and stopped being friends? What if he had a falling-out with Sharky? I never felt free to speak one hundred percent authentically. My guard was never down. I met all these interesting characters, but who did they meet? A frazzled, somewhat crafted exterior, an outer shell of who I was. Small wonder my friendships weren't very deep.

And small wonder why I was so good at this job. It enabled me to continue being closed off. It put me squarely in the fray of someone else's life while hiding in plain sight. It gave me an uncontestable reason to be here, to be among them. To be part of the club. But it didn't feel real. In a sense, I was still wasting away in the Babbo basement. And it didn't really have anything to do with my outer world but how I wielded my outer world from within.

I had to get a handle on my fear of intimacy and close relationships, and I couldn't keep blaming it solely on the job. The isolation was becoming more painful than the risk of rejection.

That was another thing: I was not making what I should for the amount of responsibility I carried and the amount of work I did. This was a delicate matter to bring up with Joe. He'd rather pay in trade—let me come along to Italy, give me free meals and wine at the restaurants.

I made fun of Joe's cheapness but wished some of it would rub off on me. I still carried the same balance on my Visa. Each month, I paid slightly more than the minimum due on my student loans, nowhere near paying them off. I didn't even know how much I owed. Last I looked, it was more than twenty thousand dollars, thirteen years after I took them out. My mother was right; I never should have taken out that kind of money. At thirty-four, I never thought I'd still have this burden. Borrowing forty thousand dollars from Sallie Mae was only the first of many mistakes.

I thought perhaps I should save up my Christmas bonus as a nest egg. But I didn't want to—I wanted to go to Paris for a few days, treat myself to a nice dress and a new pair of good shoes to wear while there. It was my second summer working from Europe while wishing I could be relaxing and vacationing in Europe.

The only liquid cash I had was my twenty-five-hundred-dollar safety net, and I didn't want to spend that. I asked Joe if I could get an advance on my bonus slated for the end of the year. He knew I was getting pummeled, so it was a great time to ask. He agreed. "Shop away," he texted.

I went to Rinascente, Italy's answer to Bloomingdale's. I picked out a black, knee-length Sandro cocktail dress with a Peter Pan collar still conservative enough for work but chic enough for Milan. Liza would have approved. I found a pair of low-heel black patent leather Ferragamo shoes with a square toe at twenty percent off, but I liked them better than any of the full-price ones.

There was a knock on my bedroom door a few nights later. I had recently instituted a rule that even though we were under the same roof, I could not be expected to do any work after 7:00 p.m.

Joe nudged open the door tentatively. "Am I allowed to talk to you about work for a few minutes?" He glanced at my laptop. On the screen was the home page for a hotel in Paris. "You're going to pay for a hotel in Paris? Don't we know someone there? Ask Marigold if you can stay at her place."

No way was I inviting myself to Marigold's home. She wasn't Fabrizio and Luca, who owed Joe a million favors. I'd only hung out with her twice, and reminded Joe as much.

"This is what you're gonna do with the money I just gave you?" he said, as though speaking to one of his kids. "Call Marigold. She has business in Milan anyway—she said she had to come back the night that Quattro mauled her, remember? You can offer her a house swap. She can take your room, and you can take her apartment."

Which was how I ended up in Marigold's darling apartment on the Rue de Lille, two blocks from the Boulevard Saint-Germain to the left, and the River Seine, the Louvre, and the Tuileries Garden two blocks to the right. Joe left me alone the entire time. I finished the latest blog for *MasterChef* the first few hours I was there, and that was it.

I was having such a glorious time walking around Paris in my Ferragamo shoes, eating quenelles, and drinking too much Beaujolais at Aux Lyonnais, Alain Ducasse's famed bistro, that I picked up the phone when Alessandro called. He and Camilla wanted to invite me to a party in Portofino the next week. "We've rented a house here for the summer. It will be just like the party last year in Forte dei Marmi. You can stay with us. You'll meet a lot of people."

I didn't want to hang out with him. I felt guilty being around Camilla, but the last party was such a good experience. I would've said no if he hadn't mentioned her, but that means he wasn't expecting a repeat of that night the previous summer. I told him I'd think about it.

***

"Did you see that email from that guy about that thing?"

Funny: I actually knew which email Joe meant, or at least had the possibilities narrowed down to ten out of the thirty that had come into his inbox in the last hour.

"Is it about that event tonight for House & Loft on Via Manzoni? The one the winery's sponsoring?"

"That's it—the one we got roped into by that starfucker guy . . . what's his name?"

Joe asked me to swing by the event to see how the wines were placed. When we donated wine to these events, the organizers agreed to promote it. They left information about the winery out for guests and displayed bottles on the bar, but nobody ever paid attention. It was more of a social thing.

I was almost there when I got a WhatsApp from Sharky. *Did ya buy yr ticket for tonight or what?*

Oh fuck. I was supposed to go to the opera. How did I forget?

There was still time to ditch the House & Loft party. Joe wouldn't care. He'd tell me to go to the opera. La Scala was just a few blocks away. I could see if there were still tickets. But I kept walking fast along Via Manzoni. I told Sharky I had a conflict—work called— and there was no backing out. I shot myself in the foot, again. Saving the day, even on a minuscule scale—on something Joe didn't even really care about superseded it all.

I arrived at what appeared to be a gorgeous old mansion. I was wearing the Paris dress with the hand beading on the Peter Pan collar and the Ferragamo shoes; if I'd had anything else on, I'd have felt entirely out of place. My look was much more conservative than how most women dressed in Milan, but I felt good. Like a richer version of me. It felt foreign to be totally at ease with what I was wearing.

I found the "starfucker guy" who'd arranged the event. His name was Tommaso. Joe's term for him was crude but true. He was over-the-top nice to me and I suspected it was because I worked for Joe. Then Tommaso said he wanted me to meet someone.

I followed Tommaso through the crowd, my eyes glued to my phone, and looked up just in time to realize I was standing too close to the man he was about to introduce me to.

"*Ciao*, I'm Jovani."

I'd heard it said that when Bill Clinton shook your hand, you felt like the only two people in the room. Meeting Jovani was like that. He had one of the most beautiful faces I'd seen—he'd give Jesse a run for his money. He had brown curls and a sculpted, lean physique. I initially struggled to make small talk because he was distracting. This soon dissipated, partly because he was kind and inviting, and partly because he told me within five minutes that he had a girlfriend (which not all Italian men did). I was simultaneously disappointed and relieved.

"I'm moving to New York in a couple of months to move in with my girlfriend. We should keep in touch. You have to tell me where all the good vegan restaurants are."

Glad to have something tangible to offer, I assured him Joe and I would help with whatever they needed in the food world.

Jovani spoke slowly and clearly, almost too slow; perhaps because he was unsure of the English language. But the more he talked, the more peaceful he seemed. He was present. His state of being was in stark contrast to my own frenetic energy. I jittered about, even when standing still.

Jovani smiled knowingly as he looked down at my hands. Each held a phone: my American cell and Joe's old iPhone that I used as my Italian cell. I was at a cocktail party, for Christ's sake, and I had both phones at the ready.

"I can tell what it is you do for work. That you are an assistant," he said, his voice deep and throaty.

"Is it that obvious?"

"Only to someone who used to be one. I was the assistant to the head of a major fashion house for eight years. And I looked just like you—always with two phones."

Jovani made his own wine now, prosecco. He was the other wine sponsor besides the Bastianich winery. He told me to call him if I wanted to have drinks before leaving town, which was just in a week, and we could swap assistant stories.

I stayed with him as long as I could, maybe twenty minutes. I felt like I was holding my breath—I didn't know what to do with this guy.

A few days later, Jovani picked me up, and we headed to Bar Basso for drinks. It was allegedly the place the Negroni was invented. I chose it because an influential friend in the culinary world had boasted about it, but we passed through the dark doorway and into the land that time forgot. It was empty, save for the burly barman, and had an air of Miss Havisham's house, had Miss Havisham's neglected, old house been a bar. I ordered a Negroni and it arrived in a cartoonishly large glass that I picked up with both hands, sucking down my drink to kill the embarrassment.

And that was when I found out Jovani was a count. Titles didn't mean anything in Italy anymore, but his family still lived in a big ancestral home in Treviso. His girlfriend was a famous American actress—*now* I understood why Tommaso called back to me, as we approached Jovani at the House & Loft party, "Have you seen *The Help*?"

Jovani told me when he was an assistant, he helped plan Katie Holmes and Tom Cruise's wedding in Rome. "We were involved in fashion, but we ended up helping with everything." Then his tone grew serious. "I want to tell you something."

He recalled a story of how once, he lost both his phones on the beach when traveling for work. He took a walk. They were in his pockets. He walked off the beach, and they were gone. He went back to look for them and found nothing. Naturally, he panicked. But he did not replace them for two weeks.

I believed he was a count, had a famous girlfriend, and helped plan Tom Cruise's wedding, but *that* was hard to believe.

"You should wish for it. Could be the best thing to happen to you."

I was flying home in the morning. I woke up later than I'd meant. I took a quick shower, dressed, and then started cleaning out every drawer in my bathroom, tossing jars of face cream, tubes of toothpaste and SPF lotion, dental floss, hair ties, and eye cream into quart-sized plastic bags. I looked under my bed, in the corners of the family room, underneath every piece of furniture for any rogue socks, underwear, or tank tops hijacked by Quattro. I packed my suitcase, slipped my laptop and notebook into my carry-on, and rolled it all out of my bedroom.

Quattro knew I was departing. He knew what a suitcase meant. I'd grown to dread leaving the apartment these last few weeks because he resorted to snapping at my ankles out of desperation when I—or anyone—tried to head out the door.

Now was the moment when, ordinarily, I'd lure him into the kitchen with a treat, toss it into the far corner, and then turn and back out quickly, shutting the door behind me, trapping him inside.

I knelt down in front of him instead. I could swear there was love in those shining brown eyes. But maybe it was hope. I picked up his two front legs and gave him a long hug. This little dog just wanted to be loved, to find his place among those he was surrounded by, but he was so afraid of it, so terrified, that he destroyed every chance he got.

I told him goodbye. He watched me roll my suitcase to the door. He didn't move as I turned and flipped its many locks, pulled it open, and shut it behind me.

I'd heard the saying *God puts people in your way for a reason.* I wondered if dogs counted.

ten

THE DREAM TEAM

Joe made good on his word about hiring help. Almost as soon as I got back from Italy, he hired Elena to be his Italian assistant and act as his boots on the ground for the opening of Orsone, the restaurant and B&B across the street from the winery in Friuli. It was slated to open in just six weeks.

Joe had met Elena for a coffee in Udine, the closest city to the winery, and after twenty minutes offered her the job. "Her English isn't perfect, but it's better than your Italian—you guys will do all right," he said.

I started her training immediately with a one-hour phone call every single morning—midafternoon in Friuli.

Elena and I did better than all right—from the spotty first phone call (network service and Wi-Fi at the winery was an ongoing issue) we worked in tandem like we'd been doing it for years. What were the odds that Joe would find us someone even more dutiful, more paranoid, and who took the job more seriously than I did? We were two good little soldiers and I reveled in having a tried-and-true partner to help navigate the ever-expanding world of Joe. Elena had worked at the Eataly Bologna store prior to moving into Corporate. She gave me insights into Italian culture and society that I'd never learn from Rosetta Stone. She was my first close girlfriend since graduate school. I never once worried that Joe would fire her and make me do it because he might have been crazy but he was far from stupid. We became best friends practically overnight.

Within a month the three of us functioned as a new and improved unit: me in New York, Joe on a soundstage in L.A., and Elena in the Italian countryside on the border of Slovenia. Joe even occasionally referred to Elena and me—in public for other people to hear—as "the dream team."

When Joe was in New York, we shifted back to doing at least half our meetings and calls at Corporate, but I still ran over to the store a few times a day. It was a habit I couldn't break. There was always some chef or GM to talk to. The boys were barely at Corporate or the store these days. Michele had been back from the Rome store for a while, but we were expanding to Chicago in two months and scouting other cities, which required him, Edo, Aaron, and Ari to travel constantly. But I had unexpected company at Corporate.

Gina couldn't work in the Babbo kitchen anymore. The cancer had come back a few years earlier, and she managed to beat it a second time. While in remission, she got tested for the BRCA1 gene, the marker for an increased risk of breast cancers, and when she tested positive, she opted to undergo a double mastectomy. Her body had been through a lot in the last five years, and the Babbo kitchen was no place for anyone who needed to heal, so Mario and Joe built her a small test kitchen on the tenth floor of Corporate, where she could recipe test a few days per week.

She was always seated at her stool whenever I walked into the test kitchen, never standing, and the first thing she did when entering my office was pull the chair from Joe's empty desk and sit down. She usually stayed at least an hour chitchatting, lecturing me on how I was making a mess of my life, and venting about the various injustices she came across on the tenth floor. The gravest injustice involved a little dog named Spam who belonged to a young woman in the design department. The woman kept Spam, a sweet, espresso-colored Patterdale mix, on a very strict diet of water and air while in the office. "I don't want him to become a beggar," she said, and forbade anyone from feeding him. But each time Gina heard his nails *click-click* on the kitchen floor tiles, she dropped him little pieces of chopped celery, carrots, or a smidge of pastry dough, quietly whispering, "You deserve it, baby."

Gina wasn't shy about noticing I'd up and disappeared from my old life, from my Babbo family. "I guess you have your *new* life and all your Italian friends now." When Joe's name flashed across the caller ID, I had to interrupt our banter. "Don't let me take up time from your lord and master," she'd say, putting both hands up.

I brushed the comments off. I wondered if she'd felt left out when Eataly opened because she'd said to me a few times back in 2010, "I would have loved to run the dessert program at Eataly—but nobody even asked me."

She had a point, though: I hadn't bothered to keep up with the Babbo crowd. All I did was work. I called them only when I needed something for Joe. What I usually did was call each one of them back-to-back every five minutes until they answered the phone because I—Joe—needed something from them immediately. I was *getting it done*. I'd even snapped at Aaron.

He'd called to push back on one of Joe's ideas—Joe was shooting yet another TV show and wanted to feature a vegan hot dog at Eataly's vegetarian restaurant, La Verdure, that was made by one of the contestants. It wasn't a big ask, but it came last-minute, and the team at Eataly were *over it*.

I listened as Aaron politely explained. After all these years, I still liked him. The old feelings came back as easily as they'd faded. The way I'd mishandled things with him in those early months was still a thorn in my side. But the same qualities that drew me to him, his sweet, quiet way of managing things, were the reasons why I knew I could squash this obstruction-led rebellion in ten seconds flat.

I hung up the phone embarrassed. I sounded just like Joe. I thought of the person I was when I first took this job. When I first met Aaron. I wished that our conversation had gone differently, as I'd wished everything with Aaron had been different. But it was more important to lock down this task—to *make it happen*, one of a hundred on my ever-growing list. A task that wasn't even important and would be all but forgotten come Tuesday.

Gina also noticed my own health taking a dive. "Why are you breathing like that?"

Like a kid caught out, I tried to steady my heavy breathing. "I have asthma."

"You've been sitting down all day. Where is your inhaler?"

"I can't find it."

"Bullshit, Kim—if it were Joe's inhaler, you'd know where it was and have two to spare."

Months passed, and Gina started coming in less and less. The group kept her on full health insurance, but she wasn't making her full-time salary and was struggling financially. Mario and Joe decided to throw her a benefit aptly named "Fuck Cancer" at Otto that February. Her peers in the pastry world all made exquisite cakes that were put up for auction, with proceeds going to Gina to help manage expenses and what health insurance didn't cover.

I showed up to Otto that night an irritable mess, hacking away like I had pneumonia. I stayed only forty minutes before going home and collapsing on my bed. Earlier that week, I'd heard Alice on speakerphone tell Joe, "Send her home!" She could hear my coughing through the line.

But it wasn't possible to take time off without getting buried. Joe was up for a new TV show on CNBC prime time that would be like *Shark Tank* for restaurant concepts. Doing the show meant shooting four in one year—*MasterChef USA, MasterChef Italia, MasterChef Junior*, and CNBC's *Restaurant Startup*. I never thought he'd actually take the gig because it required him to invest his own money: real capital. But he didn't want to cut himself off from any unforeseen opportunities, which usually involved collecting more interesting people. So despite the fact that I was barely breathing, I felt that same old rush hit my bloodstream when he called to tell me it was a done deal. His already absurd schedule had but a sliver of wiggle room, so it was arranged that he'd shoot *Restaurant Startup* while he was out in L.A. shooting *MasterChef USA*, on his days off. But the real work for Elena and me kicked off almost as soon as production wrapped. Promotion needed to be carefully folded into everything Joe did and planned out on all social media platforms, and his brand was already a muddled mess.

Though he didn't say, Joe must have known I was falling apart. After the success of adding Elena to our duo, we'd batted around the idea of getting help in the New York office, but he didn't seem to be serious about it until he got *Restaurant Startup*. Knowing that it might take Joe anywhere from twenty minutes to six drawn-out months and multiple interviews for him to decide on someone, I got to work interviewing candidates.

My breathing worsened. I started feeling weak at the gym—I couldn't finish a fifty-minute barre class. Sometimes my chest would feel tight, and when I stood up, I felt like I was going to pass out. I'd get heart palpitations just from running over to Eataly, sometimes even when sitting down. It felt like there was no air inside my office unless I opened the window and a gust swept over my face. I Googled my symptoms—shortness of breath, weakness, dizziness, feeling seasick—and frequently the search results showed two things: *panic attacks* and *early signs of carbon monoxide poisoning.*

I scoffed at the idea of a panic attack—I didn't feel like I was dying. In the course of ten minutes, I became convinced that my little yellow office was trying to kill me. There had to be a slow leak of carbon monoxide coming from somewhere. That was where I sat for at least ten hours a day, every day, and I never had the symptoms at home in my apartment. *This had to be the problem.*

I stopped Paul, the CEO, on his way to the elevator one day and asked if we had any issues with carbon monoxide in the building. His brow furrowed. He turned his head to the side and asked softly, "No . . . why do you ask, Kim?"

I quickly recounted my symptoms, the search results, pausing only to ask if we actually had carbon monoxide detectors on this floor, and if so where, and how often did we change the batteries, only to continue on with my hypothesis without allowing him to answer. When I did stop talking, it was because I was out of breath.

Paul stared at me like I'd just told him there was a bomb under my desk, his face awash with concern. As he slowly and clearly disclosed the various detectors in place on all floors of Corporate, it started to sink in that he was using the same gentle but firm tone he adopted when Joe was really agitated and going off the rails. The creases in his forehead deepened.

I announced that I was going to Duane Reade to buy a carbon monoxide detector and marched out of Corporate. By the time I returned, I knew I had momentarily gone a little nuts, and tossed it unopened into a storage cabinet.

But the dizziness, the pressure in my chest, the heart palpitations had become my everyday normal. I went to see a cardiologist, who gave me a stress test. I took him literally when he said, "Run as hard as you can," and ended up throwing up in the bathroom.

The cardiologist couldn't find anything wrong with my heart. As a precaution, he ordered me to wear a heart monitor twenty-four hours a day for two weeks. I had to stick electrodes all over my chest and even wear them to bed. They were attached to a small black beeper clipped to the waist of my pants.

The damn thing beeped every five minutes, but I interviewed candidates left and right regardless. I had to lock someone into the role before Joe changed his mind.

Then we met Charlotte at the Soho Grand Hotel, at the birthday party for jewelry-Donna's little sister. The guests were all part of an expat community from Sydney—a gorgeous pack of young, tanned Australian women in their early thirties, most on the hunt for a work visa so they could stay permanently—this was their white whale. They were making the most of their time in the big city, not glued to their phones. They were not wearing practical shoes should they need to spring into action for work on a Saturday night. I felt plain and conservative in my J. Crew flats and jeans next to their short cocktail dresses and tiny Chanel clutches. I had my work bag with me, inside which were papers for Joe to sign.

"You're the guy from *MaaahhhsterChef*," a thick Aussie accent boomed from across the hotel's garden bar.

Christ, who's he talking to? I thought. I felt frumpy and irritable and wasn't in the mood for any of this; I went out of loyalty to Donna. But three minutes after speaking with Charlotte, I knew I wanted to be her friend. There was something slightly off about her, the same oddball sense Mario had touched on when he'd called Joe and me strange all those years ago at the Otto bar. She had to be six foot two, gregarious and unafraid of Joe, nor was she shy about needing a job.

Then Charlotte and Joe randomly ran into each other a week later outside Becco, Joe's restaurant in the theater district, and we figured it was fate. Joe offered her the job a week later.

Since I'd met Charlotte at the swanky Soho Grand Hotel, I took her to the equally chic Jade Bar inside Ian Schrager's Gramercy Park Hotel to reiterate the offer and finalize the details. We each hopped onto a teal velvet barstool and ordered overpriced rosé, and I told her about life in New York and the crazy world of Joe.

Part of me didn't want to hire her. I just wanted a friend. The old fear came back: what if we hired her and then Joe made me fire her? But I liked her too much to protest. And I was in no position to turn down high-level help.

I knew Charlotte was perfect for the role on her first day, before she even had a chance to take off her coat.

"Heeeyy! I'm ready—and legally eligible to work. What do you have for me?"

I took a deep breath and tried hard to suppress a smile. "Dildos."

"What?" Her blue eyes were bulging.

Both of us were smiling now, trying hard to hold back laughter. "He said he wants you to go buy two dildos, ASAP."

She opened her mouth, but I wasn't finished.

"He said he wants one with all the bells and whistles—the one from *Sex and the City*. He's going to send them to the head writer and showrunner of *MasterChef Italia*. I have no idea why. I stopped asking why a long time ago."

And off she went and got exactly what Joe required.

Charlotte got on board fast. After two months, I was feeling relieved. The issues with my breathing were lessening. It was springtime, and with Elena and Charlotte kicking ass and taking names, I started planning a real vacation.

It was around this time I got an email from Hans, a German restaurateur and hotelier. We'd met years earlier when the head of the culinary department at Boston University called the office, asking if someone could give a "VIP tour" of the store while Hans was in New York.

When we met in 2012, Hans invited me to stay at one of his hotels in Hamburg the next time I was passing through Europe—as if I passed through Europe all the time. Now he was back in town and wanted to know: Could I help him with a Babbo reservation, and would I have dinner with him?

He was much older than the men I usually liked, but very handsome. Salt-and-pepper hair, tan skin, broad face. I'd had trouble gauging his age back then because he'd shown up to Eataly for our tour with his then-girlfriend, who couldn't have been more than twenty-eight.

I needed to put myself out there. I needed to listen to Gina. I made no time for romance or even friends outside of work. So I met him at the Michelin-starred Estela for a dinner of small plates later that week.

What Gina meant was do more of *this*—say yes to dinner dates, join a dating app—but a month after our dinner at Estela, I ended up flying to Europe to hang out with Hans instead.

I didn't *just* fly to Europe to see Hans; it was on my way to the winery. I decided to go back to Italy for my vacation. This time, I'd enjoy it without having to be on the clock. Elena was urging me to come and see her and Orsone, and Joe offered to put me up in the family house on the winery property—a little place we all called the Foresteria.

I realized while riding the metro from the Hamburg airport to Hans's hotel on the edge of St. Pauli, Hamburg's answer to New York's gritty East Village, that this was extreme, no matter how you looked at it. But it was too late to turn back, and I let the excitement bubble up in me instead.

Hans was waiting at the front desk when I arrived and had the whole day planned for us. I was exhausted from the flight but had only two days in Germany before heading off to the winery.

We zipped through Hamburg's immaculate streets in his red Ferrari convertible, catching glimpses of the glimmering water every few turns. "Hamburg has more bridges than Venice," he told me, his face looking more bronzed in the natural light. He said he'd take me to all his restaurants, but first, we headed for the home of one of his favorite employees, the GM of his flagship seafood restaurant, Ocean. It was on the River Elbe, along the harbor.

We walked into his employee's home and it became clear that Hans was friends with his staff, just like Joe. As we settled into a nice conversation on their front porch, Hans pulled the GM's acoustic guitar out of the foyer and started to play.

There had to be a special place in hell for people who forced others to listen to them play guitar. As Hans strummed along and sang, leaving us to awkwardly halt our conversation, it slowly started to sink in. I'd flown to Germany to hang out with the German version of my boss. Suddenly he'd become like a dad, an authority figure.

This was the kind of guy I wanted to be friends with, not date. They knew everyone and were masters at commanding attention.

They were fun. I sure didn't mind one signing my paycheck and sending me all over Europe, but the thought of dating one made my skin crawl. It was obvious Hans's employees liked him. I understood completely: he was the *fun* boss. But they didn't challenge him. I wondered if he realized here in this arena, he was still the boss. No one asked him to stop playing.

Hans flew off to Mallorca the next day, but not before taking me around to several of his restaurants and a dinner at Ocean with a few other friends. The next night, I ended up at a restaurant he'd recommended—Bullerei. I sat at the bar under a large skylight, in the open, warehouse-like space, eating ravioli with bluefish and beets that stained my teeth. The sky was a dusty pink as the sun finally started to set on what felt like an extremely long two days. My phone read 9:45 p.m. This was the farthest north I'd ever been.

Before he'd departed, Hans showed me his favorite room inside his hotel—his office.

He walked me down a dark, quiet hallway and pulled back the door to his office. All four walls of the large, open room were covered almost floor to ceiling with rows of restaurant menus. Hans traveled constantly and collected menus from everywhere he ate. There were menus from Johannesburg, Paris, New York—plastic ones, paper, even gorgeous leather-bound beauties like our menus at Babbo, which were made exclusively from Coach leather and cost a few hundred dollars apiece.

"I wanted one from Babbo," he said. "But your server was too fast. The trick is not to hesitate. You have to be patient; wait for the right moment."

I ghosted my fingers over a menu printed in Afrikaans. "Have you ever been caught?"

"A few times. It's very embarrassing. But when you walk out the door, it's exhilarating."

The next morning while checking out, I noticed a server whiz by the front desk toward the restaurant, a brown and gold canvas menu in his hand. I felt a strange compulsion take over.

When I arrived at the Foresteria a few hours later, I pulled the brown and gold menu from my bag and propped it along the edge of the front porch overlooking the hills of vines. It looked like Alba, but with thick swaths of hunter green from the clusters of old evergreens intermixed. I snapped a picture and sent it to Hans.

"Well done!" he texted back. "You little thief."

He was right. Never had my heart pounded so hard.

Then I trotted down the hill into Orsone to meet my best friend for the very first time.

In person, Elena and I picked up right where we left off over the phone. It felt like we'd known each other for years. Always doing our duty first, we quickly synced on updates to Joe's agenda, and then Elena gave me a tour of the restaurant and the six guest rooms upstairs. Lidia and Joe's Michelin-star ambitions were apparent. Everything was done high-end, but simple. *Elegante.* The large kitchen was like none I'd seen in NYC. Spacious, covered in shiny new stainless steel. Sparkling copper pots and pans hung from multiple surfaces and still appeared unused. A large rectangular window overlooked the classic but chic dining room, with wood-beamed ceilings and rich leather furniture in shades of beige and mahogany and a fireplace at one end.

Joe had transplanted top chefs from Del Posto to run the kitchen, and it was good to see some fellow New Yorkers. Elena and I then trekked up the hill to the winery office to greet the staff, most of whom I'd already had long email relationships with.

"Let's get a coffee," Elena said. I followed her into the back of the office where the barrels of wine were housed, to a Lavazza coffee vending machine. Elena pulled a denim change purse from the pocket of her dress. It accented her freshly manicured red nails. Her hawklike attention to detail extended to herself. This wasn't New York; it was a rural part of the country on the border of Slovenia that most American tourists had never heard of. There wasn't a nail salon down the block. She took the time to do her nails herself.

"You have to pay for coffee?" I gasped. "Lavazza doesn't give you this for free?"

"Kim, we are a little place out here in the middle of nowhere," she joked. "We aren't as important as you New Yorkers."

Spoiled New Yorker I might be, but this was absurd. I couldn't wrap my head around Elena having to pay for coffee at the office—one she never left. Corporate was stocked with Lavazza vending machines and they shipped us free replacement coffee pods by the caseload.

"Why don't you just walk over to the Foresteria, brew a Moka pot, and bring it back here?" I pressed.

Elena's dark, arched eyebrows shot up. "Kim, we winery employees cannot just walk into our boss's house and use his kitchen like it is our own."

But that was exactly what I did. After four and a half years of Joe dragging me around and spending summers under the same roof, actually sharing a kitchen, I guessed I'd taken these liberties for granted. If you were an employee Joe liked, if you made it into the inner circle, then what was his was yours. He might have balked when it came time to give out raises, but with his possessions and connections he was extremely generous.

I walked next door to the Foresteria, made a Moka pot, and brought it back to the office for us. I felt guilty for snapping at Joe and Charlotte for pummeling me with emails when I was trying to tool around with Hans uninterrupted. I deserved a real break. I also knew it was my choice to take a vacation and not turn off my phone. I could have disappeared on a catamaran and sailed around the British Virgin Islands for ten days, but I chose to take Joe up on his offer to stay at his family house on his property. Twenty emails from Charlotte was part of the package.

I let myself sleep in the next morning. I woke up to the caretaker, Ida, knocking on the front door. She held out her cupped hands. She'd brought me two fresh eggs from the chickens kept around back, still warm from the hen's body. I sat on the porch for a few hours, breathing in the warm, fresh air and drinking my coffee while wasps bounced against the wooden roof. Just like in Alba, they didn't trouble me.

I checked my incoming emails, which had finally slowed, but my calendar reminded me that Florence Fabricant, otherwise known as Flo Fab, the veteran food writer for the *New York Times*, was arriving at Orsone today. What a different morning I would have had if Elena had not been hired. Flo Fab was her responsibility. But as Joe's long-time proxy, I still needed to go pay my respects to the grand dame of dining. I took a shower, narrowly avoiding contact with the daddy longlegs spiders in the corner, slipped on my patent leather Ferragamos and a black silk sundress, and made my way down the hill.

Flo Fab and her husband were already having lunch at a table in the tavern. They were the only guests in the small barroom. I'd met them both only once before but had fielded calls and emails between Florence and Joe for years now. Flo Fab was her usual polite, reserved self, her chin-length gray bob smooth and in place, but her husband was very animated. They invited me to join them for lunch. I said I'd sit down for a glass of wine but had to get back to the office and do some work. It was a lie—not that they weren't good company, but I had a burning desire to a bike over to the tiny medieval town of Cividale del Friuli, about eight minutes away. It was shaping up to be a quiet day and I wanted to explore before some task sucked me back into work.

While I sipped Friulano, I noticed how nervous our waiter was. Hands shaking, he started to top up Florence's glass with Friulano instead of the Vespa Bianco she'd been drinking. A controlled but stiff-looking Elena swooped in and corrected him, pouring Florence a new glass. She couldn't hide the disappointment on her face, as if the waiter had made the gravest of mistakes.

"It's all right," I said in a low voice, turning toward her. But Elena flashed me a look that said otherwise.

It dawned on me then that I was sitting with one of the most influential people in the food world, an industry I'd worked in for thirteen years, and my biggest concern was whether or not the chalky-gray mud on my Ferragamos would wash off. Who passed on lunch with Flo Fab? Especially in this gorgeous place where Elena and I called all the shots. What did it mean, that I barely cared anymore?

eleven

A FLY ON THE WALL

Joe was flying to São Paulo. His trip was only four days long; he was going to check out the new Eataly store before they opened later that spring, meet Oscar's partners down there, and do some press. It was a welcome respite for Charlotte, who'd had a pretty intense first couple of months.

I'd promised myself I wouldn't answer my phone. It was Sunday, and in three hours Joe would be in the air. I'd been trying to integrate what my cardiologist told me about shutting off and decompressing, because though the breathing problems had lessened, they hadn't gone away. I was still working too much, too wound up.

But then I saw Joe's name in big white letters on my phone screen, three hours before his flight to São Paulo. I was on my way home from Union Market and decided to wait to answer him until I got home. He likely wanted me to send his flight information and itinerary yet again—I'd sent it by text and email the night before, and that morning, like always.

But wait. I'd never checked him in. I hadn't sent his boarding pass. How could I have forgotten to do something so ingrained? So much for decompressing.

Joe called again. I put my paper bag down on the edge of the sidewalk, on top of a snowbank.

"Hi, Joe, I just realized I never checked you in. I'm five minutes from home. I'll do it as soon as I get inside."

"It's okay, Kim. I'm on my way to JFK right now. I tried to do it myself, but . . . " His speech was slow. Something was wrong. His voice sounded hollow, like the last time he spoke of Jesse. "They're saying I need a visa to board my flight to Brazil. Do you know anything about that?"

It was as if the sky had turned black. All I could see was the sidewalk stretching up 7th Street, lining my path home.

I don't know what I said to him. I called Delta and asked the rep if this was true—if a visa was needed for an American to fly to Brazil, and if so, why was it not mentioned when I booked the flight over the phone?

"Well, it's not our responsibility to inform you, miss. We assume that you know this if you are, in fact, flying to Brazil. Had you booked the flight online, you would've been prompted to request one. So maybe you should book online next time."

Next time, I thought. *But this* is *the next time.*

This was not the first time I'd left Joe stranded at the airport, unable to board his flight to a foreign country because I had no idea he needed a visa. How completely fried was my brain that I could let this happen not once but twice? I even had a vague memory of Ari sitting in his office on the ninth floor, saying to me, "You know you need a visa to go to Brazil, right?"

The first time, we had just planned a last-minute trip to Hong Kong. Joe technically needed to fly out there once a year to visit our Lupa restaurant concept we'd opened a few years back. It had come together quickly, maybe in ten days. We decided to tack on a few days to the front of the trip so that he could swing by China.

Our director of operations in Asia had been bugging Joe to meet prospective partners in Macao who wanted to put an Osteria Mozza inside their casino. Joe's partner at Lupa Hong Kong was supposed to book his flight. After some very confusing back-and-forth with the partner, Sachin, he sent a flight option and not a booked flight. When he asked me a few days later if I needed him to book Joe any flights, I assumed they were additional ones and that this one was already bought.

"It's Sachin's fault," our ops director said defiantly, out of loyalty to me and because he couldn't stand Sachin.

As much as I wanted it to be Sachin's fault, it was one hundred percent mine—no way did I ever let a third party book a flight for Joe and not call the airline to double-check that they got every detail correct. But with the China trip, we literally had no time. Joe called me from the Cathay Pacific terminal at LAX, so angry he could barely speak.

It was the hollow sound of Joe's voice on the phone that told me he was going to fire me. I went into the office the next day feeling like a live wire.

That morning, I got on the subway and was suddenly hyperaware of every person around me. I went to any and all lengths to be kind to those near me, as if my self-worth depended on it.

Then Joe called the corporate number and said he was coming in. He asked if Paul, our CEO, was in.

Afterward, I hung up the phone and told Charlotte that Joe was on his way in.

She blinked. "Isn't he in Brazil?"

I relayed what had happened the day before.

She groaned in sympathy. "Kim, we've both been working to the bone—it's been a complete madhouse. I know he's mad, but he'll get over it. You do everything around here—it'll be okay."

Then I told her about China. Her expression tightened.

"Oh. Oh, Kim."

I made a mental note to stop working at 5:00 p.m. and switch to writing up a transition document for Charlotte, if I was still there. I didn't want everything getting dumped on her.

Ding-clap-clap—Joe walked in and didn't say anything. He sat in the leather chair in the corner of the little yellow office, then finally told me to call Paul. I bet they were going to use the office of the director of operations in Asia, right next to ours. I needed Charlotte to leave so I could get on the chair and listen against the HVAC vent. If I pulled a thick cookbook off the shelf and placed it on the seat of the leather chair, I could stand on it without leaving any telltale shoe prints. Two books put me at ear level with the vent, and I could hear everything in the room next door without having to strain.

This was my way of eavesdropping on meetings I wasn't allowed to join. Such discussions were few and far between; Joe held most conversations, even highly confidential ones, right in front of me—talks with HR, lawyers wielding a summons or crafting an out-of-court settlement.

My presence triggered looks of alarm among these professionals. "Should I step out?" I'd offer, as they looked for a place to sit that wasn't the ugly orange couch.

Joe would just wave his hand, shaking his head in annoyance. "She already knows where the bodies are buried," he'd say, and carry on with whatever they'd gathered to discuss.

These were the moments where Joe inadvertently set me up as an authority. They signified a trust reserved only for executives, fellow owners. But what if it wasn't about trust at all? What if I'd garnered this place of pseudo-exaltation because I was disposable? What if I was just a fly on the wall, so insignificant and powerless that had I dared repeat anything, he'd simply squash me like a bug?

Over the next few days, I heard snippets of Joe's conversations with Paul through the vent.

"I'm very angry, Paul."

I could never make out our CEO's soft voice clearly, but Joe came through no matter how quietly he spoke. I'd trained myself to detect even a whisper—I could pick up his voice from a block away.

Paul seemed to be trying to talk him out of it, which his kind eyes confirmed when he and I rode the elevator together from the tenth floor to the third the next day in silence.

When I met with our CFO, Fran, in her office, her gentle expression told me the same thing.

A young woman named Samantha had recently started working on the tenth floor. Fran knew her personally. I'd seen her filing and performing other clerical work. Someone told me that Fran had found her the job.

Samantha approached me two days after hell was unleashed and asked if I would make time to talk to her about my role assisting Joe.

Samantha was a horrible liar. She shifted in her seat, played with her hands, looked down at the floor or her lap when I asked her, "What is it about my job that you'd like to know?" She emailed me twice the following day and meekly approached me in the ladies' room while I was washing my hands. She couldn't answer my basic questions because she didn't really want to know about my job. She didn't want to do this.

It took all the restraint I could muster not to step in and help her find her way through. I wanted to cut her off midstumble and tell her how exactly she should play this: *Say you've always wanted to be an executive assistant; that it is your dream to do this kind of job! Ask me if there is a project that you can work on with me—that you'd love to shadow me for a day.*

I thought of Joe chiding me in the past, saying, "You lack the killer instinct." But heaven help him if he was thinking of replacing me with Samantha. I respected the fact that she had a hard time lying. It reminded me of a time when I did too.

The whole situation prolonged my constant state of fight-or-flight-level stress, the horror slowly unfolding over days instead of minutes. The daily spikes of cortisol and adrenaline couldn't be good for my already strained heart. In the end, the cardiologist didn't find anything wrong with me. He said my symptoms could all be attributed to stress, but that stress over time could cause a heart attack.

No one had a good handle on what I did because the role had expanded to include an amount of work that should have been managed by four people, by my best estimate. I'd known it was too much to manage responsibly for years but hadn't realized how big it was until onboarding Charlotte. She needed to understand the shifting political landscape of every partnership, business deal, and restaurant, right down to planning a random dinner party or selecting the right birthday gift. She needed to know how to deal with Mario and Lidia. If she did something they didn't like, Joe would be mad because then he'd have to deal with them. I'd always known how to deal with them both, and this meant crafting what I said and did for Joe so that I didn't have to very often. There was a lot more work to this sort of juggling than most people realized.

I got along with Lidia. She was particular about how she liked things done. She was a tough businesswoman—raised in a refugee camp along the Italian border of what was then Yugoslavia, when communist revolutionary and statesman Josip Broz Tito slaughtered eighty thousand of her fellow Italians for their heritage. Early on in my role, she invited me to have dinner with her uptown at Felidia. She didn't know me from Babbo and needed to give me a once-over. She said that I could always come to her if I needed help or advice in dealing with Joe.

"When he gets fresh, you've got to give it right back to him—that's what I do," she said, her expression stern as she pumped her fist out toward me.

This was shortly after I achieved *we* status, so by that time Joe and I were in a pretty good groove. But I appreciated her offer just the same.

As the week wore on, I knew Fran and Paul were scrambling. I saw the worry on their faces as we passed one another in the office. It was becoming tough to avoid dropping another big ball, having to work like this. I took deep, fast breaths, forcing in as much oxygen as possible to stop my palpitations, which had returned with a vengeance—my heart felt like a trapped bird beating against its cage.

I couldn't help but think that if I was so important, why was I only making seventy-five thousand dollars a year? If what I did to keep the wheels on the bus was so essential, so multifaceted, and so complex that no one had a firm handle on it, and that I could not simply be fired outright? What if I had, before this, just one day walked out?

The real fuckery lay with me because there was no saving my job. It was just a matter of time before they got themselves organized. Joe probably needed another week to wrap his head around it—this was what he did when about to fire someone important; he needed to work up to it psychologically.

Why was I still working so hard? Shouldn't I have gone home, drunk some Friulano, and scoured Monster.com and Craigslist? Why wasn't I doing something to help myself? Why was I still sitting in this little yellow office? Even then, I was addicted to reading and answering my emails. I couldn't bear to leave one loose thread or have even one ball out of hundreds left sitting in my court. I could not focus on anything else but work so long as there was work to do, as if my sense of worth was wrapped up in this job. I'd always thought I'd lose my sense of self if I stopped working, and even though I knew I was losing my job, I still couldn't stop.

"Are you okay, Kim?" Michele sent three emails in this vein before I finally answered him. He was down in Brazil with the rest of the Oscar show. Everyone knew I'd fucked up.

"No. They are going to fire me. They don't know that I know. So don't say anything."

I tried to remember what Jovani the count said about losing his phones on the beach, and that he'd been in the same boat as I was. This couldn't be true. No one knew what this was like. No one was in my boat.

Friday came, and this was when we usually fired people. But it was after 7:00 p.m. and everyone had already gone home but Paul and me. I wished I had someone in my life to talk to about this. Someone to go home to and tell me it would be okay. I'd been sitting hunched over in my chair all day, and suddenly I became acutely aware of how badly I needed to be held by another human. It reminded me of the last time someone had wrapped their arms around me: 2012, a few days after Hurricane Sandy, standing in a stranger's Chelsea apartment with square-jawed Noah. That was more than two years ago. I hadn't even kissed a man since and could count the dates I'd had on one hand.

At Heights and Boerum Council, we used to encourage the volunteers not to shy away from taking an elderly client's hand if offered or putting a hand on their shoulder. There was a lot of talk about the healing power of human touch from something as simple as a hug. Isolated homebound older people, the folks who received our home-delivered meals, suffered from a chronic lack of human touch. I never understood it when I was practicing, but I understood it that evening. My body ached for it.

On Monday morning, Joe called me from the store first thing. "Stay there. I need to talk to you."

I pulled the packet I'd prepared for Charlotte from the bottom of my desk drawer and placed it in hers, right on top so she couldn't miss it.

Ding—but no *clap-clap*. It was Joe, but he moved into our office slow and quiet. Even when he wasn't speaking, I could usually tell when his mind was going one hundred miles an hour, even before he opened his mouth and let it rip. But today he seemed uncharacteristically clear.

I heard the blood pulsing in my ears. We went over the day's business and a few emails that had just come in. He didn't sit down. He didn't take off his coat. He didn't walk out of the office while still speaking to me and then return as if he'd never left. He just paced back and forth in the small space.

This went on for what felt like hours, until I slowly realized he couldn't do it.

He stopped pacing. Then he said, "Okay, good talk," and walked out.

And somehow, I knew the matter was closed. He hadn't done it, and now he never would.

I dried my palms on my jeans. I couldn't figure out if I wanted to laugh or cry at the realization: if I ever decided I really wanted out, I'd have to do it myself.

twelve

CAFFÈ CORRETTO
ON CHRISTMAS

My most cowardly encounter involved a man named Brandon. The summer before I left for New York City, I was still working as a residence counselor at the house on McCarroll Street but picked up some shifts at another home in Albany to earn as much as I could before the move. This house was markedly different. Most of the residents dealt with significant physical impairments. Several were quadriplegics and needed assistance with almost all activities of daily living. They could not eat solid food. Counselors needed to be specially trained and certified to feed them. Both men and women lived there.

The house had good energy to it. Everyone gathered in the kitchen and family room for dinner, and together the two rooms created an ample open space where everyone could see one another and talk. Wheelchairs took up too much room for the group to meet around the table. Counselors would pull up a chair next to whoever needed help. Brandon, one of the residents, usually claimed a spot at the kitchen counter, which marked the middle of the combined space.

Another counselor, Cameron, and I often shared shifts. He had been there a while and seemed to have gained everyone's trust. He was attentive, empathetic, and disciplined. He was also a better cook than I was and helped make dinner for the group.

I rarely cooked growing up—my mother pretty much forbade anyone else to use her cookware for fear of scratches. If I summoned the bravery to use one, she usually circled, whispering, "Don't scratch my pans," leaving me with no motivation to cook. But at the Albany house, I was free to learn as I went, and was surprised at my interest.

Since I was only working there temporarily before heading to grad school, it didn't make sense to take the training on how to safely feed the residents. Instead, I did the cooking and got a head start on cleanup while Cameron and the other counselors mixed glasses of puréed spaghetti and meatballs or chicken fried steak and macaroni, then carefully spooned the mixture into the residents' mouths. Just looking at the liquid food in the glass made me queasy, but for Brandon and some of the other residents, this was all they'd ever known.

Cameron was always after Brandon to drink more water. Brandon's doctors reiterated at every checkup that he was dehydrated. But if even a drop went down the wrong pipe, it took so much effort for Brèndon to cough it out.

Brandon made everyone laugh. He had a hard time controlling the muscles in his face, which hindered his speech, but it didn't take more than a few conversations to understand him. He was a smart and good-natured young man with dirty-blond hair. He loved to go outside to the large pond in the development, which left his face and forearms browned from the sun, and frequently asked me to take him. He was very observant, playful—even flirtatious with the female counselors. Brandon enjoyed calling me out when I did or said something that reminded everyone I was a clueless twenty-two-year-old. He was significantly smarter and more mature than I was. He listened as I told him about my upcoming move to the city and how I could not wait to explore Greenwich Village and Soho. I brought in a large map and guide of downtown to show him the shops, streets, and restaurants I planned to check out as soon as I arrived. He'd give me a hard time for lighting up a Parliament. He loved to listen to Anne Murray on an old record player in his room. I knew all the words because my mother loved Anne Murray too. I told Brandon that the song "Snowbird" was my favorite—"And if I could, you know that I would fly away with you."

One night, Cameron insisted Brandon drink more water. They'd been to the doctor that week, and the dehydration was causing Brandon other issues. I got in on the coaxing and told Brandon that he could forget about our nightly stroll to the pond unless he finished the entire glass. Not content with letting Cameron and me have the last word, Brandon gripped that blue striped straw between his lips and sucked down every last drop.

Later that night, Cameron and I were in the family room watching television when we heard Brandon call out for help. We rushed into his room. It was hard to understand what he was saying, but his expression was horrified. He scrunched his face as if in pain. And he was a mess—literally. He had diarrhea all over his lower body; his pajamas and sheets were soaked.

I helped Cameron carefully lift Brandon out of bed. We carried him into the bathroom and started to remove his soiled clothes, taking care to hold him up over the large pink marble sink. The smell was almost unbearable. We had to gently clean around his stiff legs, making sure nothing was trapped in the folds of his delicate skin. My elbows and wrists were crushed into the hard marble under the weight of his body and were starting to hurt. It was one thing to change a baby's diaper; it was another to clean a person the size of an eight- or nine-year-old child. I thought of the parents of the ladies at McCarroll Street.

"What do you think happened, Brandon? Do you feel warm or like maybe you have a summer flu?" Cameron asked.

Brandon's mouth broke into a crooked smile, and out came one word: "Water."

This was my fault. Entirely. His body couldn't handle that much water. But he drank it anyway because I pushed him. Because I'd made it a part of our playful banter. He wasn't going to do it for Cameron, but he couldn't refuse me.

If Brandon was embarrassed, he didn't show it; he just laughed while I apologized profusely.

A few weeks passed, and I was counting down the days before I'd leave for New York. Brandon seemed particularly eager to get out to the pond one evening, and as soon as we did, I realized he had something to tell me and had wanted to get me alone. He was serious. No fun banter. The more it seemed to mean to him, the less I wanted to hear it. I interrupted him and rushed us back inside. I figured he wanted to say some sentimental goodbye, and I'd always had a hard time with those. I preferred a clean, cold break, even at the cost of another person's closure.

I busied myself with dinner prep back at the house, then cleanup, and avoided Brandon.

As bedtime neared, I went out to the back porch to smoke a Parliament, and there he found me again. He blocked the sliding glass door with his wheelchair and wouldn't move aside.

"I love you," he said. He was looking right at me. His hazel eyes totally unafraid. He was such a physically small man, but he didn't seem small in that moment.

I didn't believe him; pretended I did not understand his words. And I was cold toward him. I began talking over him feverishly. But I remember the look he threw me just before he gave up. It was pure disappointment.

Opening himself up was such a brave thing to do. No one had looked at me that way before, with such sincerity. *I bet he says this to all the pretty young counselors*, I told myself. But I knew that wasn't true.

The night of my last shift, I waved goodbye to Brandon unceremoniously and walked out the front door, like he was just another client—as if we'd never become real friends.

Fifteen years later, I wished I'd found a way to let him down gently and salvage our friendship. I understood how it felt to be on the other side. I also knew the damage it did to keep things bottled up, to dance around one's feelings for so long until it took up all the space in your body and mind.

Brandon was heavy in my thoughts as I made my way to meet Aaron at a coffee shop on 18th Street. I had a feeling Aaron knew why I'd summoned him. I had told Michele a few days earlier that I was going to tell Aaron I'd always liked him. I didn't say anything about the tapping and the prompting, that I knew there had once been *something* on Aaron's end that he never voiced no matter how much his brother prodded him.

"Don't do it," Michele said, and his concern was genuine. "Aaron is weird with these things, and it will make the office very awkward." But things were already awkward and untenable for me. After the Brazilian visa incident, I'd lost close to ten pounds.

I'd never gotten close to Aaron the way I had with Edo and Michele. We never became actual friends. I wondered sometimes if I'd have liked him as much as I liked the idea of him. It wasn't like I'd been thinking about him nonstop all these years; I'd been way too busy screwing up opportunities with other men. But there was a nagging feeling of regret whenever I saw him.

One night a few months earlier, in the fall, I was in the store for Identità Golose, a two-day series of lectures, cooking classes, and dinners celebrating Italian food and ticketed to the public. It was the fifth we'd hosted at the store; each year Oscar flew in all the top Italian chefs. We—the staff, Joe, the boys—were over it, but we still showed up at the store on the first night to kiss cheeks and otherwise pay our respects.

I moved through the crowd and slipped inside the narrow doorway to La Scuola, our small cooking school, and ended up with Ari in front of me and Aaron directly behind me.

"Hi, guys," I said.

Before Ari even answered me, he turned his head around and glared right over my shoulder at his brother, as if I weren't even there. He held Aaron's gaze until I heard that familiar, soft "Hi, Kim."

That was it, the last straw. I wanted to scream at both of them, *I can see you!* I hadn't witnessed their absurd interaction in so long I'd almost forgotten about it. All those years of taps, looks, nods, and nudges, followed by Aaron's somewhat strained hello, had chipped away at me. I had to know what it meant.

I needed it out of me. I didn't even want to be with Aaron. I only pictured him *knowing*. But I couldn't get rid of the weight of the regret—it was as if I needed Aaron to take it from me. As though something needed to be killed. And the only way was to make sure he knew. All the tapping, nods, nudges, head turns, and prompting merged not just with the regret of Aaron but of all the guys who'd come after, who I handled in similar ways. I wanted to completely change my behavior around men and to close the door on the way I'd acted before.

Aaron appeared unusually calm as he pulled up a stool beside me in the coffee shop. "What did you want to talk to me about?" He looked me in the eye, not at the floor. Not a phone in sight.

Michele had told him. That might have been my real motivation for telling Michele in the first place. Michele would never let Aaron walk into this cold.

I didn't know what was real and what had been an illusion. So I told him only what I knew for sure was true.

When I spoke, it was as if someone else were talking. As if my future self had taken over my body to make sure that my current self didn't fuck it up. I didn't even feel nervous, though I must have been—I felt like I was being led. "I have always liked you," I told him.

He was so still and unsurprised. And kinder than I'd been to Brandon, though my declaration was much less dramatic.

Aaron told me that he had just gotten back together with his old girlfriend. "I feel bad for you," he said in his warm voice, now looking at the floor. He did not sound condescending. He sounded like he meant *I'm sorry you are too late*. Something about him seemed satisfied.

I walked back to the office feeling sad, but as though I'd shed a large weight.

And yet that was not the most difficult experience I had arranged for myself on Christmas Eve 2015. I walked the two blocks up to Corporate along Fifth Avenue, my jacket tied around my waist. It was a bizarre seventy degrees out.

Although Gina was the strongest I'd seen her in years the last time we met, two months earlier for brunch by her apartment in Washington Heights, she'd gone in to have another surgery the following week, and things took a turn for the worse. She was at Mount Sinai again. We were told she had a matter of weeks.

Someone organized an email chain among Gina's friends and industry contacts, and we signed up for shifts to visit her in the hospital. I had to stay in town for the holiday to live-tweet from Joe's Twitter account. The season premiere of *MasterChef Italia* was on Christmas Eve, and the next episodes would air on New Year's Eve. So I took the Christmas Eve evening shift. The chart showed that Gina's mother and sister would be seeing her during the day, but I could not bear the thought of her alone that night.

I was useless at work after my conversation with Aaron. Still out of it, like a stunned bird. The day kept on. There'd be no bonus this Christmas because of my Brazil fuckup. Last year, I had been stuck in town away from my family and had spent the holiday live-tweeting for Joe during the two-hour airing of *MasterChef Italia*. On Christmas Day, I'd worked from the back bedroom of the Farinetti house with Edo and Michele, who also were unable to go home. Joe had felt bad about it and slid an extra two-thousand-dollar check on my desk. But this year there was no Edo to cook for me; no drunken, gleeful Michele pouring Barolo, and I was again away from my family.

Joe, Alice, and the kids stayed in the city instead of flying out to Venice and then driving to the winery or the Dolomite Mountains. They all came into the office in the early evening to say Merry Christmas before heading to Felidia for family dinner with Lidia.

The Bastianiches showed up in the middle of the *MasterChef Italia* episode. One tweet every sixty seconds, and I was already dealing with a time delay on the iPad. I could not break my concentration or turn my attention from it for even one minute.

Everyone talked in the small office. Joe yelled to someone in the hall from a few feet in front of my desk. The kids each gave me a hug. Then Joe asked how the live-tweeting was going while watching Twitter on his phone and offering unhelpful advice: "Did you see what Bruno tweeted? You gotta get on that; we should answer that tweet."

Keeping my voice even, I said, "Guys, I have to pay attention," but they all stayed in the small office, chattering. I was falling further and further behind. Joe, still watching the Twitter feed, pointed out something else funny I'd missed. I snapped, "It is really hard to follow along with all of you in here."

"Okay, okay, okay," he said, as he ushered the kids out. "We'll leave you."

"Sorry, Kim," said his youngest son.

And then it was finished. 5:15 p.m., but already pitch-black outside. I gathered myself together and got in the elevator. Never had I wanted a drink so badly. I didn't have any wine at home except for the bottle of Dom Perignon that Jay the novelist had mercifully gifted me, but I was bringing it to a dinner I'd been invited to on Christmas Day. I didn't want to go into Eataly Vino, not because I was afraid of running into Aaron but because I loathed the idea of getting cornered by Ari, who was no doubt updated. I had just enough sanity left to get me through Gina's hospital visit, and I couldn't risk getting into a situation where I had to actually feel something.

I ducked into a random wine shop on 23rd Street, grabbed a bottle of pinot grigio from an Italian producer I didn't know, and was grateful for it. I thought about opening it the whole ride up to 96th Street on the 6 train. Would it really be so bad to be one of those New Yorkers drinking on the subway?

At Mount Sinai, Gina was half asleep, alone. I pulled the chair in the corner closer to her bed and put my things on the floor. She was pale and thinner than she'd been just two months ago at brunch.

A nurse came in. She woke up Gina to give her medicine in her IV. Gina smiled wryly and asked the nurse if this was the one that caused nausea.

"Yes, dear."

Gina seemed weak and not in the mood to talk. I asked her if her mother and sister had been by yet. She said earlier, and that Evan, one of the chefs at Babbo, would be coming tomorrow.

I thought maybe I should tell her about Aaron. The last conversation we'd had before she went in for surgery had been about trying online dating.

"You're wasting time!" she'd yelled, as though she shared some stake in my fate, standing on the steep incline of her Washington Heights street—so slanted that it made her much taller than me. The thought of online dating turned my stomach like Babbo men. She didn't want me making the same mistakes she did, ending up alone. But I already had.

As I hesitated, Gina jerked her head up off the hospital bed and pulled the yellow kidney-shaped plastic bin the nurse had given her up to her mouth, and spit into it.

"Do you need anything?" I asked.

She didn't answer, so I checked my phone to give her privacy as she pushed herself upright, chest heaving. When the time came, vomiting seemed to require a great deal of energy. The physical act itself seemed almost too much for her weak body to perform. She'd been battling cancer for seven years, but I'd never seen her like this. And I understood she was going to die.

The nurse came back and took the bin. After a minute, Gina asked me if I would bring her some black tea tomorrow. I said I would.

Within minutes, she was asleep. I stayed for another half hour.

The next day, I pushed aside the remains of last night's bottle of pinot and pulled out the Dom Perignon. Then I headed back to the Upper East Side to bring Gina her black tea.

I walked into Gina's hospital room and found it crowded with people sitting around the bed. Evan's teary eyes were almost too much for me. I felt guilty, and mentioned more than once that I was there last night, to excuse why I was rushing now. I put the black tea down and got out.

The fact that this was how her battle ended, a seven-year-long fight, made me want to shut down. I couldn't wait to get lost in the crowd at the party and listen to other people talk. Numb myself.

The party I'd been invited to was hosted by Gloria, who worked under Edo at the store. It was at her gigantic rent-controlled apartment on the Upper West Side, which took up an entire floor in a building her husband's family had the good sense to hold a lease on. The space would be filled with people: Italians from the store who weren't able to make it home for the holiday.

There were thirteen of us around the table, and the champagne was just enough for everyone to have three sips—a toast at the start of the meal. Edo was there. I hoped he didn't know about Aaron; I didn't want to talk about it. Gossip sure did fly fast between the Eataly boys. But if he did know, he didn't say anything.

Four days later, I exited the subway car at Seventh Avenue in Park Slope and when my phone got service back, an email notification popped up on the screen. Gina had died. I felt relieved. She was supposed to have a few more weeks, but maybe this was better. She had really been suffering.

I continued to feel relief until the night of Gina's wake. I caught a ride up to the chapel in Yonkers with one of her former pastry chefs.

I walked into the sparse, white-walled chapel and back through time—the room was packed with familiar faces, some I hadn't seen since my first few years at Babbo. I waited in the line that formed leading to the front of the room, where her mother and a few other family members were seated.

A former Babbo server I'd been friendly with was in front of me. What began as small talk turned into a stream of uncontrollable tangential commentary about nothing significant—the room, who else had shown up that night from the old days—they tumbled out of my mouth from sheer nerves. To his credit, he stood quietly listening.

As the line approached Gina's mother, my body started to shake. I couldn't stop twisting my hands together and could barely hold back the flood of tears. I thought about turning around and heading back to the lobby just before it was my turn. I told Gina's mother that her daughter had meant a great deal to me.

I stepped away, and the floodgates opened, tears pouring down my face. It was terrifying not being able to control my emotions.

Evan, who had been in Gina's hospital room when I dropped off her tea on Christmas Day, ushered his wife and me, both of us sobbing, into a pew. Mario went up to the podium and delivered the first two lines of his eulogy in his usual showman shtick. Then he looked out at all of us filling up the chapel pews and standing along the edges of the room. And I watched as the showman left his face. His voice changed. Any semblance of his shell was suddenly gone. The switch was palpable and jarring. I'd never before heard him speak in his real voice all the years I'd known him.

I was resolved to learn from my mistakes, from Gina's mistakes, to heed her warning.

The year before she'd passed, I'd felt so lonely that I had taken to crying on the subway ride home several nights per week, and this worsened during the first few months of 2016. Some days I managed to hold it in until I was inside my apartment building, where the act of putting my key in the door triggered a massive wave of tears.

On the days I could not hold it in, I was *that person* on the train. Some people glanced at me with empathy and looks of concern. Most people did not stare. To my fellow passengers' credit, they said nothing.

I'd seen people on the train like this before, totally lost in some event. I had once said to a crying woman, "It gets better," but I had no idea where that came from. I just wanted to give her some comfort without making her have to talk to me—I said it as I was exiting the train.

The crying incidents were some of the few times I really didn't care how others perceived me. There wasn't a shred of embarrassment or self-consciousness. The sadness and regret of how I'd managed my life outside work were all-consuming.

After almost getting fired, I realized that one mistake could shatter everything I'd worked so hard to achieve. All I thought I'd built for myself was rented—friends, status, opportunities. I didn't even have much in the bank. I had wanted so badly to get out of that Babbo basement, but what did I do once that happened? I was given opportunities, personal and professional, and let them all slip away. I thought of myself as braver, more adventurous than my coworkers at Babbo and Heights and Boerum Council—like I was going out and making things happen, like I was going to see and experience all the things everyone came to New York for. But all I did was watch.

thirteen

OBSTRUCTIONIST

Ari called me the Monday we were all back in the office after New Year's. "Are you okay?"

We talked, but not about Aaron. We both knew why he was calling, but I didn't give him an opportunity to bring Aaron up, and he didn't push. Still, I appreciated the call.

The next day, I piled into the elevator of Corporate with the boys for the last time. Eataly was moving out of the building. They'd found new space down the block from the Flatiron store on 23rd Street.

For months I'd practically begged Ari and Michele to take me with them. I was overstepping, but I didn't care. We hadn't worked together like we did that first year and before the store opened, for a long time. But knowing they were near, just underneath me, hearing the squeaks of their sneakers as they stomped up the stairwell, had always been a comfort.

I was not sure if it was me that they didn't want to make room for or if it was Joe they wanted to keep out. The days of the boys snapping to and standing at attention when Joe gave an order were such a distant memory; as if that period never happened at all. My going was important to me because it was as if being surrounded by them again would resurrect the spirit of the old days, better days. It wasn't just the boys; I'd made many friends at Eataly. I'd be surrounded by friends there. Maybe I'd develop close friendships if I sat among everyone. I'd get invited to drinks.

The real issue was that I didn't want to do the job anymore. This was a daunting prospect; like I had to find a whole new life. Eataly moving out confirmed what I'd long suspected: I lived and died for this job partly because it solidified my place among them. The collective band and the energy of creating the store was what I always loved most about this circus. What the boys represented in my mind— people I wanted to be like, places I wanted to go—whether they'd earned that place of exaltation or I elevated them and the store to it simply because I didn't have much else going on didn't matter. They were what I got out of bed for in the morning. Without them to stir me, I knew things would deteriorate.

I lost Charlotte, too, in December. She put in two and a half years, though they whizzed by like six months. That was a smart amount of time to stay in a role like this: enough time to benefit, but not enough to leave you burned out, which I absolutely was.

Without the boys, there was no buffer from Joe's roughness. All I saw now were his shortcomings and faults. I didn't like the way he managed, the decisions he made, or how he handled situations. This had never bothered me before, certainly not when I was vying to get out of the Babbo basement or talking him into letting me work from Italy.

The truth was, Joe hadn't changed. He was the same volatile Joe/fun Joe he had always been. I was just over it. Like Sebastiano's wife being over life, I was over *this life*. I could barely mask my disapproval at his quirks, his big ideas. I'd become the most dreaded of all things: an *obstructionist*. It was only a matter of time before he found out. He might know already.

Eventually, I started looking for jobs. I didn't know what I wanted to do, so I searched for openings at companies I was interested in—Google, Facebook, Instagram. There was a user experience/content strategy role open at Google, which involved writing. It seemed junior, but I had no experience in UX. The job description read that candidates needed experience in the dining scene. With ten years at Babbo and six years as Joe's executive assistant, maybe I had a chance.

I remembered I knew an Italian guy working as an engineer at Google, a friend of Santos's. Quietly, I asked if he'd refer me, and he submitted my application.

It was possible Joe knew of the application. The office within Google I'd sent my résumé to was Zagat, which Google acquired in 2011. Before everything went digital in the very early aughts, no one in New York left the house without their copy of the Zagat restaurant guide. Joe wasn't close with the Zagats, but they had spoken over the years. They knew how to reach him, how to let him know that his executive assistant was looking elsewhere, even though I'd made it *very clear* on my application that I did not want my current employer called.

My survival in Joe's office over the years rested on my ability to observe, then decipher everything Joe did and said, from a squint in his eyes to the tone of his voice to the choices he made. These were my instructions, my main source of information as to what he was thinking, not what actually came out of his mouth. My observations proved more reliable than any direct instruction from him. Body language, pitch, tone, and emotional response helped me get ahead of him and predict what he'd do next. At this point, even a subtle change in an established pattern of his behavior glowed red to me.

A UX liaison at Google reached out to tell me that my application was being reviewed, and the morning after, I heard a disturbance in Joe's voice. A change in his pitch I had a nasty feeling had to do with me.

Then Meredith called. She asked for Charlotte's phone number. Charlotte, who had moved back to Australia. I remained silent as she anxiously fired off excuses as to why she needed it, giving herself away.

Joe called me on the office line around 5:00 p.m. the following night. "I'm meeting the guys"—meaning the Wild Ramsons—"at Bar Jamón. You and that new assistant we just hired, what's her name? Amanda? You and Amanda are welcome to swing by and have a drink with us."

I always said yes when Joe went out with anyone from the Wild Ramsons. It was like a silent signal that fun Joe had surfaced. And tonight at Bar Jamón, it would give me a chance to scan for further clues of Google's possible treachery. It wasn't illegal in New York State for a company to contact a candidate's current employer, even if the candidate explicitly stated not to.

Amanda was smart, but she wouldn't last. Fun Joe didn't make an appearance often these days. The job held almost none of the perks it once did for me. I lobbied hard for Joe to send Amanda to Italy for ten days so she could help Elena run a music event in Milan, and I succeeded. If she got into a good groove with Joe, then I could leave.

Sometimes when Amanda was on the phone with Joe, she broke out into laughter, tossing her head back, cheeks flushed red, and then I knew he was being nice, funny, probably making fun of someone, and a little glimmer of hope would rise up in me.

Amanda and I headed to Bar Jamón, a tiny barroom around the corner from Casa Mono where we fed people *pan con tomate* and Txakoli wines while they waited for their table. The next twenty minutes were the most uncomfortable I'd experienced around Joe. Those daggers that flashed briefly during my interview back in 2010 were out, and not going anywhere. He went through the motions of being nice. He was even drinking, but the wine did not appear to have its usual effect on him. If you'd have asked Amanda if she'd noticed, she would probably have said no. But she didn't read him for a living— not yet, anyway.

A few days later, I received word from the UX liaison. *Unfortunately, we are unable to move forward with your candidacy at this time, as we did not find a perfect fit with our current business needs.*

Maybe I imagined it all—the daggers, the change in pitch, the meaning behind the call from Meredith. Most likely, Google was not going to hire someone for a UX and content strategy role who had zero experience in UX or content strategy. If I were smart, I'd have waited for an executive assistant position to open up and applied for that. But I found the idea of starting over with a new person and doing this kind of job again incredibly overwhelming.

The Google rejection left me feeling hopeless. I liked the idea of working for a tech company: something different. I felt skittish about applying for more jobs but had to do something for myself. I thought about what else I enjoyed. I liked blogs—Into The Gloss, Byrdie, and

All the Pretty Birds—but they were run by fashion experts, which, despite Liza's best efforts, I was not.

I decided to create a blog where I'd interview assistants who worked for high-profile companies and people—*the jobs a million girls would kill for*. It had to look sharp. I wanted to use high-quality photos. And I wanted to use only original photos shot for the interview. I couldn't afford a photographer, but Joe had taught me well. I thought about who I knew who might want to shoot for free or would help me learn the basics so I could do it myself. I was going to need pictures of myself for the site, so I could practice with that.

"Someday, I'd love to be a photojournalist," Michele declared, looking up from his camera lens as he squatted on the pavement of Gramercy Park East. "This is my dream."

Michele had been taking pictures for years, and to my surprise and delight, he was eager to make time for me. We planned to shoot that Saturday. He'd done a few photo shoots with his girlfriend, so he told me to bring a few different jackets or a change of clothes, different shoes.

Liza connected me with one of her top makeup artists, who kindly walked me through exactly what I should use on my face for shooting portraits. It was such a lift to have a project that was just for me, and also a little strange.

Michele and I spent a few hours in Gramercy Park. People stopped and watched quizzically, as if they should know who I am.

"They think I'm a real photographer," Michele stage-whispered. "I think it's the hat."

We moved on to the Lower East Side and shot there before calling it a day.

"You're wrecked," Michele told me over beer and fries at Boulton & Watt bar.

I didn't know how models did it—after an hour or so, holding poses was grueling work.

We shot again a few weeks later, this time at Michele's house on Charles Street. I started to prod about when he thought he'd make his dream of becoming a photojournalist a reality.

"Maybe when I'm fifty. I can't do anything until then. It's not possible."

It reminded me of something he'd said a while back. We'd been talking about the future of the company and his brothers, and he remarked, "I am not the smart one, that's Flavio. I am the worker."

"You're smart!" I'd assured him. But I heard people at the store say the same—that Michele was the family workhorse. That Oscar was hard on him. He'd been his dad's boots on the ground in so many countries, I'd lost track. I wondered if he felt like I did, only as good as his last project, his last task. Like there was no way out. He was only thirty. I hoped he didn't wait to do what he wanted.

At the house on Charles Street, I sat next to him while he went over the basic functions of the used camera I'd bought. I had trouble following. The English he chose wasn't quite right, but that wasn't why. He was breaking it down in such a clear and thoughtful way that it should have been easy to grasp. We sat close enough that I could feel the heat coming off his shoulder, and it dawned on me that it'd been years since I'd been this physically close to a man. His knee pressed into mine as he leaned in to explain the function of some little knob. I could smell his clean hair and his last cigarette.

When I got home, I lay down on my bed and cried until my head pounded.

I wished I could tell him how I was drowning and couldn't stand the job anymore. The afternoons we spent shooting brought me to the edge of all I'd neglected to let into my life. A man, yes, but also just a close friend to confide in. Those days illuminated how long I'd been locked away, even if it didn't look like it from the outside.

Truthfully, Michele was the last person I should vent to about the job, although he'd understand more than most. He was not only Joe's partner; he was technically Joe's boss when it came to Eataly. I trusted Michele; he'd never tell Joe if I unloaded on him. But what if he told someone else? I could lose everything just repeating nonsensitive information, low-level company gossip. Rarely could I join in when co-workers vented. I sensed them pulling back from me when I didn't contribute. This was how work friends evolved into real friends, how close connections were forged. But I sidestepped every opportunity out of equal parts fear and a warped sense of duty. This was the trap of being an executive assistant. The job was an island.

Most executive assistants had access to their boss's personal and work inboxes; we saw everything. We knew who was about to get fired, if the company was going under, if we were about to be sued, how much money everyone made, the out-of-court settlements that never reached the light of day, who had a coke problem. If it got out I'd said even one thing I shouldn't have, or participated in gossip Joe would otherwise expect me to shut down, I'd be done.

A year earlier, I was having dinner at the restaurant Parm by the Major Food Group with a few people who orbited Joe and Mario, and someone started laying into Joe. One of my friends at the table finally said, "Guys, come on, Kim is his assistant." He was the only one who saw me sitting there, shrinking. The staff at Parm had the names of every person at our table—I had to tell them who I was coming with, including everyone's title, to get the reservation. They knew exactly which "Joe" we were talking about.

I had a client at Heights and Boerum Council who had debilitating depression. The day I met her, she was crawling on the floor of her apartment. The front door was propped open when I arrived. I knocked, called her name, and then pushed it open just a few inches. I saw her about fifteen feet back, kneeling on the floor. I thought she'd fallen.

She said, "Come in," then crawled a few feet until she reached the end of her couch and pulled herself up. She asked me if we could do the assessment while she lay down. She was a retired narcopharma-cologist; she knew exactly what her situation was and articulated it well. She crawled when she didn't have the energy or motivation to stand.

I was depressed, but not crawling on the floor. But the lack of mo-tivation she cited, the inability to muster through something? I un-derstood that now.

Charlotte did end up coming back from Adelaide, but only for a few days to clean out her apartment and close out the lease. Joe wanted to see her, so late one afternoon the three of us met for a drink at Mario and Joe's latest restaurant, La Sirena.

Joe got us a table on the terrace, and some guy he knew showed up. They got lost in their own conversation, which usually I'd follow fe-verishly, should this be someone he was currently working on or some-thing he'd not yet told me about. But I got lost in my phone instead. I felt bad I was not in a better mood for Charlotte, but it was hard to be happy in general those days. To extend the energy. To be fully present for someone; good company. I thought about her time in the office and wondered if I could have been a better friend and why I was so quick to sacrifice becoming a better friend, as I'd hoped to be when we first met at that party at the Soho Grand. Why I was so willing to do what was right for the role instead of what was right for me.

I sat and waited. Waited for Charlotte. Waited for the server to refill my empty glass with cold rosé, which went down too easily.

Waited for my phone to *ding* and tell me to pick it up. Waited to go home and crawl in bed. Waited to die. That's what it felt like. Ice crunched and water sloshed behind me; the server pulled another bottle of rosé from the ice buckets in back of our table.

My ears perked up, as they always did, when I heard Joe mention the boys or the Italians. He said something about the guys from Alba. The Alba mafia. For a moment, I forgot myself. Forgot I was with my boss and that we were talking about his business partners, and I said, dreamlike, "I love them."

"You don't want those kinds of Italians, Kim," Joe snarled. "They're communists with dirty teeth."

Oh. I knew what *that* meant. He'd said that about Michele and the guys from Alba before, but usually when going for a laugh. There wasn't anyone he didn't make fun of or assign a nickname to. But he wasn't trying to make me laugh today. He said it in the tone he used when I was slow to get onboard with him.

Joe didn't like Michele and me taking pictures together, which we'd splashed all over Instagram, was how my brain interpreted his comment. Maybe because Michele had power. Joe had tried to subtly push me toward guys before—he'd genuinely tried to help me in the past—but they were all employees or people he had power over; not men that if I got together with them seriously, they would cause me to leave the job. What did he think, that I was going to be his good little soldier forever? That I was going to be his version of Jakov, the Croatian guy who lived and died for Lidia? Jakov had done every job imaginable for her, from answering the phones at Felidia to looking after Nonna, Joe's grandmother. He moved into the guest house above the garage on Lidia's property in Queens for a time, even though he was six foot three and the apartment had only a bathtub the size of a kitchen sink. He brought me chocolate candies filled with espresso that he picked up on his short trips to the motherland. But he would never leave Lidia. Whatever she needed, he was her guy—*for life*. I wasn't knocking his loyalty. I just didn't want the same thing for myself.

But maybe I already was Jakov and was the last one to know it.

I still did my duty, of course, but the steam that once powered my engine vanished. I no longer clutched my seat at the table, and Joe knew it. He knew me as well as I knew him.

I had gotten what I needed out of the job, more or less. I took advantage of some of the opportunities it afforded me and squandered others I'd never get back.

When I was in the running for the role at the end of 2009, I thought, *Just get me out of the Babbo basement, and I'll make something of myself. I will stop working two jobs, and I will craft a real life for myself, like other people do. Just give me more access to men my age, peers, people with common interests, and adventures to go on, and I'll have a full life. I'll be happy.*

I gained much out of this role. But the real things, the important things that really mattered on that list, continued to elude me. And I had no one to blame except myself.

I didn't want to be at Babbo, but Joe baited me with white truffles, old Nebbiolo, and the promise that Wild Ramsons and friends from Italy would join—Serena and Angelica from *MasterChef Italia*, the dildo recipients—so I caved. I'd always enjoyed these decadent, boozy dinners at Babbo over the years. Seated beside Alice, I watched the staff maneuver through the absurdly cut-up, crowded space like dancers, their hands grasping pricey bottles and arms full of hot white plates precisely stacked from fingertip to elbow as they zipped up and down the steep center staircase and squeezed in and out of the pickle, the way I once did. Home, yet not home. It was time to leave.

I would email him first, so he'd have time to digest it. He could choose when he wanted to talk.

I'd given Joe my notice once before, or tried to. I sprang it on him in our little yellow office, shortly after Charlotte left. I was jealous she'd gotten out.

Joe handled it pretty well for someone who didn't like change. "Leave and go do what? Where are you going to go?" Then he became understanding and wanted to help me. "We know everyone—you can break into any industry you want. I will help you. You just need to figure out what you want to do."

But I didn't know what I wanted to do. I only knew I wanted to make more money, and I told him this, thinking he'd let me go easier. But after six weeks of me still not knowing what I wanted to do, Joe settled the matter by giving me a twenty-thousand-dollar raise.

"You can be like Meredith now," he said.

I could have thrown him into oncoming traffic.

"I *am* like Meredith," I hurled at him. "I do Meredith's job, Tim's job, and Diana's job. I am already *there*—I've been *there* for years."

"Okay, okay, okay," Joe said, as he pumped his open hand toward me. "Are we clear now? Is this finished?"

His words did nothing to unclench my locked jaw and hunched shoulders. It came too late.

"Yes."

And we went back to business as usual.

"He used you a little, didn't he?"

That was a lot out of the mouth of my mother. Though Joe possessed qualities that she and my dad abhorred—a foul mouth and rough demeanor—they loved him. They thought his sharpness, which they only witnessed watching episodes of *MasterChef,* was comical. But the truth was, I used him too.

"You can tell he likes you," they'd beam, after he spent an obligatory ten minutes with them tableside at Becco or Babbo.

I responded quizzically each time, *"How?"*

Regardless of our differences, which had always been present but suddenly were intolerable, I owed Joe a good transition. *I'll email him next week, when he's in Milan and has time to process it,* I decided.

And then the scandal hit.

fourteen

FLIP THE SWITCH

"You'll like Marcus. He's like a less hot version of Aaron," Joe said.

Marcus was the crisis PR rep we hired to manage communications relating to the scandal.

"Pull up that email with his invoice and send it to me. Don't pay it yet."

This was pretty much the extent of my discussion with Joe these days. I got all the information on the scandal from Joe's inbox. He knew I saw everything, so we didn't need to talk about the details. I asked him to let me know when it was okay to tell my parents what was happening. I'd worked for B&B Group in some capacity for sixteen years. This was the lens most people saw me through.

The major players in food media had a love/hate relationship with our group over the years. I'd always been defensive when stories came out. What did they say? Was it positive? Did they get it right? How much snark was in the piece? For big stories, the outlets sent Joe a list of facts to check before they went to print. As I waited for this particular email from the fact-checker, I thought about how odd it was to be rooting for them. To be one hundred percent behind them as they prepared to go to press with a story that would alter the company forever.

The email from the fact-checker hit Joe's inbox. I scanned the list of allegations for hints of the handful of alleged incidents I'd heard so long ago when I was a hostess at Babbo. But none of the stories that had been whispered to me, warnings I'd been given, were on this list. Every single allegation was new to me. How many more were there?

Eater broke the story on my thirty-ninth birthday: Mario was accused of sexual misconduct and abusive behavior by former staff and female journalists spanning back to the late '90s. Immediately, he was banned from entering the group's restaurants. B&B Hospitality Group put out a statement that Mario " . . . will step away from the company's operations, including the restaurants, and has already done so."

Mario's response included "much of the behavior described does, in fact, match up with ways I have acted. That behavior was wrong and there are no excuses."

The same morning, Joe needed to get his passport renewed, and took me with him. I recalled checking the expiration date during my first week on the job and thinking I wouldn't have to worry about it; I wouldn't still be there in eight years.

I shlepped down Varick Street looking for the entrance with a visibly shaken Joe. I really didn't need to go with him, but he insisted because he and Alice planned to take me out for a birthday lunch at Lupa, just across the neighborhood, immediately following.

While Joe waited in line, I checked on Elena to see if she was ready with the translated version of the company's statement on the scandal, and Joe's personal statement for the Italian press. I watched Joe pick up his phone, "*Ciao*, Oscar."

Elena told me, "Eh, Kim, it will not be such big news here. In Italy, these things aren't such a big deal . . . *sfortunatamente.*"

Elena was excited about our upcoming trip to Miami. In her world, everything was still normal. She'd worked out a spokesperson deal for Joe on a new European cruise line, and they were flying the three of us to South Beach for the kickoff.

In the following days, my workload tanked. I came in at 9:30 a.m. and left at 5:30 p.m. There were no requests for Joe to appear on *The Today Show* or CNBC; the only story was *the* story. No more special projects, dinners, music shows. It all halted. Calls and meetings with the attorneys and our crisis PR team took up most of Joe's time. For the first time, I was not invited. Also for the first time, I didn't want to be there. I was sure my simmering anger, which I barely kept a lid on, had something to do with it.

More stories came out. Other women shared their stories on social media. Every day I showed up angry. It'd been bubbling up since the Harvey Weinstein scandal broke back in October. That was around the time I'd gotten wind of a complaint against Mario by an employee at one of the restaurants. I saw the notice come into Joe's inbox, but when I went back to read through it later in the day, it had vanished. I wondered how bad it could be, if I wasn't allowed to see it. I thought I saw everything.

I tried to get rid of my anger. I reminded myself that I had a plan for what was next for me. But some days, what I felt was pure rage. I was angry for the women—who I believed completely. I was angry for a lifetime of little things that all of a sudden we were allowed to talk about.

When my father called immediately after my text, I knew what he was going to ask.

My throat constricted. I answered the phone.

"Oh my God, Kim. This sounds awful. It sounds like . . . is Mario really a bad guy?" The disbelief, the shock in his voice made him sound almost childlike as he tried to reconcile the situation.

I filled my parents in on the basics of what they could expect to see in the press. I hated that I needed to have this discussion with them. Then I thought about the call I didn't have to make. The calls the women had to make to *their* parents, their family members, their friends and coworkers. How did those conversations go? How gut-wrenching was it to make those calls? They had mothers and fathers too. Those women were someone's kids. Someone's sister. Someone's mother.

Aside from a comment I made to my parents during their last visit, I never let on that Mario had a bad reputation.

"When you next see Mario," my mother had said back then, "be sure to tell him how much we're still enjoying the places. He's not around when you go to the restaurants after work?"

"No, not really. I don't drink with him. People have always said he's a mean drunk. Crude."

"Really?" said my dad, saucer-eyed.

"You never told us that!" whispered my mother.

"Well, I'm telling you now."

Back in the waiting room of the New York Passport Agency, I sighed. "A lot is happening here, Dad. I have to go—"

"Wait now . . . he didn't . . . did he ever . . . "

"No, Dad—he never touched me. I've barely seen him these last eight years. I'm sorry. I really do have to go. I'm sorry I have to tell you guys this."

"We're just glad you're okay," my mother chimed in from the background.

Aside from a handful of what I'd consider inappropriate comments scattered over the years, Mario really didn't bother me.

"Hee hee—here comes Joe's *other* wife," he'd yelled across the room at the opening of Eataly Downtown.

"Hee hee, go fuck yourself," I said—only in my head, of course. *I wouldn't dare.*

All Joe kept saying over the next few days was, "Jesus Christ. I can't believe this," over and over again. "This is a nightmare."

Joe asked me to put up a sign in the Corporate elevators listing his cell phone number and inviting staff to call him directly if they were upset and wanted to talk. I appreciated the gesture but pitied the fool who dialed that number. Joe was not a nurturer. He'd been going around to all the restaurants to talk to the staff. This was the kind of thing I generally orchestrated, but I stayed out of it. I was glad not to see it. I wished I could be a source of support for people, or just help manage this situation so it went as smoothly as possible for everyone, but I was lucky if I didn't start crying at my desk—or yelling. The urge to yell at almost everyone I spoke with was something I was actively managing.

Joe was heavily criticized in the media. Eater reported that he helped create a "boys' club culture" within the B&B Group and could not corral Mario's behavior.

I had never thought about that until I read through the story. I shut my laptop and thought, *That sounds about right.* If someone had asked me years ago if I worked in an oppressive, boys' club environment, I probably would've answered no and meant it. Scanning through the article made me realize that not everyone had fun working for Joe, and it seemed I'd had a wildly different experience than what some of my coworkers were reporting.

Joe told the press that he had "heard [Batali] say inappropriate things" to employees and that he "should have done more" to criticize Mario. He said, "I'm proud of what our teams accomplish every day, and I've always tried to show respect for them and their work." He said in a statement, "It pains me that some employees feel differently, and I'm reexamining my own behavior to ensure that everyone I work with feels that respect."

I was good at being a social worker. Helping people came easy. To sit with someone else's emotions—often raw or volatile emotions—in a professional capacity, when the situation had nothing to do with me, came easy. I always knew what to say or when not to speak and just listen, how to garner trust and put them at ease. Sometimes the most vulnerable just needed to know that there was someone out there who cared. No one's problems could be solved in one hour, but my clients trusted that I would do what I could to help them. That we were in this together.

I didn't know what happened to Mr. Stein. He was so vulnerable. I was one of a handful of people with whom he came into physical contact at the end of his life, and I didn't even know what happened to him.

The last I remembered was that his daughter flew in from Nevada when Mr. Stein started to deteriorate fast. She called me before flying out. For the first few minutes, she was stoic, like her dad. Then she broke down.

"I'm an alcoholic," she said. "I haven't had a drink in ten years . . . but this is the kind of thing that . . . "

Her voice cracked. She took a few quick breaths, like maybe she was crying. We stayed on the phone for a while.

I answered the door the day she came to the office.

"I'm looking for Ms. Reed," she said.

"I'm Kim," I replied.

She looked confused. Her face fell. And then she gathered herself, shook my hand, and said, "I'm Dana—Dana Stein. George Stein's daughter."

We moved from the lobby into my office.

"I'm sorry. When we spoke on the phone that day, I thought you were forty years old."

Her age also struck me. I hadn't done the math. She looked to be in her late fifties—my mother's age.

It felt good to help someone, but heavy. I was twenty-four.

And I left them all. I didn't look back once. I left for castles in Barolo, mornings in the *Today Show* green room, summers in Italy, and the promise of a social life. When people asked me what I did for work back then, I almost always spoke of Babbo. That was what I was proud of: my insider status there. It felt powerful.

I left social work because I wanted power. It wasn't just about the money. I wanted to feel important, to play a bigger role in something sought after by so many. I did not appreciate what my colleagues and I did for our clients. I didn't see that I was much more valuable at Heights and Boerum Council than I'd ever be running after Joe. It was that little girl who knelt by that damned, dying bird that steered me to social work. I hoped that a part of her still remained in me.

Not that all my clients were saints. Everyone got old. There were some people you didn't want to help. Once, during a home visit, a client started to tell me about his first wife, who he'd been married to for one year in the 1950s.

"I covered these walls with her blood."

The words came with no warning, out of the mouth of an Irish American man in his early nineties—one of Rosie's boyfriends. "He's so cute, I want to put him up on my china cabinet," she'd say.

"That whore," he'd continued. His voice trembled.

I'd been distracted when he uttered the first line. But now, I had tunnel vision and was unable to move. He was only four foot eleven and weak, but he still had bulk to him. I was acutely aware that I was in this apartment, in a back room, alone with him. I didn't think he would hurt me, and I wasn't sure he could, but it was frightening to be alone with someone who talked of violence so easily.

"The guys from the neighborhood told me. She'd been working as a prostitute; can you believe that? Sellin' herself. She gave it up to all of them the same night, right in the bar—they came and told me."

I felt sick. Did he really not understand what likely happened that night? Did that sound like something a 1950s housewife with a husband would do?

I sensed the same ignorance, the same gullible idiocy, in some of the men I talked to about the #MeToo movement and what was happening at B&B Group. It seemed like every man I spoke to after the news broke had some bullshit layer of defense packed around him. There seemed to be a *Yeah, but* out of every man's mouth when the subject came up, as they shifted to look visibly annoyed. "Yeah, but doesn't she have a coke problem?" "Yeah, but I heard she was a little crazy."

The majority of these guys weren't just agreeing to agree with one another, sticking up for their fellow bros—*they were*, but it was deeper than that. They actually believed the crap they said. Because this was what we'd all been taught, all of us—as women, we were taught this too. Men are to be believed. Men were not to be questioned. Men should never have to explain even the most glaring bad behavior. Men had the privilege of being judged as individuals. They were given the benefit of the doubt. They were assumed virtuous, even if their past behavior screamed the opposite.

"But you're not going to write about this on your blog?" one restaurateur and chef with ties to the group asked me, looking like a deer that'd just heard a twig snap. "You shouldn't comment on it. Just leave this period out." What he was really saying was *Don't make it inconvenient to be friends with you.*

"She was not a good person, that one," is how another male friend who worked in the group described a former female employee who dared to speak to the press. "She really was a bitch. Not great at her job. You shouldn't bother with her." His brown eyes narrowed as he warned me. He spoke worse of her than he did Mario, a man who was banned from his restaurants and was accused by more than a dozen women of sexual harassment and assault.

This pattern repeated itself in the weeks and months that followed: Devalue. Discredit. Shun. Even some women said disappointing things. I stopped by one of the restaurants about a week after the initial piece broke and ended up in conversation with a longtime server who used to be at Babbo. I asked her if she was okay. She struggled to find the right words. She put her hand on her forehead and was quiet for a moment. Then she said, "Well . . . I mean, um . . . Mario's a genius . . . "

"Ugh, God," I said.

"I think they're all afraid," Joe announced after a meeting with the women who worked under Meredith. "They're acting like they are sad he's gone. Like they hate me. I don't get it."

"They're shell-shocked. I always had the impression Mario was good to his admin team."

When you'd worked for someone for so long, it could be hard to flip the switch right away, to stop drinking the Kool-Aid, especially if you built your name on theirs. It was easy for me to say how I felt to my coworkers because I didn't want to be in the job anymore. I wasn't staying in the industry. I'd gotten what I wanted and no longer had anything to lose. I imagined how I would've felt if the scandal had happened in 2011 or 2012 when I was riding high, when I would have clawed anyone's eyes out had someone tried to take this job from me.

A female chef in our group told me that she was being shunned by a few female food journalists because she didn't leave the company right away. She chose to stay in her role—a role she'd worked her ass off for. I wondered if those same journalists were also giving the male chefs in our group a hard time.

I waited three months to give Joe my notice after the scandal broke. I sent him an email on a day when he was in L.A. He didn't acknowledge it, so I brought it up the following morning. Even then, he didn't say much. He'd known it was coming.

fifteen

FRUIT ON THE TABLE

My new boss, Sharon, and I were going to get along just fine. She didn't know how to cut and paste, let whatever was in her head fall right out her mouth, and slung the word *fuck* down the hall at least ten times per day.

I'd taken a temporary job out on Roosevelt Island with RIOC, the Roosevelt Island Operating Corporation. It was supposed to be temp-to-permanent, but I told the recruiter who placed me that I'd only agree to it until I found a senior-level role with a higher salary. This didn't sit well with Sharon, but since her last assistant quit with no notice, she didn't have a choice. The pay was only $26.00 an hour, but I was guaranteed five days per week and health insurance.

Main Street on the island looked like you'd expect to see a tank rolling down it any minute. They had their own police force, the Public Safety Department, who didn't carry guns. Americanos at the deli were only $1.50.

It was all very *damn the man* there. Like there was something in the water or maybe the ghosts from the old asylum, now crumbling on the other end of the island, that sent residents a subliminal dose of resistance to anything, good or bad, RIOC was behind.

There were a number of people I could have reached out to, to find work, but I couldn't bear to speak to anyone who knew me from the group just then. And that was how everyone in New York knew me. I wanted to be somewhere where I wasn't *little Kim* and wasn't at the whim of people's dueling agendas. Where I was just me.

It seemed like everyone I spoke to had an extreme opinion. Joe's friends, who'd morphed into mine over the years, seemed to see Joe as a victim, a line I couldn't go along with if my life depended on it. Others eyed me warily, one even warning me, "You'd better have a good reason for still working there."

I could not have picked a better place to disappear from my old life. It was low-key—a good place to recover from burnout. Even writing cover letters was difficult. I had to practice focusing every day, something I never did before.

"You'd better start looking for a real job," my mother said, when I told her what the temp work paid.

She was right, but I couldn't. Most days I felt like I was drunk. My body felt heavy, as though it were made of lead. I only had five thousand dollars in savings and another five thousand in my 401(k). After seventeen years, that was all I had. I was thirty-nine years old. At least my student loans, at long last, were gone. My parents had ended up paying off the last ten thousand dollars two years earlier. I would never have gotten out from under otherwise, and the relief outweighed the shame after a while.

Just before Joe gave me that twenty-thousand-dollar raise a few years back, he told me that hundred-thousand-dollar jobs didn't exist for assistants. That I would have to do something else to make that kind of money.

I wanted to choke after my first meeting with a recruiter. "Someone with your résumé is worth $120,000 in today's market. It varies between industries—in finance you're worth $150,000 base. And why did you list Executive Assistant on your resume? This is a textbook job description for a Chief of Staff role."

To make matters worse, just before I left, I'd learned Meredith's base salary was $30,000 more a year than mine. A young man who was our intern in 2010 and had a decade's less experience than I in the workforce, and in my opinion, a fraction of my responsibilities, was paid a base salary $9,000 higher. Thirty thousand dollars was *real* money. They were worth every penny, but so was I. Joe gave me some experiences money could never buy. He was generous in other ways. But I never needed the free Barolo. I would rather have had the money to buy my own. To make a down payment on an apartment. Freeze my eggs. Seeing Meredith's salary lined up next to mine on an Excel spreadsheet in Joe's inbox was wrenching. I didn't talk to Joe about it for fear I'd explode, but I raged to Paul, who sympathized but retorted that Mario and Joe paid their teams differently.

Letting go of my anger about my old salary was an ongoing struggle, but slowly it began to subside. I told myself that Joe was so far removed from these details, I doubted he even knew. But he should've known. *I should've known*—should've gotten my ass to a recruiter years ago. Why would I believe Joe? He didn't even know how much he got paid—Maury and I managed his income. When I'd trained

Ari's assistant a few years prior, the first thing I told her was that Ari was her number one priority—and not to rely on any third parties to take care of him as she would.

"No one will ever take care of *your person* like you will," I warned. I should have told her to take care of herself. Whose person was I? I was too busy taking care of everyone else—my clients, Joe and all his crazy dreams—that I never built anything for myself. I didn't even get paid market value.

I decided to be my own person. To look out for myself like I'd looked out for Joe. I was going to get myself back together. Make smarter decisions about where and how much I worked. I stopped checking my phone every twenty minutes and slowly got out of the habit of checking it before bed. Eventually, I got back into the swing of interviewing, left RIOC and kooky Roosevelt Island behind for an assistant role at a hot new financial technology company in Greenwich Village—but not before scouring the internet and Glassdoor for any red flags—accusations of abuse, even bullying.

"You must have your hands full supporting Jeremy" was something I heard often from my new colleagues, but it wasn't remotely true.

During a meeting in my first few weeks on the job, I was running through tasks I'd taken care of that day and listing off emails he ought to look at in his inbox. Jeremy sat there watching me, blue eyes unreadable, his hands, painted with dark blue nail polish, resting on his black jeans. At six foot four, even when we were sitting down next to each other, he still towered over me.

I couldn't read him and thought maybe he didn't like how I'd organized everything. Stomach twisting, I stopped talking.

"You make it look so easy," he said, tucking his long blond hair behind his ears.

Jeremy was in a completely different stage of his career than Joe had been when I took over his office in 2010. Joe had a decade more entrepreneurial experience than Jeremy. That was a lot of hustle and grind, of which the cumulative effect was to get rid of things. To pare down. To do as little yourself of the day-to-day as possible. To get things out of your orbit and free up space in your brain. Only then was I beginning to have sympathy for the 2010 we-don't-need-a-fucking-meeting Joe. He was more than happy to throw me chunks of his work so long as I could catch them.

Jeremy, on the other hand, just said a polite "No thank you" when I asked if there was something I could do on some matter that came into his inbox, which clearly needed a well-thought-out strategy to tackle. A leadership change. Drafting communications to the press or to the board of directors. Certainly, it was my job as an assistant to read, digest, fold the information into its proper place among competing professional and personal priorities, and remind him to carve out time to figure out how he was going to handle it. But I couldn't handle it for him. I couldn't go that extra step and do his work, like I did for Joe. I couldn't create a solution to something I knew nothing about, involving people I'd yet to analyze and make quasi-paranoid assumptions about. I couldn't wrap it up in a bow and ask yea or nay, taking up no more than ten minutes of his time.

Jeremy kept me busy, but it was a workload for one. Personal tasks and the usual admin calendaring, inboxing, small projects, travel, expense reports. They didn't need someone like me there. Jeremy didn't really need a little lieutenant. He already had an army. He didn't want anyone drafting his updates; he needed to figure out what to write himself. I sat in on the meetings with our executive recruiting team, but so did our in-house head of recruiting. The most I could help with was booking a flight for a potential candidate based on the West Coast, while trying not to feel useless.

There were no profanity-laced tirades and no little yellow office to have them in. There was no leather chair to stand on. No vent and

HVAC duct to strain my face up to. No one told me, "Find out what they want," giving me the green light to pick up the phone and call people who ordinarily did not conduct high-priority business with someone's executive assistant. No one sent me stumbling into some diamond mine of a situation for which I was unqualified, sans flashlight, expecting me to come out the other end holding a stone.

The upside of working what I was slowly realizing was a "normal" job was that I had time to do all the things I'd promised myself I'd do. I finally accepted an invitation to spend the weekend at a friend's country house in Washington, Connecticut, where there was almost no Wi-Fi—because I no longer felt compelled to feverishly check my phone at 7:30 a.m. on a Sunday. I said yes when Edo invited me to his last-minute dinner parties, which always began promptly at 7:00 p.m. I joined a social club, and if I couldn't dig up one of my married friends to go with me, I went by myself. I became a board member of Heights and Boerum Council. Board meetings were held every other month at 6:00 p.m. sharp, but I knew the commitment would not be a problem.

There was only one missing piece of the puzzle at my new job: the absence of an equivalent to the Eataly boys.

The CFO was adorable: around my age, mild-mannered, no ring. He was a former hedge fund guy who showed up in old sneakers with dirty shoelaces and a faded hoodie. I soon learned he was getting married the next year. Most of the men my age were married or in the thick of long-term relationships. The rest were all young. I was one of the oldest people there.

My mind was finally starting to feel like my own outside working hours. Now that my outer environment was not a distraction, suddenly I could think clearly. Suddenly I thought about myself all the time, the way I used to think about my and Joe's inbox. And I wondered if I would ever be with anyone again. I was very angry with myself for not doing better in this area. I could "make anything" happen for Joe, jump into industries I knew nothing about, learn how to do my job in a foreign language with virtually no time to study, plan music shows in European countries, but for the middle and latter half of my thirties, I couldn't get myself what I needed and so desperately wanted. As if pursuing a sex life, a romantic life, was too much for my body and mind, both of which had been running on fumes for years.

I felt embarrassed too. I was afraid that my dates would know. That they'd be able to tell how long it had been. That it would be painful, like the first time. Over the last few years, I'd begun to dread my annual visits to my gynecologist, particularly the question that Dr. Sean never failed to ask: "Have you been sexually active since your last appointment?" I could only say no for so many years before believing that something was wrong with me.

He shook his head and set my medical file on the counter. "I've been telling you for years, Kim—straight men are *crazy*. Lots of my patients go through dry spells."

I began trying online dating, but the idea of meeting a stranger based on their photo and a few lines in their bio for the purpose of deciding whether you'd like to be intimate with them at some point was a lot for me. I couldn't think of anything more frightening. I not only feared my own emotional experience, but I was afraid to take in what I assumed was their emotional experience; I got caught somewhere between too much empathy and the drilled-in notion, the automatic response, of constant people pleasing. To be nonthreatening to a man, no matter the circumstance.

I had tried recently anyway, meeting a man I'd connected with on Hinge. I chose the George Washington Bar at the Freeman Hotel for our date because I'd wanted to check out the room, which looked like an old library, for some time. I arrived first and grabbed a stool at the end of the dark wooden bar and ordered a glass of white wine.

The guy was French Canadian. There wasn't a lot of chemistry, but he looked in person exactly as he did in the photos on the app, and I was interested in his work, which had taken him to South Africa. I even forgot for a few minutes, as the conversation picked up, to be nervous.

At one point during our second drink he said, "I usually look for women who are more intellectually compatible to me . . . but the fact that you learned Italian for your last job—"

Was he actually saying this to me?

He went on to repeat the line, " . . . *But* the fact that you learned Italian for your last job," as if it didn't fully sink in the first time. I was glad he repeated himself; had he not I might have thought I was hallucinating.

But the real horror lay in the fact that I took it. I sat there smiling, sipping my glass of Chablis, and not knowing how to get out of there, how to end the date gracefully. So I ordered another round.

The bartender moved near us and my adrenaline spiked. I was doused in shame—he was going to hear what this French-Canadian fuck was saying to me and see that I was eating it.

I understood that my demeanor, my pleasing girlishness, hunched shoulders, and unfocused speech might not scream high intellect, but it didn't scream "moron," either.

How different the world felt sitting next to Gareth or Michele or even Jesse. But ultimately, I couldn't be at the whim of others. I had to bring my real self to play. But putting it into practice was still hard, even as I was so done being *little Kim*.

I didn't let this guy deter me. I kept swiping right and hoped for the best. I chalked him up to practice, which clearly I needed.

Alexey was the young guy charged with onboarding me. He'd started off in the company's finance department but was tapped to run special projects for Jeremy, and then got roped into supporting Jeremy fully after they'd let the last assistant go.

He was good at being an assistant, for someone who'd never really been a bona fide assistant or had any desire to be. He didn't make me feel stupid for asking a thoroughly stupid question.

He insisted on taking me to lunch at the Elk on my first day, even though I knew he was underwater planning Jeremy's upcoming trip to South Beach. Sitting across from each other at a small wooden table, we took each other in. Alexey's eyes widened; his pupils fully dilated. He pushed himself up against the banquette, sitting up straight, and pulled off his green knit cap and ran his hand through his hair. He kept on his trademark black leather jacket. I liked watching him fuss.

"I do other things, too," Alexey said. It seemed important to him that I know this. He was a DJ. He had started an event planning company and executed events in several countries. I got the sense from him and others that to be the founder of a company was the end-almighty. He told me that he lived in the apartment on Hudson Street in the West Village where the Beastie Boys used to live, and that his mother and little brother lived there too. I advised him to stay as long as he could, and that if my parents lived as far as Westchester, I'd be commuting and saving on rent. I barely knew him, but the way he watched me made it easy to open up. When he asked, I told him what a shitshow the last six months at the group were. It was a relief to speak openly for once, without fearing some sort of retribution or risking an argument. Since leaving B&B, I'd had to be careful about how much I disclosed to whom; the boys' club ran deep.

Alexey looked young—younger than he actually was. He said his little brother was nine years old. *How old was his mother?* I had been thrown off while he interviewed me by how young he appeared compared to how old he sounded. He seemed confident, sharp but kind.

But there at the Elk, talking over arugula salads, as he leaned over the table, eyes alert, he appeared vulnerable.

Alexey had recently developed a pain in his left foot and was walking with a limp. He went to a few doctors, but no one really knew the cause.

"It might be psychosomatic," I told him. "You don't really want to be doing what you're doing." Now that I was in place and fully operational, Jeremy was trying to find a role for Alexey within the company because he was all-around too good to let go.

I hadn't realized the tension between us or understood why it was important to Alexey that I knew he "did other things" until one day when I felt his fingers graze the underside of mine as we parted in the office kitchen. It felt deliberate, but subtle enough that I dismissed it, knowing full well my tendency to assign meaning to things that had none.

But the second time it happened, I had to acknowledge it was real. It was too specific a move to be otherwise. I had taken him out for a drink at Del Posto. My new work friends were not foodies and I knew the gang at Del Posto would send out the works. I'd brought in a few people some months ago and they had the same reaction as Alexey—how did they not know this place existed? We stretched our legs at one of the tables in the lounge as he looked around the room, up at the ceiling, and marveled at how in the world we were enjoying such opulence all to ourselves. There was barely anyone in there; the scandal had done a number on the place.

As we sipped our drinks—tequila for Alexey, a glass of Vespa Bianco, Joe's flagship wine, for me—I realized if I were still working for Joe, if the scandal hadn't happened, he'd probably be here at some point in the night. He'd plop down at the table, interrupt us to introduce himself, call out to a busy server to bring us "the works," call in Sharky or the Wild Ramsons and tell them to get over here, and then proceed, in his irreverent way, to make fun of everyone at the table until we were all about to pee our pants. Fun Joe. I almost forgot he existed.

When we were bidding our goodbyes at the front door, Alexey did it again. *Oh, he's good*, I thought. How did he manage to find my hand in the split second after I'd turned away from him, but before stepping out of reach?

Part of me wanted to go with it. Alexey was sweet, quiet, smart, the kind of man I was drawn to. He reminded me of Aaron in that way. But the slick maneuver with his hand reminded me of Jesse. I deserved to have a fun fling—but I had also promised myself that I would not get caught up in the easy allure of phantom gestures, no matter how innocent their intent. He was darling, but he'd be a complete waste of time.

Alexey left the company in March. Jeremy couldn't find a job for him. This was an unexpected blow, triggering a familiar ambivalence of being left longing, and I wondered if I'd made the right decision not pursuing him.

He came to the company happy hour a few months after leaving. His limp was gone. We stood in the middle of the room, talking, and when another colleague approached, he stopped just short of joining us.

I looked at him, a bit taken aback by his hesitation.

"Am I interrupting?" he asked, as though he'd just stumbled upon us alone in a dark stairwell.

Until then, I didn't think anyone had noticed the tension between us. "No!" Alexey and I both cried out, a little too enthusiastically. We both relocated our gazes to the floor as we ushered him toward us.

And then Jeremy stepped down. They hired a new guy, a serial CEO.

You never know where he might take you, my mother texted.

My heart plunged. *Where he might take me.* How about I take myself somewhere? I didn't want another master to serve. I still liked being an assistant. It was what I was good at. I just didn't want to get lost in someone else's life and then be left with nothing. There were people who found a happy medium. Helped someone else achieve their dreams while still making time for their own. That was the goal, and I'd been slowly making progress. I wasn't getting too excited about the new guy anyway because chances were he'd come in and just fire everyone—including me.

The new guy was sharp and abrupt—he had more Joe in him than Jeremy. The staff wasn't used to this type of CEO. But when I caught him taking a blink-and-you'll-miss-it deep breath, I was reminded that he was really just a guy my age, in the first days of his new job.

All I could contribute to the board meetings was to set up refreshments. I wiped down the tables, getting rid of any crumbs or mustard stains; picked up the boxes of coffee from the Elk around the corner; put out an assortment of fruit I'd bought at Gourmet Garage along with a stack of clean plates; labeled which pastries were gluten-free and dairy-free.

After the meeting, I got an email from the new guy that said I'd done a *great job with setup; no issues whatsoever!* and that *the room looked amazing!*

I almost spit out my coffee. *Come the fuck on*, I thought. Wasn't this guy listening when I told him I'd worked in the restaurant industry for seventeen years? *I'd put fruit on the table.*

Talk of layoffs had been swirling around the company since Jeremy announced he was leaving. It wasn't uncommon for a massive sweep to follow a big leadership change. I should have been terrified; executives were known to want to bring in their own admin help. My colleagues jittered about when the new guy was around—the way I used to if I hadn't checked Joe's inbox in ten minutes—but

I was relatively calm. I couldn't help but think of the old me. Had I lost the job at B&B, it would've shattered me, shredded my self-esteem, but the thought of losing this one felt like little more than an inconvenience. I was surprised by how unconcerned, how unattached I felt. The possibility of losing my income was daunting, but it didn't feel like I'd lose part of my identity. Could it be that I no longer weighed my worth in completed tasks? Was it possible that I did not give a shit?

I did a good job for the new guy and continued to help Jeremy transition out, but I began leaving the office at 6:00 p.m. at the latest. I headed to the gym or the social club or went to Edo's house and drank too much wine. I took time off for medical appointments. I started visiting my parents every other month, where the guest bedroom had several neatly folded piles of my mother's latest Boscov finds. Whatever happened, I'd be okay.

sixteen

LIKE MAGIC

I was sure it would be my last visit to the old place. The governor had lifted the city's ban on indoor dining a few days before, but there was already talk of a second wave of the virus about to hit New York. All the group's restaurants took a beating after the scandal, Babbo included. Since the onset of the pandemic, hundreds of thousands of restaurants had gone under, and I was afraid Babbo would become one of them. I wanted to go back and see it while I still could, all dressed up. I didn't plan on staying long. *I'll have a glass of Vespa at the bar*, I thought. Say hello to everybody.

I headed downtown on the F train from 58th Street. I'd just accepted a new job in finance that paid market value and was invited by my new employers to have a look at the office I'd be working in post-vaccine. It was an executive assistant role, but I chose wisely this time. The person I'd be supporting was an entrepreneur, but *he's reasonable*, the recruiter said. I was suspicious, but after spending five minutes with him on Zoom, I could tell she was right. He was incredibly kind, and balked when I asked if I'd be managing personal tasks as well.

I pulled myself out of the running for another, separate role. It was exactly the kind of job I used to want—like being Joe's assistant, on steroids. And I was exactly the kind of candidate they were hoping to find—someone who had already served a term as mayor of Crazy Town and was ready for reelection. It would have paid more than I'd ever made, but the real lure was the opportunity to be scooped up again—the job was a guaranteed adventure. I could jump back onto that moving train and lose myself in someone else's dreams and wild ideas. But I'd rather make my own this time. I'd found a new master to serve—me.

I got out at 23rd Street because there were too many people on the train not wearing masks. I walked down Fifth Avenue, frigid in my spring trench coat with no gloves. I'd only been in Manhattan once in the previous eight months and it felt good to be back. It was quiet along the street for being a quarter to six at the start of the holiday season. Though there wasn't any snow on the ground, it reminded me of the last time Fifth Avenue was this silent.

Maybe I'll swing by the Blind Tiger, I thought. I hadn't been since that night of the blizzard with Gareth, Jesse, Jimmy Day, and Peter. Not before or since had I known the city to feel like it did that night in the snow. The streets of Manhattan were magic for a number of reasons, but mainly because I was right there with them, living my life in the moment, paying attention to what was right in front of me.

It took me longer than I cared to admit, but what I'd learned was I could have a night like that every night, or I could have nights like the ones spent in the Babbo basement. I got to choose. I didn't have to wait for things to happen—I might be waiting a long time. I could let people in. I had some say in the matter. I could stay up all night walking around Rome with a good man and not check my phone. I could say yes to that dinner invitation, say no to too much work.

I wondered where I would be right then if I had done just one thing differently over the years. If I had gone to law school. Married Liam. Ignored Jesse's invitation to play Scrabulous. Said no to working coat check the night of the blizzard. Kept my part-time job at the Bobst Library instead of leaving for Babbo. Where would I be? Who would I be? Would I be someone's wife? Would there be a child tugging at my pant leg? Would any of those things have made me happier than I was? I was happy. I knew who I was.

I pulled on the door to Babbo, and it flew open as easily as a flimsy screen door with a broken closer. It was never heavy. The hinge had been tight. After more than twenty years of opening and closing, it had finally come loose.

The maître d' was right at the entrance, and though it wasn't George, she seemed to know me. I looked over her shoulder, past the empty pickle and out into the dining room. Table twenty-four had two guests, and a few suited, mask-wearing staff members stood around, waiting. I took another step in and she redirected me to the left, where I saw a temperature monitor. I tipped my face up to it.

"You're fine," she told me, and I headed in.

It was darker inside than usual. No one was working behind the bar and there were no stools out. The maître d' and a man who I guessed was a floor manager hovered. It was off-putting, but I knew that they were probably just happy to finally be back at work. I could have sworn I saw one familiar, longtime Babbo server standing by the center staircase when I first walked in, but now she was nowhere in sight.

A wooden chandelier hung above the center table. It looked like deer antlers, with a small elflike figure lying across them. I recognized it from the winery in Friuli. One of Joe's long-lost art projects, resurrected. We never used to hang anything from the ceiling in Babbo, and it looked strikingly out of place. But that was not what was really different that night. I had expected it to feel like going back to a place from childhood as an adult and being instantly transported back in time, slipping into my old skin.

But none of this happened for me. The room looked familiar, but it felt strange.

I didn't even make it past the podium. I turned around, told the maître d' I'd come back another time. But I didn't think I would. It was almost as if the place was spitting me out. Repelling me. *This isn't where you belong anymore. You won't find that old comfort here.*

I went to Torino my second summer in Italy. I read up on its history before going and learned that the city itself is considered a place of great spiritual and magical significance. Allegedly, Torino's position on Earth is said to form an angle in not one but two "magic triangles." Along with Prague and Lyon, it forms a triangle representing good, a center for "white magic." With London and San Francisco, it forms one representing evil—a center for black magic.

I had immediately thought of Babbo. There was something about the energy of that restaurant. There was potency—for both good and bad, for bliss and pain, as though it too served as some sort of meeting place for all of us who worked there. I had felt compelled to say goodbye, as though it were a living thing. But when I got there, it was already gone.

All the way home, I thought of the old guard at Babbo. George and Gina. Jimmy Day, Jesse, and Cillian. Everyone else who gave so much of themselves to that place. Those who chose to stay for all its allure and blessings and punishments.

I had so much love for the whole lot of us; so much more respect than I did when we had actually worked together. That was missing from my heart while we toughed it out night after night. If I could go back, I'd tell them how special they were. That they were worth far more than their last table, last plate, last ring around the dining room, last check. I could see Jesse placing his magazine and lotto tickets on the bar; Gina bringing out a plate for me; Cillian sweeping past, rushing to put out some fire as he shouted a triumphant "Kimmy!"; Jimmy Day telling me how nice I looked with my new short haircut. I could envision George's game of Tetris playing out across his face as he surveyed the pickle, just before he tugged my right arm and pointed into the crowd with the end of his pencil, and said, "Gentleman in the green sweater, table fifty-one, please."

I thought of the young woman I used to be, who hemmed her pants with safety pins. She walked through that door thousands of times, slowly but surely becoming someone different. I'd tell her I was proud of her for not dropping anchor in the Babbo basement, for not giving up, no matter how long it took to figure things out. I'd say, *Keep going*, and tell her how proud I was of how hard she was trying, instead of feeling angry and frustrated for not having it all together the first, the second, or even the eighty-eighth time. I'd tell her that she didn't have to work so hard. I'd tell her, *Girl, I should've loved you more.*

I didn't see much of anyone from the store at that point. Edo was the only one I still talked to. My first friend at the store, and my last. I hadn't seen Aaron and Ari since I left the group, but I thought of them even if just for a second, every time I walked by Eataly.

Eventually I might run into them there, but the two young men in blue button-downs who I once got out of bed for in the morning wouldn't be there. They lived only in my memory.

Michele slowly stopped answering my texts and emails. I ran into him—almost literally—on Spring Street about an hour after I was let go by the new guy at the tech company. He didn't even stop. He just shouted a quick greeting as he rushed past me. His life shaped itself around the group, and so I slipped out of his. I was glad I didn't have to see him every day. That I didn't have to see him look at me with dead eyes that once shimmered with love and had pulled me out of dark places.

Gareth was a film producer out in California. He continued to be a good support. I couldn't decide if it was a good or bad thing we didn't live in the same city, but didn't waste my time worrying about it.

Jesse was happily married and a proud father. He'd worked hard to rebuild his reputation and learn from the mistakes of his early twenties. If you know his real name, perhaps pretend that you don't.

Alexey went on to cofound a sexual wellness app. Maybe I should have spent more time with him.

I stepped off the train at Seventh Avenue, walked up the stairs leading to quiet Park Slope. I put my key in the door and began my ritual for entering the apartment since the second week of March. I took one step in, slipped off my shoes, dropped all bags onto the floor, and without touching anything, walked to the bathroom sink to wash my hands. I'd made a mental note to clear my head when I got home, so I wouldn't get distracted and rub my eyes, wipe my nose, or otherwise touch my face. I was counting to twenty when suddenly it dawned on me.

I didn't know a soul in that place.

ACKNOWLEDGMENTS

A special thank you to Mom, Dad, and my sister Kelly, for your unwavering support for all my big ideas, for always being a safe harbor, and for raising me right.

To my agent Jane Dystel of Dystel, Goderich & Bourret LLC: you believed in me before I believed in myself, and this made all the difference.

To my wise-beyond-her-years editor, Mollie Weisenfeld at Hachette Books, you treated this book like it was your own. I will always be grateful for your guidance, for not pulling any punches, and for the care and reverence you showed my story.

To everyone at Dystel, Goderich & Bourret LLC and Hachette Books who worked on shaping this book.

Thank you to Cisca L. Schreefel and Carolyn Schurr Levin for your kind words and attention to detail.

To Elena, Charlotte, and Natalie, no one else will ever know those absurd, awful, and often ridiculously wonderful days.

Thank you to those who took the time to read early chapters and give valuable feedback: Mike Seay, Julia Segal, Jay McInerney, Chris Fischer, Bob Guccione, Jr., and Will Mavronicolas.

To Joe Bastianich. I sometimes wonder where I'd be if you hadn't hired me.

To Edo. You had me pegged on day one.

To Michele, for being a light in dark places.

To all of the current and former volunteers, employees, supporters, and board members of Heights and Hills. Thank you for devoting yourselves to empowering others and keeping valuable members of the community in the community. I am a better person because of this organization.

To the old guard at Babbo:

You were the true treasures of that place.